The Known Economy

Why do critics *and* celebrants of globalization concur that international trade and finance represent an inexorable globe-bestriding force with a single logic? *The Known Economy* shows that both camps rest on the same ideas about how the world is scaled. Two centuries ago romantic and rationalist theorists concurred that the world was divided into discrete nations, moving at different rates toward a "modernity", split between love and money. Though differing over whether this history is tragedy or triumph, they united in projecting an empty "international" space in which a Moloch-like global capitalism could lurk.

The Known Economy tracks the colonial development of national accounting and re-examines the ways gender and heteronormativity are built in to economic representation. It re-interprets the post-WWII spread of standardized economic statistics as the project of international organizations looking over the shoulders of national governments, rather than the expanding power of national governments over populations.

Colin Danby received a Ph.D. in Economics from the University of Massachusetts Amherst in 1997 and is currently Professor of Interdisciplinary Arts and Sciences at the University of Washington, Bothell. He has published articles in Post Keynesian theory, Feminist Economics, and Economic Anthropology.

Culture, Economy, and the Social
A new series from CRESC – the ESRC Centre for Research on Socio-cultural Change

The *Culture, Economy, and the Social* series is committed to innovative contemporary, comparative, and historical work on the relations between social, cultural, and economic change. It publishes empirically-based research that is theoretically informed, that critically examines the ways in which social, cultural, and economic change is framed and made visible, and that is attentive to perspectives that tend to be ignored or side-lined by grand theorizing or epochal accounts of social change. The series addresses the diverse manifestations of contemporary capitalism, and considers the various ways in which the 'social', 'the cultural', and 'the economic' are apprehended as tangible sites of value and practice. It is explicitly comparative, publishing books that work across disciplinary perspectives, cross-culturally, or across different historical periods.

The series is actively engaged in the analysis of the different theoretical traditions that have contributed to the development of the 'cultural turn' with a view to clarifying where these approaches converge and where they diverge on a particular issue. It is equally concerned to explore the new critical agendas emerging from current critiques of the cultural turn: those associated with the descriptive turn for example. Our commitment to interdisciplinarity thus aims at enriching theoretical and methodological discussion, building awareness of the common ground that has emerged in the past decade, and thinking through what is at stake in those approaches that resist integration to a common analytical model.

Markets and the Arts of Attachment
Edited by Franck Cochoy, Joe Deville and Liz McFall

The Known Economy
Romantics, Rationalists, and the Making of a World Scale
Colin Danby

Coming soon:

Film Criticism as a Cultural Institution
Crisis and Continuity from the 20th to the 21st Century
Huw Walmsley-Evans

Unbecoming Things
Mutable Objects and the Politics of Waste
Nicky Gregson and Mike Crang

The Known Economy

Romantics, Rationalists, and the Making of a World Scale

Colin Danby

Centre for Research on
Socio-Cultural Change

First published 2017
by Routledge
2 Park Square, Milton Park, Abingdon, Oxon OX14 4RN

and by Routledge
711 Third Avenue, New York, NY 10017

Routledge is an imprint of the Taylor & Francis Group, an informa business

© 2017 Colin Danby

British Library Cataloguing in Publication Data
A catalogue record for this book is available from the British Library

Library of Congress Cataloging in Publication Data
Names: Danby, Colin, author.
Title: The known economy : romantics, rationalists, and the making of a world scale / by Colin Danby.
Description: 1 Edition. | New York : Routledge, 2017.
Identifiers: LCCN 2016055255| ISBN 9781138123496 (hardback) | ISBN 9781315648811 (ebook)
Subjects: LCSH: International finance. | Banks and banking, International. | Economic policy–21st century. | State, The.
Classification: LCC HG3881 .D326193 2017 | DDC 330.15–dc23
LC record available at https://lccn.loc.gov/2016055255

ISBN: 978-1-138-12349-6 (hbk)
ISBN: 978-1-315-64881-1 (ebk)

Typeset in Times New Roman
by Wearset Ltd, Boldon, Tyne and Wear

MIX
Paper from
responsible sources
FSC
www.fsc.org   FSC® C013056

Printed and bound in Great Britain by
TJ International Ltd, Padstow, Cornwall

For Martin Diskin

Contents

PART III
Opening up 159

Illustrations

Figures

Table

Preface

The germ of this book was a paper for Eiman Zein-Elabdin and S. Charusheela's 2004 edited volume *Postcolonialism Meets Economics*. I had been troubled since I was a graduate student by the way macroeconomic analysis assumed that national economies were much more self-contained and discrete than they really were, and puzzled by the disjuncture between J. M. Keynes' international economics, which was deeply aware of transnational overlaps, and the national-scale analysis that bears his name. In my 2004 paper I drew on Foucauldian concepts of governmentality and surveillance to explain what happened after WWII, and why a standardized national-scale analysis suited the international organizations established after the war.

It became apparent that after the world was reimagined as a collection of self-contained national economies, two things happened to the left-over space of the "international." Initially it was conceived as an empty space through which goods and finance flowed. But then, within a few decades, it was converted into a "world economy" with its own personality and voice. I began to see the International Monetary Fund (IMF) as a ventriloquist, a sophisticated cultural actor, and not just a lender. This opened up the history of statistical representation, in particular the development of national income accounting – what made this strange project persuasive? What explained its reception? In turn, this inquiry led to the recognition that among the people most impressed by the IMF's cultural productions were contemporary radical critics of globalization. An influential stream of anti-globalization literature had bought in, enthusiastically, to the IMF's carefully devised depiction of the world economy (or global capitalism or international finance or neoliberalism) as an implacable and powerful dispenser of discipline.

Once I noticed this resonance I looked for the underlying structure, which sent me back to figures like Goethe and Coleridge and the more than 200 years of entanglement between a cosmopolitan/rationalist Economics on the one side, and a nationalist/romantic Economics on the other. Though noisy in their mutual opposition, these two streams of thinkers have collaborated in promoting modernity as a social ontology.

Modernity scales the world to *individuals* and *nations*, and grounds a range of political and ethical positions. Economics has played a key role in generating the modernist scaling of the social world that is now so widely taken for granted. Hence this book's effort to ask how economic knowledge is made, and to understand the romantic-rationalist opposition as a squabble about knowledge that hides more substantial and troubling agreement about history and social ontology. I write as a heterodox economist working in an interdisciplinary space that has been largely evacuated by the way modernist assumptions channel scholarly conversations.

My non-modernist priors are that we inhabit a world in which production, consumption, commerce, and finance are undergirded by a wide variety of institutions: familial, customary, religious, governmental, and legal. Culture and economy, the symbolic and the material, are densely intermingled. *Household, firm*, and *nation* are terms associated with powerful political and ideological projects *within* the world, but they are not obvious units forming it.

This book presents a genealogical account of modernist Economics, in Foucault's sense, attentive to the difficulty and contingency of knowledge. However Foucault is clearer about what one should *not* do in this kind of investigation (assume the result was inevitable; project its categories back in time) than about what one *should* do, apart from a bracing exhortation to "relentless erudition" (Foucault 1999, p. 370). I have tried to be attentive to disjunctures and disputes, and where there has been genuine continuity, to work out its institutional underpinnings.

I am also working from a Foucualdian sense of the relation between power and knowledge, which I have found liberating in describing the growth of economic knowledge in the twentieth century. One of the things I do for a living is teach Economics, including the system of national accounting that will be critiqued in this book. To learn these accounts, and work with the data that fills them, can be genuinely illuminating. Limited and theory-laden though they are, they are useful windows into the material world we inhabit, and no discussion that ignores the sheer *pleasure* of wielding these instruments will understand their power. Foucault's approach to knowledge helps us avoid a simple dichotomy between pure truth and abject swindling. To say that knowledge serves power is not to say it is a ruse. Still, many of my students and colleagues believe that measures like Gross Domestic Product *are* a swindle and a scandal, and it is worth asking why they believe this. A little like Foucault in the first volume of *History of Sexuality*, I want to ask *not* how a true economy came to be repressed by a false one, but how it is that we come to speak in these terms, how people come to believe they are deceived and a fairer, happier economy lies behind the visible one, how we come to overload representations of economy with cultural burdens, how we come to think of economic representation as scandalous.

Acknowledgments

Thanks to the University of Washington Bothell for making available sabbatical leaves for research, to the Political Science Department of the University of Hawai'i at Mānoa for hosting me during the first of those leaves, and to the Departments of English and Political Science at UH for hosting colloquia that gave some chapters their first airings. I have benefited from the opportunity to teach and work in a non-divisionized interdisciplinary unit, and owe much to my students, whose questioning helped me rethink what I was teaching. For help and critical support throughout this project I am deeply grateful to my partner S. Charusheela. Friends and colleagues who have provided valuable feedback include Suzanne Bergeron, Bruce Burgett, Vrinda Dalmiya, Monisha Das Gupta, Stephen Gudeman, Yahya Madra, Jon Rieder, Bill Seaburg, Eric Shultz, Glenn Willmott, and Eiman Zein-Elabdin. Gillian Murphy and Karun Adusumilli at the London School of Economics provided generous help with archival photographs. Colleagues at conferences and workshops have patiently listened to draft chapters and prodded me to do better; I want to particularly thank Kathy Ferguson and Mary King for organizing talks. I thank Tony Bennett, Penny Harvey, and Kevin Hetherington of the CRESC series, and three anonymous referees for their help shaping this book.

Introduction
Sarkozy versus GDP

Glory and mourning

Nicolas Sarkozy became President of France in May 2007. In February 2008 he formed a special "Commission on the Measurement of Economic Performance and Social Progress" co-chaired by two economists with international reputations, Amartya Sen and Joseph Stiglitz. The Commission, which delivered its final report in September 2009, described its charge as examining "the limits of GDP as an indicator of economic performance and social progress" (GDP is Gross Domestic Product, the most standard measure of national income) and proposing alternative measures (Stiglitz *et al.* 2009).

Sarkozy ran and governed as a cultural nationalist with a hard line on immigration; he is usually described as a politician of the "right." But his Commission was a cosmopolitan group whose deep interest in inequality is visible in its report. Most were not French; its twenty-two members included two prominent feminist economists. Why did Sarkozy choose *these* people, and enthusiastically endorse their work? One view is that he wanted to harness left-wing energies and ideas. Sociologist Geoffrey Pleyers (2010, p. 10) wrote that "right-wing French President Nicolas Sarkozy didn't hesitate to appropriate alterglobalization slogans." Libertarian economist Anthony de Jasay (2008) argued that because Sarkozy realized he could not redeem campaign promises of 3 percent GDP growth, he "invited the two most prominent economists of the worldwide Left, Amartya Sen and Joseph Stiglitz" to design measures that would make him look better. Stiglitz himself (Press 2011) contended that "the fact that two governments of the right – Sarkozy and [UK Prime Minister] Cameron – have embraced [the report] so strongly and yet it's an agenda that has been advocated most vociferously by the center-left suggests it has broad appeal." Stiglitz, Pleyers, and de Jasay all ignore Sarkozy's nationalism, and understand him as an opportunistic right-wing politician grabbing popular left-wing ideas. I propose an alternative interpretation.

As a government minister under Jacques Chirac, Sarkozy developed an aggressively nationalist profile, supporting limits on immigration and requirements that immigrants acculturate (Thomas 2013, pp. 59–88). Part of this stance was an ardent defense of France's colonial past. In a February 2007 campaign speech in Toulon, Sarkozy eulogized the "Mediterranean dream" that "once sent knights from all of Europe down the roads of the Orient … a dream shared by Bonaparte in Egypt, Napoleon III in Algeria, Lyautey in Morocco." He acknowledged "crimes and injustices" but insisted that "most of those who headed south were neither monsters nor exploiters" but builders, farmers, healers, teachers. He then turned to his central point:

> We must stop blackening the past…. I would like to say to all the adepts of repentance, who rewrite history and judge yesterday's men without acknowledging the conditions in which they lived and the challenges they faced, I would like to ask them: by what right do you judge them? I want to say to them: by what right do you ask sons to repent for the faults of their fathers, for sins that were committed often only in your imagination?
>
> (Mbembe 2011, pp. 107–108)[1]

The speech – delivered in a city with a large population of French colonists who fled Algeria after Algerian independence in 1962 – went on to re-affirm France's "moral debt" to those colonists. Sarkozy was inserting himself in a national debate about French responsibility for colonial abuses, especially in Algeria.[2] His rebuke of "adepts of repentance," who appear to include academic historians, was a recurring theme of the 2007 campaign. Sarkozy addressed his French supporters as people whose good will and suffering had been disdained by knowledge-making elites, a failure of recognition that denied them not only pride in their achievements, but the chance to mourn their losses.

Discourse in Dakar

Soon after his election, Sarkozy delivered a speech in Dakar that expanded on these themes. Though ostensibly addressed to young Africans, his audience was clearly French (Shohat and Stam 2012, p. 247). Sarkozy repeated the themes of his campaign addresses, balancing acknowledgment of colonial pillage with claims about the hard work, sincerity, and "civilizing mission" of many colonizers.

During the Dakar address Sarkozy set out an explicitly modernist framework, which is to say he embraced the ideas that (a) human history moves from the traditionalist past to the modern future, and (b) the world is divided into discrete nations, which are at different positions on the track from traditional to modern. It will be a central contention of this book that this framework supports *both* an optimistically modernizing *and* a nostalgically traditionalist discourse, and that each discourse requires the other. Sarkozy demonstrated this. On the one hand he spoke from the position of a "European civilization" that offered reason, science, democracy, and justice to an "African civilization" that lacked those things. This is the rationalist, modernizing mode. But on the other hand, Sarkozy slid easily into romantic praise for tradition:

It is by drawing from the African imaginary world that your ancestors have left you, it is by drawing from their stories, their proverbs, their mythologies, their rites, by drawing from all these forms that, since the dawn of time were transmitted to and enriched generation after generation, that you will find the imagination and the power to invent a future for you.

(Gielis 2014, p. 87)[3]

Here are echoes of romantic thinkers like Johann Herder and Samuel Taylor Coleridge. This led Sarkozy to the standard romantic lament about the burden of modernity for the fully modern:

I have come to tell you that you don't have to be ashamed of the values of African civilisation, that they do not drag you down but elevate you, that they are an antidote to the materialism and the individualism that enslave modern man, that they are the most precious of legacies against the dehumanisation and the "uniformisation" of the world of today.

(Gielis 2014, p. 87)

This illustrates a point that will be argued in later chapters: in the twentieth century "alienation," "dehumanization," "uniformization," "consumer society," and so forth function as a convenient grievance, a way for the prosperous to feel sorry for themselves. To be fully "modern" is to be able to lament one's own modernity, and claim a psychic wound from one's loss of the "traditional." The "traditional" is modernity's pet self-critique. There follows the best-known part of the speech:

The tragedy of Africa is that the African has not fully entered into history. The African peasant, who for thousands of years have lived according to the seasons, whose life ideal was to be in harmony with nature, only knew the eternal renewal of time, rhythmed by the endless repetition of the same gestures and the same words.

(Gielis 2014, p. 88)

He continued in this vein at some length. Sarkozy therefore embraced with neither hesitation nor irony a high modernist theory of history, featuring an immobile traditional past rich with stories, myths, and rites, and an uneasy modernity that is wealthy, rational, and progressive but nonetheless suffers from its materialism and individualism. It is here that the connection to economy comes into view.

Purchasing power

The distinction Sarkozy made between "civilizations" guided not only his view of Africa but also his policy on immigration. He argued forcefully that immigrants (in particular Muslim immigrants) represented an alien civilization, that they were a burden on the state and a threat to French jobs.[4] French jobs, especially rural and artisanal jobs, represented not just a paycheck but essential French subcultures (Sarkozy 2007a). Agriculture, for example, was more than raising crops: "France has an almost carnal relationship to its agriculture ... the word 'land' has a special significance in France."[5] Repeatedly, Sarkozy invested elements of the French "economy" – labor, production, consumption – with national culture and values, and segued to the argument that anything that threatened part of the French economy threatened the distinct culture of the nation. Economy was the nation's vulnerable body.

During his campaign Sarkozy promised to be the "president of purchasing power." The phrase "purchasing power" (*pouvoir d'achat*) functioned as a technical reference to what economists call "real income," but also as a metaphor for what the French people were entitled to and had lost. During the campaign Sarkozy accused the official French statistical agency INSEE of underestimating inflation, and his language sharpened once he took office: in November 2007 he charged that the French were being "told nonsense" (*racontait des fariboles*) about inflation.[6] INSEE stood accused of failing to respect and reflect the economic distress of the French people. This bears comparison with his rebuke, quoted above, to "adepts of repentance, who rewrite history" of colonialism. The common thread is resentment toward authoritative accounts that refuse to salve the wounds of nationalism.[7] Revisionist histories of colonialism dishonor the grandeur of the colonial enterprise, thus denying nationalists the ability to mourn it properly. Official economic statistics fail to show what is special about the French economy, *and* fail to highlight the distress of ordinary French people. These speeches show a "structure of feeling," to borrow Raymond Williams' concept, in which scholarly or technical precision is felt as insulting because it reflects neither glory nor loss (Williams 1977, p. 132). I will return to this point later in the book: romantic nationalism functions allegorically; efforts to nail facts to the nation puncture the ambiguities nationalism needs.

This was the context in which, in early 2008, Sarkozy recruited a group of internationally luminous economists for a special "Commission on the Measurement of Economic Performance and Social Progress." I will say something below about the content of the report they wrote, but to keep the focus on Sarkozy for now, I want to emphasize the continuity between his earlier statements and his public reception of the economists' document. Sarkozy delivered a speech in Fall 2009 upon the release of the report, which also appears as a foreword to a condensed version published in English under the title *Mismeasuring Our Lives: Why GDP Doesn't Add Up.*[8] In the speech he emphasizes the "gulf of incomprehension between the expert certain in his knowledge and the citizen whose experience of life is completely out of synch with the story told by the data."

> In February 2008, I felt the urgent need to do away with the set ideas and dogmas that had locked in all our thinking and action, and that were making us lie to ourselves. I felt the urgent need to stop giving the response to all

those voicing their troubles, difficulties, suffering, doubts, and anxieties: "You are wrong: our statistics prove the contrary."

(Stiglitz *et al.* 2010, pp. x–xi)

This suggests that published data should show more suffering and *less well-being* than they do. But Sarkozy also argues:

If we refer to a representation of the world in which the services people render within a family have no value compared with those we can obtain on the market, we are expressing an idea of civilization in which the family no longer counts for much. Who could imagine that this won't have consequences?

If leisure has no accounting value because it is essentially filled with non-market activities such as sports and culture, this means that we are putting the criterion of high productivity above that of the realization of human potential, contrary to the humanist values that we proclaim. Who could imagine that this won't have consequences?

(Stiglitz *et al.* 2010, p. xiii)

These critiques suggest that published figures should show *more well-being* than they do.[9] This is not a disabling contradiction! Instead it points to a deeper disquiet with statistics and representation. And indeed Sarkozy carefully *theorizes* this disquiet. He argues that the essential social project is collective, and therefore the way the collective perceives itself matters:

the commission … is clearly reflecting on the conception we have of what we call civilization, the basis on which we are going to judge what we accomplish.

(Stiglitz *et al.* 2010, p. xiii)

"Civilization" is a keyword for Sarkozy, functioning as a general term but also, always, as shorthand for *French* civilization. It follows that:

The kind of civilization we build depends on the way we do our accounts quite simply because it changes the value we put on things. And I'm not speaking just about market value …

The market gives us valuable information. But a project for society or for civilization cannot be built based solely on the market. A project for civilization is born out of a collective will, a collective effort over the long term. It is not the fruit of the instantaneous confrontation of supply and demand.

(Stiglitz *et al.* 2010, pp. xiii–xiv)

Here Sarkozy distinguishes between two kinds of information: the price information that markets provide, and the *national* civilizational values that, he contends, official representations ought to re-affirm and reflect back to the populace.

The "we" evoked by Sarkozy can only keep our civilization if we perceive it, and so its values must be reflected in our common representations. Romantic thinkers like Coleridge and Ruskin would approve. Like Sarkozy, these thinkers were aware of the economist's argument that prices convey useful information to buyers and sellers. But in their view that was trivial information solving a trivial problem. For them, as for Sarkozy, the more important problem was the community's ability to see itself in shared representation.

This is how GDP ends up accused, not just of being abstruse or inaccurate, but of malign deception, of "making us lie to ourselves." Sarkozy's argument is about representation and knowledge: if culture functions through signs, then the wrong signs are dangerous. Representations of the "*national* economy" should properly represent the nation. Trivial technicalities and philistine technicians have usurped the place of moral and civilizational discourse.

Seeing like a state[10]

It is not difficult, then, to work out why Sarkozy wanted an economists' document critical of national income statistics. What of the economists? Their work certainly cannot be called national*ist*. Their report's introduction notes that it "is not focused on France, nor on developed countries" and affirms that the Commission was given complete independence in its work (Stiglitz *et al.* 2010, p. xviii). Its discussion of the limits of GDP is measured, technical, and in line with six decades of academic writing on that subject. Most of the work of the document is a discussion of measures of "quality of life" and "sustainable development and the environment."

The economists' document does, however, have a relentlessly *national* focus in the sense that it assumes a world divided into discrete nations, and assumes that its advice is directed to national politicians and technocrats. There is, for example, no discussion of ways balance of payments data might bring remittances and other cross-border transactions into better view. While immigrants are mentioned a few times, they figure as contributors to social and economic inequality within the nation, and people lacking a political voice in the nation (Stiglitz *et al.* 2009, pp. 15, 50). The Commission members assume a world made up of governments, citizens, and national polities and economies, all neatly lined up.

During 2009 and 2010, despite widespread criticism across Europe, Sarkozy ordered French police to arrest and deport more than 10,000 Roma, people also known as Romani or Gypsies.[11] What are the statistics appropriate for measuring the well-being of Roma, more than ten million of whom live across Europe (Judah 2010)? Should those measures be national?[12] The populist critique Sarkozy articulates, that GDP does not adequately express national truth, forecloses questioning of this kind. The Roma lack commissions of prominent economists. The question in which Sarkozy enlisted the economists is: how can a national government hold up a better mirror to its people, its citizens? The Roma fell outside that question.

We are thus confined to a quintessentially modernist debate, holding the national unit sacred, committed to the idea that the world is divided into discrete social units that are closer to or farther from full modernity, and confining itself to a stereotyped back-and-forth between (rationalist) modernizationists and (romantic) traditionalists. The back-and-forth works for everyone: rationalist economists get to create new measures; romantic traditionalists get to keep their permanent grievance against economists; politicians get to empathize with suffering citizens. These performances license both earnestness and cynicism about statistical representation.

The encounter between Sarkozy and the economists, therefore, had little to do with "left" or "right." It was built on a shared commitment to the nation as a unit, to the idea that culture, polity, and economy line up in discrete national units, and that individual well-being is a problem with national origins and national solutions. The shared commitment allowed each to play a role in a stock modernist drama of tradition versus modernization. The expelled Roma are invisible to both wings of modernity: they figure neither in the traditionalist narrative of French civilization, nor in the modernizationist vision of a world composed of rationalized, compartmentalized, national societies.

I have tried to explain why economic statistics made such a convenient foil for Sarkozy, and why his resentful nationalism meshed so readily with anti-globalization discourse. We might ask further:

- What explains the economists' dedication to the unit of the nation, especially when it comes to generating data?
- What are the underlying connections between Sarkozy's nationalism and the Commission's technocratic cosmopolitanism? Why, for example, does a certain rhetoric about gender and family move so easily across both discourses?
- What is the relation between GDP and colonialism?

In this book I undertake a dual genealogy, working out the sources of both Sarkozy's and the Commission's discourses, and demonstrating the modernist frame that unites them. The argument in brief:

1 Modernity is not *just* the doctrine that human societies tend to move from solidaristic, locally rooted tradition to individualist, functionally divided modern society. It is *also* a stylized ritual combat between two variants of this story, the rationalist and the romantic. Ideas about economy have played key roles in the shared doctrine, and in the ritual combat between its two variants.
2 Central to the shared doctrine is heavy emphasis on the nation and the national scale. Both camps assume correspondence between the social organization of the nation and the psychological organization of its individual members. This emphasis produces a thin and socially evacuated conception of the global, understood as a space of pure flows.[13]

3   This structure has guided the development of economic statistics and the participation of those statistics in claims to nationhood. The statistics in turn make nations, and a world composed of national compartments, appear obvious. A theory of scale is written in to the numbers at a very basic level. (This does not mean the numbers are wrong, but it does mean they enable some projects and thwart others.)

4   This structure has licensed international organizations, in particular the IMF, to invest the thin space of the international with its own spirit. That spirit has been variously named the "world economy," "global capitalism," "international finance," and "neoliberalism." This is a consequence of the way modernists imagine scale.

5   Because it is an integral part of this modernist framework, neo-romantic anti-capitalist and anti-globalization writings *reinforce* these underlying conceptions of scale and agency, and credulously accept the IMF's view of the world.

6   Modernity is a particular and historically specific power-knowledge complex, and like any such complex, capable of producing powerful knowledge. But when it is treated as the obligatory social ontology and the necessary basis for cross-disciplinary exchange, it becomes an unwarranted restriction on the study of society.

I ask you to start by thinking about material life in the broadest sense: all the ways you produce, distribute, or consume goods and services. These activities happen in varied institutional contexts. These institutional contexts include kinship networks, households, small firms, large firms, governments, and charities. Markets (competitive, oligopolistic, monopolistic, regulated, unregulated) financial systems, and legal systems enable or thwart different kinds of production, distribution, and consumption. Different kinds of institutions interpenetrate. You might get a mortgage from a bank with the help of a loan officer who is a relative's friend, or find business contacts among co-religionists.

Institutions that undergird economic activity typically exclude some people in order to include others. Kinship networks exclude non-kin, governments discriminate against non-citizens, ethnic and religious solidarities are defined against outsiders, participation in labor markets is often conditioned by how you present along such axes as class, gender, sexuality, and race. I say this both to name obvious social facts and to warn against simple ethical reductions. Kinship networks, business firms, charitable organizations, and governments are fascinating and varied institutions. They may do good or evil things. While I posit that the material world we inhabit is messier and more variegated than modernist accounts admit, I am not implying that it is therefore a nicer and cozier place.

My beef with modernity is that it reduces this shaggy social world to individuals and nations. Modernists are fascinated with the *individual's* psychology, mentality, rationality, and culture. When they recognize larger institutions like firms and households, modernists prefer to theorize them as though they were individuals. Modernists rely on the *nation* to explain how individuals came to be the way they are. The nation embodies the individual's "culture"; it guarantees and provides the rights that the individual needs to act freely; its government is called on to provide whatever individuals cannot manage.

Modernity assumes that humanity exists in discrete societies, and that such societies can be described by a simple typology: "traditional" societies are face-to-face, solidaristic, and have little functional differentiation; fully "modern" societies are impersonal, bureaucratic, exhibit sharp functional differentiation, and contain only little islands of face-to-face, personal ties in the form of nuclear families. Modernists assume that all societies start as "traditional" and then move at different speeds toward full modernity, driven either by internal dynamics or competition with other societies. They assume that more "modern" people or societies enjoy some advantage over their more "traditional" counterparts, an advantage that more or less explains history. This theory of space and time functions for adherents as a *social ontology*, which is to say something you assume *before* you begin to study society.[14]

Beyond these points of agreement, modernity divides into two sub-discourses. Both may be articulated by the same person (as we saw with Sarkozy's Dakar speech above), but theorists and academic disciplines tend to adopt one or the other. For want of better labels I call the sub-discourses *rationalist* and *romantic*. Their difference boils down to whether the modernist narrative is told as triumph or tragedy. Rationalists are unimpressed with traditional knowledge and anxious to escape obligations to kin and clan; in their view full modernity frees us to pursue our disparate ambitions.[15] Modernization theory is a good example (Latham 2003). By contrast romantics are deeply impressed with the psychological integration and deep understanding they attribute to "tradition." In the romantic view, traditional society was solidaristic and attuned to nature. Goods and services bore meanings that expressed the culture everyone shared. (While romantics might appear attuned to intermediate institutions like family and church, they treat those institutions mainly as mechanisms by which individuals are taught the single shared culture.) This leads to the second difference. While romantics and rationalists agree that their imagined "traditional" society is gone, romantics mourn it as a tragic loss. Some romantics believe there is no way out of an alienating and fragmented consumer society. Others hope that a new solidarity can replace the lost one. The most obvious example is romantic nationalism, which argues that the *nation* can re-knit frayed societies and redeem our alienated souls.

What does all this have to do with economy, Economics, or economic statistics? First, the development of "Economics" over the last two and a half centuries is central to the intellectual history I have just sketched. Rationalists and romantics fought over markets, trade, consumption, and commodification. Markets figured as the emblem of full modernity and the solvent of traditional society. Not only did economic ideas make the modernist theory of history seem plausible, but also the internal dispute between modernity's rationalist and romantic moieties spurred the elaboration of *both* a rationalist and a romantic political economy. Part of the work of this book is to demonstrate this combination of repulsion and attraction, this bad-tempered collaboration.

Second, Economics and economic statistics led the *scale-making project* of making the social world appear to fall naturally into individuals and nations, leaving an evacuated "international" scale. "Scale-making project" is a concept developed by Anna Tsing and a theoretical key for this book.[16] One of this book's central concerns is the way this modernist scaling of the world, shared by rationalists and romantics, has become so intellectually embedded. One reason to pay attention to data, to technical challenges and debates, to the fraught *crafting* of representation is that in this practical work the contingency and difficulty of scale-making becomes clear. So while this book contains a lot of intellectual history, it is not just a tour of big ideas. Numbers, as scholars like Mary Poovey (2008) remind us, have a rhetorical history. If numbers work rhetorically, they can also *not work* rhetorically. What made certain numbers persuasive at certain moments?

Third, we have been left with an academic division of labor between rationalists (powerful in Economics, Psychology, and parts of other social sciences) and neo-romantics (powerful in the humanities and interpretive social sciences). Neither moiety reads the other's work. Space for trans-disciplinary investigation of material life is limited not just by the difficulty of bringing literatures into contact, but also by the ways each relies on reductive stereotypes of the other's knowledge. Thus in Economics, orthodox and heterodox, "culture" tends to mean a single coherent set of values and ideas that a bounded group of people all subscribe to – a kind of social operating system with no internal tensions. Little space is left for cultural theory. Meanwhile in the humanities and interpretive social sciences, "economy" tends to be regarded as a coherent system operating according to a single principle, and "Economics" is treated as a completed project which, having divined the single core principle animating capitalism (individual gain), is done with its research.[17]

There are two ways, then, of describing what is at stake. One is a simple appeal to the idea of doing better social science: why make such vast presumptions about the nature of the social world, about which units matter? Modernist scaling encourages a sentimentalized approach to the spheres of family and community because it understands them as fundamentally solidaristic and loving, and downplays relations of exclusion, abjection, and violence at the micro and meso levels. Modernist scaling licenses a thin and bloodless understanding of capitalism, turning it into the trans-historical unfolding of a universal principle, rather than a series of contingent and varied developments whose nature we probably do not yet understand very well. Modernist scaling cannot *see* the nation and nationalism properly because it is too close to it, cannot see the state properly because it is too fond of seeing like a state (J. C. Scott 1999).

Another appeal is more political. Think back to the Roma, who became invisible in the Sarkozy story. The modernist answer to exclusion, abjection, and dispossession is to turn people into modern rights-bearing citizens of a modern state. This ignores the possibility that the state *itself* excludes, abjects, and dispossesses, that it is a cause of the condition it purports to cure. The world of the early twenty-first century is sharply divided according to the kind of citizenship you can claim, and a global underclass of refugees and migrants is dying by the thousands while polities in the wealthy countries turn against them. To point this out is not to reject out of hand the modernist project of turning people into modern rights-bearing citizens of modern states, but it is to suggest that it should be understood skeptically as one of many possible projects, not as the necessary course of history and only route to human flourishing.

If modernity is *not* the inevitable expression of How Things Are, but is instead a fraught and contingent knowledge-project, then its creators and developers deserve more credit than they get. I have tried to bring theorists as varied as John Ruskin, Alfred Marshall, Werner Sombart, Maynard Keynes, and Fredric Jameson into a single framework, and to highlight the technical creativity of economists like Simon Kuznets, David Horowitz, Phyllis Deane, V. K. R. V. Rao, Milton Gilbert, Richard Stone, and Jacques Polak. To displace modernity – as a peculiar scale-making project – we must appreciate it. This book aims, therefore, to contribute to the history of "modernity" ... with the proviso, again, that by "modernity" I mean simply a project whose success requires explanation.

I leave it to the introductions to the book's two main sections to do most of the chapter-by-chapter overview. The first part of this book traces the rise of rationalist economic knowledge with particular attention to ways that rationalists represented economy, and to the complex ways rationalist and romantic discourses interconnected. The second part emphasizes romantic responses to this process. Chapter 11 returns to the themes of this introduction with a few more words on what a non-modernist and trans-disciplinary Economics might look like; Chapter 12 concludes.

Notes

1 Mbembe credits the translation to Janet Roitman. Original in Sarkozy (2007a).
2 Shohat and Stam (2012, p. 247). See also Mbembe (2011) on the anxious "refusal to repent" and Nettelbeck (2009).
3 The original is in Sarzkozy (2007b) and may also be found in Gielis (2014).
4 Sarkozy's speechwriter Henri Guaino attributed the phrase "politics of civilization" to sociologist Edgar Morin (Haski 2008).
5 Quoted in Thomas (2013, p. 79).
6 Charpin (2010, p. 384). During the campaign Sarkozy's socialist opponent made the same charge. In a country with France's technical tradition (Picon 2007), this is remarkable. INSEE is the Institut National de la Statistique et des Études Économiques. See Goldhammer (2007) on Sarkozy's economic rhetoric.
7 Mbembe (2011) is especially insightful on this wounded nationalism. See also Thomas (2013) and Shohat and Stam (2012).
8 A title which presents the report as a much more aggressive critique than it is.
9 Sarkozy refashions a long-standing feminist critique of national income accounting into a nationalist critique, via the category of family.
10 J. C. Scott (1999).
11 *Economist* (2010); Fichtner (2010).
12 See Shalhoub-Kevorkian *et al.* (2014) and Tsing (1993) on other categories of people who do not fit the nation.
13 The phrase "space of flows" is due to Castells (1989); I wish, though, not to use the concept, but to put it under pressure and trace its origins.

14 Fabian (1983). For examples of the argument that modernity is a pre-condition for social science, see the symposium responses to Englund and Leach (2000).
15 I hope I can be clear that I use terms like "full modernity" or "tradition" to refer to images in an ideology, not to the actual state of the world. It remains a discursive hurdle that "modernity" is often used by adherents to mean *both* the specific assumptions described above *and* the entire thinkable social/historical horizon, a "how we are" with no conceivable outside. I follow Latour (1993) and Fabian (1983) in denying the reality of "modernity" as an historical stage and finding it counter-productive both as a category of social science and as an ethical guide.
16 Tsing (1993, 2000, 2005). Her work provides a language and theoretical context for thinking about a world that is unevenly globally connected, and a way to re-conceptualize culture and economy so they are not opposites of each other.
17 My economics is heterodox, but whatever limits my mainstream economist colleagues might be working under, this stereotype does no justice to their work either. One reason I avoid the term "neoclassical" is that it smuggles the erroneous assumption that one can deduce contemporary mainstream Economics from some small set of theoretical axioms (Lawson 2015). Much contemporary mainstream work, for example, clashes with "neoclassical" assumptions about rationality and information.

Part I
The voice of economy

Introduction to Part I

The first six chapters track the development of persuasive representations of the "national economy" and "world economy." There are three conceptual stages: (1) the splitting of human activity into "economic" and "non-economic" parts, (2) the collecting of the "economic" parts into a representable "national economy", and (3) the confecting of a "world economy" summing across those "national economies" and structuring the empty spaces between them. Each stage builds atop the previous stage and absorbs its assumptions.

Anyone can build an abstract system. What made this particular system persuasive? What got it the backing of governments and international agencies? How does a project move, in a few years, from being the hobby of a few academics to a tool of a powerful global apparatus? I have tried to surface something of the strangeness and contingency of this project, with particular attention to places like 1930s Palestine and British colonies in Africa where the "nation" of national income accounting did not yet exist.

Chapter 1 examines the economy/household distinction, with special attention to the romantic-rationalist struggle in which that distinction figured. It will be a central argument when we get to the second part of the book that this initial struggle remains embedded in contemporary discourses about economy. Chapter 2 examines a fascinating pre-WWII case, in which both romantic and rationalist tropes figured in the statistical construction of a Jewish economy in British-ruled Palestine. Chapters 3 and 4 bring the focus to Keynes and Britain, and aim at a non-technical exposition of some core features of the Keynesian macro framework, and the way those features in turn shaped postwar representations of the "national" and "international" economies. Chapter 5 examines the working out of these ideas in British colonies in Africa, a project important to the globalization of national income accounting.

Chapter 6 turns to the International Monetary Fund and its use of these understandings of national and international economy. Its drama centers on the IMF's death and rebirth in the 1970s, which transformed it from an obscure technical agency to an ambitious promoter of a new understanding of the international economy.

For reasons of narrative compactness I follow the thread of the development and generalization of national income accounting, and its persuasiveness as a representation of the nation. I will have relatively little to say about academic Economics or economic theory. My interest is in the technical and the representational, and in the moments when this became fraught or difficult, when choices had to be made and skeptics persuaded. Foucault and his legatees have perhaps been too ready to read "Economics" ideologically, too attracted to marquee theorists like Bentham, Hayek, and Becker, too bored by workaday Economics.[1] In the Foucauldian literature on medicine and psychiatry, for example, we are used to the idea that routine technical practice mattered. It is this focus that I want to extend.

Note

1 Tellmann (2009) offers an insightful explanation of this gap.

1   Love or money

Overview

This chapter tracks the breakdown of Adam Smith's unitary vision of social life into a split between household and business, and its implications for measurement. The next two chapters will examine the way the split-off "economic" parts were gathered and shaped into a standardized "national economy."

The household/business split was strongly affected by the romantic reaction to the Enlightenment. Adam Smith (1723–1790), in good Enlightenment fashion, developed a holistic theory that did not hive economy off from the rest of society. Romantic critics found this work tediously dry, lacking in religious faith and feeling, patriotism, and national culture. The rise of modernity over the nineteenth century can be thought of as a breakdown of the Enlightenment project, its partial dissolution into rationalist and romantic streams.

Unable or unwilling to carry on Smith's holist project, John Stuart Mill (1806–1873) fenced off a limited "business" sphere for the new science of political economy. In this limited sphere many of Smith's analytical insights could be preserved and extended, even if his larger vision was discarded. This can be interpreted as a retreat, but we can just as easily argue that Mill took advantage of the romantics' pugnacity to re-found political economy on narrower and easier ground. In any case, the twentieth century was bequeathed a sentimental division between a loving and self-sacrificing household sphere, and a competitive and rational business sphere. For twentieth-century modernists this division became not just a background assumption, but an imperative: once you accepted household/business as an essential divide, as a condition of civilization, then you had to take care lest either compartment contaminate the other.

The exclusion of housework from contemporary measures of national output is often regarded as a scandal. What this chapter shows is that this exclusion – scandalous or not – is baked into the cake. The exclusion of love is the *constitutive* taboo upon which a visible "economy" has been brought into being.

Smith, Coleridge, Mill

In his 1759 *Theory of Moral Sentiments* (1976), Adam Smith worked out a psychology based on sympathy. Socialized humans judged the actions of others, and learned that others judged their behavior. As they came to understand this interplay of assessment, people developed a deep and abiding *interest* in behaving in ways others would find admirable. The result was a Stoic ethics updated for the eighteenth century, stressing dignity and self-restraint.[1] Smith's 1776 *Wealth of Nations* (1979) thinks within that ethical system. Smith is routinely quoted about appealing to the self-love of "the butcher, the brewer, or the baker" to get our dinner, but the less-recognized context of that quotation is the contrast Smith was drawing between commerce and begging. Begging embarrasses everyone. *Commercial* transactions are ethically better because both parties keep their dignity. For Smith the "other" of commerce is feudal servility (and feudal generosity). So, assuming as Smith did that people are already well socialized, "self-love" lets people manage their own affairs without unduly troubling others (Muller 1995). Whether or not you find this ethical vision persuasive, for our purposes the important fact is that Smith developed a *single* psychological theory to explain people's actions across all spheres of life. He proposed no *separate* market psychology. In Stoic fashion Smith approached wealth, trade, and production as integral parts of a single social and natural order.[2]

The Enlightenment crested with Kant. The European romantic movement that rose after and against it was too disparate (and too romantic) to be easily summarized, but it gathered force from recrudescent nationalism, from religious revivals, from unease over commerce and fashion, and from alarm over the social, moral, and aesthetic effects of the industrial revolution. (Chapter 7 discusses romantic political economy as a positive doctrine.) In Britain it was given particular force by nationalism kindled by the Napoleonic Wars. Poets like William Wordsworth (1770–1850) and Samuel Taylor Coleridge (1772–1834) foreswore their youthful cosmopolitanism for zealous patriotism. They had little patience for Smith and his followers. "What solemn humbug this modern political economy is!" wrote Coleridge in 1833. In a passage that epitomizes romantic political economy, he continued:

> You talk about making this article cheaper by reducing its price in the market from *8d.* to *6d.* But suppose, in so doing, you have rendered your country weaker against a foreign foe; suppose you have demoralized thousands of your fellow-countrymen, and have sown discontent between one class of society and another, your article is tolerably dear, I take it, after all. Is not its real price enhanced to every Christian and patriot a hundred-fold?
>
> (Coleridge 1884, pp. 186–187)

Unfettered markets encourage strife between people and between classes within a nation, dividing people and classes who should be united in common purpose by patriotism, religion, and national culture. This was the standard nineteenth-century romantic critique: self-interest undermines national interest. Smith wanted to build community *out* of carefully tuned self-interest; romantics thought self-interest was community's nemesis.

Smith's key nineteenth-century successor was John Stuart Mill (1806–1873), whose 1844 *Principles of Political Economy* sought to update and systematize *Wealth of Nations*. In the 1830s and 1840s, Mill staked out a defensive position against romantic criticism of political economy. In an essay published in 1836, he wrote that

> "Political Economy" … does not treat of the whole of man's nature as modified by the social state, nor of the whole conduct of man in society. It is concerned with him solely as a being who desires to possess wealth, and who is capable of judging of the comparative efficacy of means for obtaining that end. It predicts only such of the phenomena of the social state as take place in consequence of the pursuit of wealth. With respect to those parts of human conduct of which wealth is not even the principal object, to these Political Economy does not pretend that its conclusions are applicable.
>
> (Mill 1948, pp. 137–138)

With these words Mill abandoned Smith's project of a single psychological theory explaining all human action, and re-founded political economy on a crude and narrow psychological ground ("solely as a being who desires to possess wealth") that Smith would have emphatically rejected.[3] Mill's rhetoric cleverly *appropriated* the romantic critique of political economy. Rather than fight the romantics Mill cheerfully conceded their central charge, that political economy assumes selfishness, and used that concession to clear a space in which his science could flourish.

In other words, several moves were open to Mill. He might have tried to rescue Smith's late-Enlightenment effort to build a single comprehensive social theory (something which, broadly speaking, both Malthus and Marx attempted).[4] Alternatively Mill could have abandoned that project completely, and joined the romantics in working everything out from tradition and national culture. Instead he split the baby in half, and thereby became a founding father of modernity.

In an 1840 essay on Coleridge, Mill wrote that Coleridge's thought "expresses the revolt of the human mind against the philosophy of the eighteenth century" (which would include Smith) (Mill 2006, p. 125). He went on to praise Coleridge at length for his insights into national culture, national character, patriotism, religion, reverence, and feeling. Then Mill's tone turned:

> In the details of Coleridge's political opinions there is much good, and much that is questionable or worse. In political economy especially he writes like an arrant driveller, and it would have been well for his reputation had he never meddled with the subject.
>
> (Mill 2006, p. 155)

This was an unwarranted affront. By the standards of the early nineteenth century Coleridge's writings on economic questions were perfectly creditable. They show a capacity for analysis and an ability to make distinctions and follow complex arguments.[5] Though by no means a first-rank economist, Coleridge was hardly a "driveller," and his economic writings rank no lower in coherence, clarity, or reference to evidence than the political and cultural writings Mill so generously praised.

Mill, therefore, responded to the romantic assault on political economy not by joining it, and not by rejecting it, but by opening the modernist split: a society divided into separate compartments with distinct rationalities and distinct sciences. The combination of generous praise and condescending dismissal of Coleridge marked a new boundary.

Marshall

Mill's most important successor as a field-defining political economist was Alfred Marshall (1842–1924). His *Principles of Economics* was first published in 1890 and went through eight editions, the last in 1920. Marshall kept Mill's assumption that the sphere of "economy" was split off from other parts of life on psychological grounds – by people's intentions and states of mind. But he made several new moves.

First, Marshall *historicized* the splitting-away of economy from other parts of life. Primitive society, he argued, had been divided between one's own community, to whom one had duties and obligations, and strangers, to whom one was hostile.[6] Modernity, in his view, put an end to hostility toward strangers, and at the same time split community between neighbors and close family (Figure 1.1).

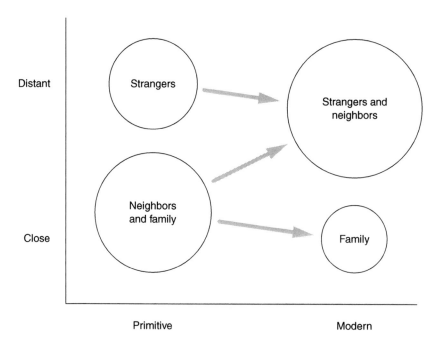

Figure 1.1 Marshall's history.

Following this historical "emancipation from custom," neighbors joined strangers in a new sphere in which "modern industrial life" could flourish, with its characteristic mentality:

> the fundamental characteristics of modern industrial life ... are ... a certain independence and habit of choosing one's own course for oneself, a self-reliance; a deliberation and yet a promptness of choice and judgment, and a habit of forecasting the future and of shaping one's course with reference to distant aims.... It is deliberateness, and not selfishness, that is the characteristic of the modern age.
>
> (Marshall 1949, p. 5)

Arguing that competition was a "secondary" and "accidental consequence" of this shift, Marshall proposed "constant forethought and restless enterprise" as the animating spirits of industrial life, which are surely more attractive qualities than the mere greed of Mill's "being who desires to possess wealth." But the real genius of Marshall's reformulation was his treatment of the modern family.

> In a modern society the obligations of family kindness become more intense, though they are concentrated on a narrower area; and neighbours are put more nearly on the same footing with strangers. In ordinary dealings with both of them the standard of fairness and honesty is lower than in some of the dealings of a primitive people with their neighbours: but it is much higher than in their dealings with strangers. Thus it is the ties of neighbourhood alone that have been relaxed: the ties of family are in many ways stronger than before, family affection leads to much more self-sacrifice and devotion than it used to do.
>
> (Marshall 1949, p. 5)

The modern age, said Marshall, is kinder and gentler *because* it has split the sphere of market and economy away from the sphere of devotion and love. He emphasized this with a swipe at the romantics:

> In every age poets and social reformers have tried to stimulate the people of their own time to a nobler life by enchanting stories of the virtues of the heroes of old. But neither the records of history nor the contemporary observation of backward races, when carefully studied, give any support to the doctrine that man is on the whole harder and harsher than he was.
>
> (Marshall 1949, p. 5)

The modern re-arrangement of society (Figure 1.1) supports not one but two kinds of virtuous activity: thoughtful planning in businesses, and loving self-sacrifice in families. Marshall supplements this with the further claim that only a modern society is capable of large-scale charity.[7] The modern society plans better and loves better. This is both an ethical theory and a spatial theory: the moral excellence of family depends on scaling it down to a private, interior "narrower area." This scaling-down clears out the larger scale, neighbors and strangers, in which economy will operate.

What had changed in the half-century between Mill's 1844 *Principles* and Marshall's 1890 *Principles*? Marshall presented a more sophisticated and confident response to the romantics. Instead of conceding loyalty and love, Marshall argued that the romantics were wrong about *both* the household and business spheres. And rather than conceding that the business sphere was governed by the selfish desire for wealth, Marshall contended that the core principle of business was thoughtful and deliberate rationality.

Marshall thus made no effort to revive Smithian holism. He accepted the modernist ideal of a society divided into separate compartments with distinct motivations. He accepted the romantics' view that some large change had occurred to move society from "traditional" to "modern," though he rejected the romantics' ethical valuation of that change. He accepted the romantic emphasis on feeling and sentiment, defining, like Mill, "economic" acts by the states of mind motivating them. What is new in Marshall is the argument that *both* rationalities are ethically valuable, *and* that each must be quarantined from each other. It is only via the modernist split, in Marshall's view, that devoted love *and* rational "deliberateness" could emerge, each on its proper scale.

Marshall mapped this split onto gender, and opposed women's paid employment. He believed women should be specialists in love: they should work within the home, as sisters, wives, and mothers, to educate and succor men.[8] On those grounds Marshall played a leading role in the defeat, in 1896, of a proposal to allow women to earn degrees at Cambridge University (Keynes 1956, p. 55). Marshall's advocacy of a gender division of labor did *not* rest on what we would now call a biological argument, that women were ill-equipped for non-household roles. Quite the contrary. Marshall mobilized to thwart the education of women *because* he recognized the possibility of mingling gender roles.[9] The militancy of Marshall's gender politics shows that his modernity was a project, and not just an interpretive schema.

From theory to measurement

We now move from theorizing an economy to measuring one. I will not provide a general history of efforts to measure national income, which go back into the 1600s.[10] But I want to highlight one historical point. In the early decades of the twentieth century dozens of researchers in different parts of the world were working on measuring national income. Almost all these researchers were individual scholars without state backing, and in consequence there was a rich range of definitions and methods. Many early twentieth-century scholars were interested in measuring housework. A 1942 survey by Arthur Bowley (1869–1957), the pre-eminent English scholar of national accounting in the early twentieth century, found a field more or less evenly split over the merits of including housework in national income.[11] Everyone appears to have agreed that the volume of domestic services was quite large: Lindahl's estimates for Sweden, for example, showed unpaid domestic work adding 20 to 25 percent to total estimates of national output. Disagreements do not seem to have hinged on the *technical* feasibility of imputing a monetized value for this output.

So it is puzzling to find Simon Kuznets writing in 1933 that "there is general agreement among students of the problem as to the exclusion of housewives' services and services of other members of the family, in spite of the very large size of the items involved" and repeating this misrepresentation of the literature in 1946.[12] It is surprising to find Milton Gilbert writing in a 1955 review that "I violently disagree, as I have argued elsewhere, that housewives' general services of cooking, cleaning, child bearing, child-minding and the like should be considered economic activity" (Gilbert 1955). What explains the selective reading by Kuznets, who was usually a careful scholar? What explains Gilbert's "violently"?

The explanation I offer is that these were ideological, boundary-policing responses. These economists were operating from the same ethical and social template as Marshall, in which the exclusion of the loving household made economy possible and conceptualizable. In different language, the taboo on housework was a *productive* taboo, because it licensed a particular vision of economy: large-scale, rational, and impersonal. Hence any suggestion of including housework in the measured economy had to be ruled out.

I turn next to a few of the figures involved in developing this concept of measurable economy, and return at the end of the chapter to the larger modernist structure of thought.

Kuznets

Simon Kuznets (1901–1985) was born in Russia and emigrated to the United States in 1922, where he studied under leading institutionalist economist Wesley Clair Mitchell (1874–1948). In 1927, Kuznets joined the National Bureau of Economic Research (NBER), which was a private think-tank founded in 1920, headed by Mitchell, and dedicated to empirical research.[13] When in 1931 the U.S. government sought data to guide policy during the Great Depression, it called on NBER expertise. Kuznets, already working on a study of U.S. national income, joined the Commerce Department from 1934 to 1936 and produced the first official estimates of U.S. national income.

Kuznets and Mitchell shared Marshall's modernism.[14] Kuznets wrote:

> The modern economic system consists of individual units whose basic purpose is to make a living; of purely business units whose main aim is the making of profits; and of social organizations whose primary purpose is to render service to society as a whole. Each of these groups contributes differently to the sum total of commodities produced and distributed, is motivated by forces of quite different nature and involves a different approach to income as an appraisal concept.
>
> (Kuznets 1933, p. 205)

But Kuznets and Mitchell differed from Marshall in one important way. They belonged to the U.S. "institutionalist" school, which had been influenced by the German "historical school" and thus by romantic nationalism. Institutionalists retained Herder's relativism (see Chapter 7), which is to say his emphasis on the difference, to the point of incommensurability, of different nations. They rejected efforts by British political economists to *deductively* work Economics out from universal first principles, preferring, inductively, to start from close observation and historical study of particular places. Mitchell and Kuznets were still modernist to the core, but they understood the modernity of the early twentieth century U.S. economy as a *particular historical fact*, a fact that licensed the construction of data in a particular way about that economy.[15]

This divergence would produce, a decade and a half later, one of the key dramas of national income accounting. It was the U.S. institutionalists' close, dedicated commitment to fact gathering that made them pioneers in national income statistics. Kuznets and his colleagues developed a high level of technical acumen and deep familiarity with data sources. Routine publication nurtured an expert U.S. audience for their work.[16] This was without parallel anywhere else in the world.[17] But on the other hand, the relativist zeal for unearthing the *particular* facts and *particular* institutional workings of a *particular* country made Kuznets' project a poor candidate for generalization across the world. As Perlman puts it, "Kuznets' blueprint did not begin to offer a well-knit theoretical system," while Keynes did (Perlman 1996, p. 214). Kuznets' successors in government service defected to Keynes' system during WWII. Kuznets did not simply lack a system: he was opposed on institutionalist grounds to systems, opposed to abstract and mobile theory.[18]

Today the terms "quantitative" and "mathematical" are sometimes used interchangeably, but economists in the early twentieth century knew the difference. The British political economy tradition, including Ricardo, Marshall, and Keynes, was mathematical in that it used deductive reasoning from first principles to build theory. Data-gathering played a minor role. Marshall defined national income and wealth in *Principles*, but made no effort to measure them. The German "historicist" and U.S. "institutionalist" traditions, by contrast, were quantitative in that they were committed to building theory out of locally gathered facts (Coats 1992, p. 331).

Kuznets' institutionalist commitments were evident in his caution against extending measures of national income across different economies. "Highly developed" economies were characterized by a sharp break between the business and household sectors. However:

> To draw a line between economic activity and economic goods on the one hand and active life and its stream of satisfactions is more difficult the greater the diversity of social experience for which the distinction is said to be valid. It would not be easy to formulate a distinction that would be valid for both the primitive tribes in the wildernesses of Africa and South America

and the nations of North America and Western Europe; or for the institutional settings of European Society in both the tenth and twentieth centuries.

(Kuznets 1941, p. 7)

For Kuznets this split was a fundamental institutional fact about the U.S. economy, and therefore *underlay* any effort to measure it.[19] On this basis he endorsed "the exclusion of housewives' services" because "these activities are motivated largely by non-economic considerations and form much more a part of life in general than of professional economic life proper" (Kuznets 1933, p. 209).[20]

But the household was not forgotten. On the contrary, Kuznets understood the "economy" as a thing standing *outside* households *in order* to provide households a flow of good and useful things. It was this flow of good and useful things *to* households that he wanted to measure. Was the flow adequate? The immediate predecessor to Kuznets' work was a tradition of inquiries from the late 1800s into the well-being of working-class U.S. families, driven by concerns about poverty among a growing urban working class (Desrosières 2003). Such work was thus directly concerned with measuring things like the food and housing households could afford. National income, in Kuznets' view, blew this welfare-measuring project up to a national scale (Perlman 1996, pp. 209–212). The focus on measuring the stream of good things to households led Kuznets, for example, to reject measuring the output of criminal enterprises, on the grounds that their illegality was a societal judgment of the badness of their output. The excluded household, therefore, stood outside the "economy" *in order* to provide the ethical standpoint from which to measure it.

The moral logic of this "welfare approach" to national income led to deeper reflections:

> All the gigantic outlays on our urban civilization, subways, expensive housing, etc., which in our usual estimates we include at the value of the net product they yield on the market, do not really represent net services to the individuals comprising the nation but are, from their viewpoint, an evil necessary in order to be able to make a living (i.e., they are largely business expenses rather than living expenses). Obviously the removal of such items from national income estimates, difficult as it would be, would make national income totals much better gauges of the volume of services produced, for comparison among years and among nations.
>
> (Kuznets 1937, p. 37)

We can see in this oft-quoted passage both the strength of Kuznets' commitment to ethical underpinnings for measures of national income, and some of the limitations that led to his defeat by the Keynesians. The list of "evil[s] necessary ... to make a living" is potentially very long, if it includes everything we do that helps us hold a job.[21] A wide range of household production and services, including the production of the next generation of workers, could be construed as functional for businesses, a point that was later pursued by feminist economists.[22] A tight focus on benefits to households also meant that activities like capital investment by firms, or all kinds of spending by government, became visible in a Kuznetsian welfare approach only if their benefits to households could be directly perceived.

Finally, though this point has not been emphasized in the literature, it must have occurred to observers that Kuznets' ethical foundations, however sincerely held, were naïve. His above-noted exclusion of criminal activities assumed that there existed a common social judgment of what is good and bad, and assumed that one could read the law as a record of that judgment. Were these defensible assumptions? Ethical doctrines are vulnerable to ethical critiques. Might it be wiser to avoid the danger of ethical critique by disclaiming *any* ethical foundation?

The scarcity argument

While Kuznets' influence receded after WWII for reasons described in Chapter 4, the modernist household/business distinction remained foundational. How to sustain it? The formulation that was increasingly adopted from the 1940s onward was to assert that (a) the "economic" dealt with any activity that required choice under scarcity, and (b) household activities were not conducted under conditions of scarcity. This is a descendant of Marshall's distinction between the deliberate rationality of the economy and the generous nurturing of the home, but more austerely formalized. The best-known version of (a) was proposed by Lionel Robbins (1898–1984) in 1932, defining Economics as "the science which studies human behaviour as a relationship between ends and scarce means which have alternative uses."[23] There are no economic ends as such, but merely economic or uneconomic means of achieving ends *of any kind*. This strikingly broad formulation is hardly an obvious criterion for excluding household production – surely it is part of most people's experience that laundering, cooking, cleaning, and child-minding consume scarce time and energy.

But ideology is powerful. To take one example, V. K. R. V. Rao (1908–1991) studied at Cambridge and wrote *The National Income of British India 1931–1932* as a doctoral thesis; it was published as a book in 1940. In his introduction Rao engaged an earlier study (K. T. Shah and Khambata 1924) that had excluded *all services* from national income on several grounds, among them that "it is not logical to include some services such as those of lawyers, doctors, civil servants, etc., and exclude others such as those of wives, mothers, etc" (Rao 1940, p. 10). Rao rejected this reasoning, responding that housework was not only *guided* by non-economic motives (as Marshall and Kuznets argued), but that it could not even be *conceptualized* in terms of choices between the use of scarce resources. In the case of childcare, he said, "the mother's service is rendered free" while "the nurse will render hers only for a payment." It followed that because mothers were willing to care for children without payment, their services could not be regarded as scarce. But he adds: "It is quite conceivable, that with the growth of civilization and the feminist movement, mothers might feel that their services must be paid for" (Rao 1940, pp. 11–12). A few years later he expanded this argument:

a good deal of human activity is indulged in for its own sake and constitutes an end in itself. Take such a thing as a man's family life. When people marry or spend time with their children, they do not think in terms of economy of effort. When individuals are acquiring friendships or listening to music or appreciating a painting, it would be ridiculous to think of their being influenced by considerations of waste or economy of means. These considerations are relevant when one is thinking of activity as a means of obtaining given ends; but all human activity is not of this kind; and to the extent it is not, it has no economic aspect.

(Rao 1943, pp. 4–5)

Rao later became a leading advocate for the global generalizability of national income accounting, arguing that the modernist household/economy divide applied worldwide (Rao 1953). He will resurface in Chapter 5.

U.S. economist Milton Gilbert (1909–1979), a central figure in the postwar standardization of national income accounting, put the difference even more starkly:

The precise difference between economic and non-economic activity is not that one is useful and the other not, but that the effort spent in non-economic activity is not available for an alternative use in the economic sphere. For example, one person may spend some of his leisure knitting a garment, while another is helping his children with their school work. Neither of these activities should be included in the national product, any more than if the persons had spent the same time watching television, since whether they do one or the other does not affect the supply of scarce factors of production ... employed women are a scarce economic resource; housewives are not regardless of their indispensable contribution to society.

(Gilbert and Kravis 1954, p. 67)

The household emerges as a space of leisure, of non-work.[24] Rao's and Gilbert's descriptions of what goes on in the household sphere – leisure pursuits, art appreciation, and loving care for children – are romanticized. They are romanticized not just in the sense of idealized, but in the sense that they draw on romantic ideas of home and art as sources of happy wholeness, safe from the strife and striving of the economic world. For example Paul Studenski (1887–1961) describes "noneconomic production" thus:

In this category belong the "hobbies" of individuals, their self-services (whether in washing, dressing, shaving, eating, exercising, or what not), the services rendered by members of the family to one another on the basis of the ties that unite them, and those exchanged by neighbors on a friendly basis.

(Studenski 1958, p. 164)

This passage moves easily from dressing yourself to "ties that unite" the family to "friendly" relations with the neighbors: the non-economic, household sphere is a place of love and mutual aid. There is no conflict, no drudgery, no trouble at home. There is only a plenitude of loving help and idle pleasure.

Both Marshall and Kuznets sentimentalized households. One might expect Robbins' expulsion of the ethical from the economic to put an end to such sentiment.[25] But the result in the 1940s and 1950s was an even *more* starkly sentimentalized household than anything Marshall or Kuznets imagined.

Sentimentalized households

Why does this romantic idea about households make sense to people? In a 1979 article critiquing the anthropological literature on households, Sylvia Yanagisako demonstrated that there is no obvious or "natural" sphere of domesticity or house-holding that holds across time and space. In other words, you can find people doing specific tasks like cooking or clothes-washing or child-minding just about anywhere you look, but the ethnographic record shows a wide range of different social institutions and arrangements structuring those activities in different times and places – who cooks for whom, who minds which children, and so forth. So as a material reality, we cannot speak of "the" household as an obvious, given category. There is no universal biological substratum that generates a universal "domestic" sphere. Yanagisako showed that efforts by anthropologists to specify terms like "domestic," "household," and "family" in universal terms were tautologous, the terms typically being used to define each other.

So where does this category come from? What grounds it? In a 1987 essay, Yanagisako and Jane Collier argued that the commitment by many anthropologists and other social scientists to "the household" and "the family" as a universal category was ideological: those social scientists had a "folk model" of their own, built on an *opposition* between love and money. In this folk model:

> the production of people is thought to occur through the process of sexual procreation. Sexual procreation, in turn, is construed as possible because of the biological *difference* between men and women. The production of material goods, in contrast, is not seen as being about sex, and thus is not necessarily rooted in sexual difference, even when two sexes are involved in it.
>
> In this folk model, which informs much of the social science writing on reproduction and production, the two categories are construed as fundamentally differentiated spheres of activity that stand in means/end relation to each other. Our experience in our own society is that work in production earns money, and money is the means by which the family can be maintained and, therefore, reproduced. At the same time, the reverse holds: the family and its reproduction of people through love and sexual procreation are the means by which labor – and thus the productive system of society – is reproduced.
>
> (Collier and Yanagisako 1987, pp. 24–25, emphases in original)

Collier and Yanagisako were asking more or less the same question that I am asking in this chapter, but starting from the side of household rather than the side of economy. They question the emergence of "household" and find that it has a required opposite in economy; I question the emergence of economy and find that it has a required opposite in households. The two halves are distinguished not by the kind of work done, but by what is imagined to be in the minds of the people doing the work. The "folk theory" that Collier and Yanagisako describe corresponds fairly closely to what I am calling modernity or modernist ideology.

Collier and Yanagisako's presentation of the modernist folk model helps describe the cultural and ethical circuitry underlying the "circular flow" diagram (Figure 1.2) that I will elaborate in the coming chapters.[26]

Cut society in two, and economy springs to life between the cut halves – something like Aristophanes' theory of gender in Plato's *Symposium*. The productive part, business, is distinguished by splitting it away from households, and its output is measured as it flows back to the household sector. As we will see in Chapter 3, this foundational household/business split generates two equivalent goods/services flows: (a) factor services (labor, and the use of capital and natural resources owned by households) from households to businesses, and (b) goods and services flowing back from businesses to households. There are matching flows of payments for these things. This is the basis of contemporary concepts of national income.

The master-concept in this diagram is *complementarity*.[27] Though divided, the two halves remain in communication, each supplying what the other needs, each completing the other. Complementarity supports a heteronormative theory of gender, but it also gets us a theory of modern society characterized by two distinct linked spheres, one for money and the other for love. What Marshall, Kuznets, Rao, and Gilbert share is the story that "economy" as an object of knowledge emerges via a modernist split of home from business, a split which in turn lets us divide the world into fully modern (where the split has happened) and non-modern (where it has not yet happened).[28]

While modernists sometimes use words like "industrial" or "urban," modernity is not about steel mills or subways. It is a folk theory about mentalities. It is an assertion that there has occurred a profound shift in how some people think and act, and in how they understand themselves, their surroundings, and their opportunities. It is the people who have made this shift who are the subjects of economic science.

This folk theory has a darker side. Social policy, as it developed in many countries in the world in the late nineteenth and early twentieth centuries, increasingly insisted on *enforcing* the separation of love and money, of household and economy. The counterpart of regulation of workplaces was regulation of households, with particular and often repressive intolerance for any mingling of the two. Badly ordered households included those in which for-market production and home-making were mingled, thus breaking the tabooed separation between home and market so ethically important to modernists. In the late nineteenth century bachelor Chinese workers who slept in their shops in San Francisco found

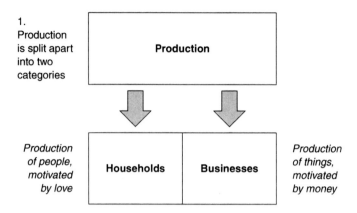

1.
Production
is split apart
into two
categories

Production

*Production
of people,
motivated
by love*

Households   Businesses

*Production
of things,
motivated
by money*

2.
The flows between these two compartments become the measure of
total output and total income.

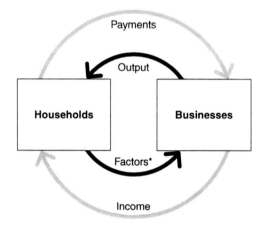

Payments

Output

Households   Businesses

Factors*

Income

*Factors of production: capital, natural resources, and labor.
The corresponding incomes are profits, rents, and wages.
In this framework households own everything businesses use,
and thus all payments for output end up as income for factor owners.

Figure 1.2 The creation of a measurable economy.

themselves accused of unfairly competing with native-born whites because they
did not *consume* enough: failing to establish (and support) separate households
and families, they worked too hard and long for too little money. By failing to
separate family and business into different sites with distinct moral principles,
went the criticism, they were doing neither love nor business properly. In the
story Nayan Shah tells in *Contagious Divides*, vigilante violence, government

regulation of housing and workplaces, and policing by social workers combined to force remaining Chinese immigrants and their descendants to enact modern domesticity, with married heteronormed couples and separate-from-work apartments and an enforced level of respectable consumption (Shah 2001; Charusheela 2010). Defining the scale of the nation, and policing its boundaries, was linked to, and dependent on, defining and policing the scale of the household. Moreover it was "economic" standards of labor and consumption that marked people as acceptable or excludable participants in the national project.

Around the turn of the twentieth century, within relatively wealthy countries, there was already developing a complex of investigation and policing of the poor to regularize their family life and make them modern subjects. Modernity has functioned as an elaborate apparatus of self-congratulation for people who think themselves modern (and can persuade the state to agree). It has simultaneously functioned to justify barriers against people who do not measure up as modern, lose the status of being fully human, and thus invite exclusion and dispossession. This is part of the story of the next chapter.

Notes

1 For a recent discussion see Forman-Barzilai (2010), whose note 16 on page 6 surveys literature on Smith and Stoicism.
2 Gallagher (2006) offers a compelling account of the how political economy got split away from natural science in the nineteenth century.
3 See Smith (1976) on Mandeville (Part VII, Chapter IV, "Of licentious systems").
4 I am asking a few key figures here to exemplify a larger and richer debate, on which please see Waterman (2003), Winch (2009), Bronk (2009), Levy (2002), and Connell (2001). Political economists neglected include Thomas Malthus (1766–1834), David Ricardo (1772–1823) and James Mill (1773–1836); among romantic critics Robert Southey (1774–1843) and Thomas Love Peacock (1785–1866) would merit attention in a fuller discussion. If we think of Malthus as trying to continue the Smithian tradition of a single broad-gauged social theory applicable across all spheres, the scandalized reaction to his theory of population likely encouraged political economists to leave family and sexuality alone. See Winch (1996) on romantic responses to Malthus.
5 See Link (1948), Connell (2001), and Kennedy (1958).
6 Marshall appears to be drawing on G. W. F. Hegel, Henry Louis Maine, and Herbert Spencer. See Cook (2009, pp. 189–226).
7 His example of charity is contributions to buy the freedom of slaves, perhaps a further swipe at pro-slavery romantics like Carlyle and Ruskin.
8 Edgeworth (1956). For further discussion of gender in Marshall see Kuiper (2001, pp. 131–147), Pujol (1998, pp. 121–143), and Groenewegen (1994).

9   It was not only in the matter of education that Marshall deprecated the identical treatment of men and women. In the most intimate of the talks … he expressed himself as opposed to current ideas which made for shaping the lives of men and women on the same model … Some loss of individual liberty, Marshall thought, should be risked for the sake of preserving the family.

(Edgeworth 1956, pp. 72–73)

10 The two essential published histories of national income accounting are Studenski (1958) and Vanoli (2005). Other noteworthy large-scale historical treatments are

Alway (2009), Mitra-Kahn (2011), Hirschman (2015), Bos (2009), and McDowall (2008). I will not survey the critical literature, but this is the place to acknowledge Marilyn Waring's (1988) pioneering critique of national income accounting. Waring has understood, perhaps more clearly than anyone, the deeply political nature of economic representation, and the way gender, race, and colonialism are embedded in economic representation.

11 He found four studies that include "domestic services rendered by wives" or argue for their inclusion, and four that exclude domestic services (Bowley 1942, p. 11). See Desrosières (1998) on Bowley's career.

12 Kuznets (1933, p. 209), and (1946). Cf. Ironmonger (1988). See also Hawrylyshyn (1976).

13 See Fogel (2000) and Fogel *et al.* (2013) on Kuznets' relation to Mitchell. On Kuznets and NBER see also Philipsen (2015), Hirschman (2015), Özgöde (2015), Carson (1975), Duncan and Shelton (1978), Kane (2012), Perlman and Marietta (2005), and Perlman (1996).

14 See W. C. Mitchell (1937).

15 See Breslau (2003) on the emergence of economy in Mitchell.

16 While he does not address this period, Holmes (2013) is invaluable for thinking about the relation between official publications and their audiences. The development of an audience stretched back to NBER's publications in the 1920s; on this see also Hirschman (2015, pp. 71–75).

17 Patinkin (1976) provides a comparative discussion of the development of U.S. and British national income estimates in the early decades of the twentieth century.

18 Speich Chassé (2011) is especially clear on this.

19 He was emphatic to the point of irritation about separating out economy in this way: "every canon of proper definition would be violated if we included almost all active life under economic activity and all its positive results under economic goods" (Kuznets 1941, p. 7). Studenski (1958, p. 178) uses similarly emphatic language.

20 See also (Kuznets 1941, p. 22) on the distinction between a household and a firm. Wood (1997) is essential reading on the production boundary, which will return in Chapter 5.

21 Wilfred Beckerman, who worked under Gilbert at the Organisation for European Economic Cooperation (OEEC), explains the implications of this argument (without naming Kuznets):

> the whole economy would be included inside the productive sector. Even the household sector would be included, since it would be simply one more industry converting inputs of food, clothing, shelter, and recreation and so on, into another intermediate product, labour, which would be inputs into other productive sectors.
>
> (Beckerman 1968, pp. 27–28)

You can think of different national income accounting schemes as different partitionings of a common, underlying, highly detailed input-output matrix. It then becomes clear why you need a separate household sector in order to generate a *single* measurable flow that you can call national output. In other words the cultural condition (a love/money split) is also a mathematical condition.

22 See Elson (1993, 1995), Grown *et al.* (2000), Walters (1995).

23 Robbins (1932). He claimed that it was only after someone else specified the ends that economists could find the means to achieve them efficiently. He thus abandoned Marshall's effort to put an ethical foundation under Economics. In this manifesto Robbins very briefly rebuked Ruskin and Carlyle for asserting that economists were concerned only with low ends, and then pivoted to a much more extended attack on (Marshallian economist) Edwin Cannan's effort to limit Economics to the pursuit of virtuous ends. Robbins drew on the mathematical innovations of continental economists like Walras and Pareto and identified with the marginalist side of the *Methodenstreit*; the late-1800s

"war of methods" between marginalists and the German Historical School. He can thus be seen as the third in a sequence (Mill, Marshall, Robbins) of efforts to delimit rationalist Economics by using romantic thought as a foil.

24 Another example: Kravis (1957, pp. 366–368) presents a relatively full and nuanced discussion of these issues, but still boils the division down to "work" (economic activity) versus "play" (non-economic activity).

25 Perhaps ultimately it did, in Becker (1981).

26 On such diagrams and their successors see Patinkin (1973), Buck-Morss (1995), Thompson (1998), Bissell (2007), and Tress (1948).

27 Please see also Schneider (1980), whose rethinking of gender and kinship also informed Collier and Yanagisako's (1987) work. Danby (2007) discusses this further.

28 See also T. Mitchell (1998) on the other of economy. Koopmans' seminal attack on the institutionalists (1947) rests on an a priori household/business split and the assumption that economists already "know" the motives of both categories of actors.

2 A Jewish economy in Palestine

Introduction

When we talk about "the French economy," the word "French" is doing a lot of work. It invokes a self-evident unit, a bordered territory with a government, language, people, art, history. An elaborate state apparatus promotes the self-evidence of "France" as a unit, supported by myriad international institutions devoted to the idea that the world is split into discrete internally coherent nations. With all that in place, it is easy to propose that this already-richly-integrated unit has an "economy."

So if we pursue the story of national income analysis via countries like France or Britain or the United States, we may miss some of the strangeness and arbitrariness of this project. It is hard not to think that a measure of the "British economy" is authorized by an essential pre-existing Britishness. We catch a better glimpse of this project as it unfolded if we look at a representation of a national economy without a nation.

One such example is the "Jewish economy" in 1930s Palestine. Britain ruled Palestine from 1923 to 1948 under a League of Nations mandate. During this period, the Jewish Agency for Palestine functioned as a British-recognized representative of local Jewish interests. But the Jewish Agency was also a proto-state: it developed its own security and social-welfare capacities, facilitated immigration, and worked to knit together a minority Jewish population that was geographically dispersed within the territory.

While the figures are contested, it is generally agreed that the Jewish population of Palestine was under 20 percent of the total at the beginning of the 1930s, reaching 30 percent by the early 1940s. If you had arrived in Palestine in the late 1930s and sought to write up its "economy" by looking around you and gathering data, you might well have described a heterogeneous colonial situation with a variety of communities (Seikaly 2015). That is not what the Jewish Agency did. Instead its economists separated, in the most finely grained way possible, the available data on production, consumption, investment, and so forth into Jewish and non-Jewish parts – down to markets in individual vegetables. Then they combined the Jewish statistics to create, on paper, an integrated "Jewish economy." This Jewish economy then became, by a gradual metonymy, the "Economy of Palestine."[1] Metzer describes the stakes this way:[2]

The "single economy" approach, adopted mainly by Arabs, was consistent with their political views and objectives, whereby Palestine was a single entity in which Jews, while entitled to individual rights, were by no means supposed to have any separate collective standing, let alone autonomy. The Jewish-Zionist position adopted the notion of a separate Jewish economy and promoted it both as a plan of action, while striving to form an autonomous body politic based on the "National Home" postulate, and as a factually justifiable distinction for reference and analysis.

(Metzer 1998, p. 1)

The work of theorizing and making persuasive this separate economy shows that a representable "economy" requires neither state power nor geographical integrity. Jewish and non-Jewish economies overlapped in space. If a Jew bought an onion grown by a non-Jewish farmer in the same town, that was as an import into the Jewish economy. Indeed, during the 1930s and early 1940s the Jewish Agency was not merely trying to persuade foreign supporters and the British government of the plausibility of a Jewish economy (and ultimately Jewish state) in Palestine. It was also persuading Jewish settlers in Palestine to act as though they were part of an integrated and distinct "economy," through "buy Jewish" campaigns and efforts to encourage Jewish businesses to hire Jewish employees (Shoham 2013).

The Jewish Agency's work is a token of a shift in the 1930s in many parts of the world toward the idea that a national economy is a coherent whole whose behavior might be influenced by government policy (Yonay 1998; Tooze 2001). J. M. Keynes, who is featured in the next two chapters, developed the *particular* theory and representation of national economies that became globally standard after WWII. But the larger project was shared by many people in different places. This episode also shows the close interpenetration of romantic and rationalist conceptions of economy, melding a romantic "agrarian ethos" that emphasized the spiritual benefits of farming with a rationalist "ethos of rapid development" which held that Jewish economic activity was distinctly modern, efficient, rational, and dynamic.[3]

Agrarian ethos

During the 1920s and early 1930s, what Arie Krampf calls the "agrarian ethos" dominated Zionist thought and policy. It "consisted not only of economic theories and policy instruments but also national normative and symbolic content" (Krampf 2010, p. 88). German Zionist Arthur Ruppin (1876–1943), a key theorist, wrote in a 1913 essay advocating colonization "firmly rooted in the soil (Ruppin 1949, p. 39) that

it is only when we shall be able to point in Palestine to "the work of our hands," when we shall have proved that we are not exploiters of the labour of others, shall we have established our moral right to the land ... our employment of Jewish workers is not connected with a feeling of animosity toward the Arabs, who are good and valuable workers; it arises solely from our desire to transform ourselves into workers and to fructify the soil with the sweat of our own bodies.

(Ruppin 1949, pp. 50–51)

And in a 1933 essay on "Settling German Jews in Palestine"

Have we been successful in enabling these Jews to build up a sound and healthy life? Let me begin [with] that part of our work ... which has always lain nearest our hearts, namely, agriculture. It is not just one of the branches of production: it is also the fountain of youth, in which we renew ourselves in the physical and spiritual sense after centuries of crippling life in the cities, remote from the soil.... For two thousand years we had had practically no contact with agricultural work, and we had to find our way back to it spiritually.

(Ruppin 1949, p. 284)

Ruppin's writings closely tracked the romantic critique of urban life, commerce, and capitalism. He accepted a central trope of European anti-Semitism – the wandering, unrooted Jew. The wholesomeness of rural life contrasted with the artificiality of the city; the idealism of the agricultural pioneer rebuked the self-ishness of the urban businessman. This contrast had a political expression in socialist Zionism. Krampf quotes David Ben-Gurion (1886–1973), then secretary-general of the Histradut, the Zionist labor federation, as taking the lesson from a 1927 recession that the Jewish bourgeoisie "did not know the secret of transformation and was not trained to the change of values which is associated in the realization of Zionism and building the country" (Krampf 2010, p. 84). Capitalism was too amoral and volatile to support nation-building.

Ruppin's advocacy of agrarian colonization was not limited, though, to a romantic rhetoric of soil, sweat, and spirit. He simultaneously took a keen interest in investment, growth, and efficiency. Ruppin repeatedly contrasted the rationality and dynamism of Jewish farming with the capital-poor, traditional farming of the Arab *fellahin*.

The combination of romantic traditionalism and rationalist modernization is one of the most noticeable features of this literature; there is no better example than David Horowitz. Horowitz (1899–1979) was born and educated in Galicia, a region now mostly in Western Ukraine but then part of the Austro-Hungarian empire. Polish victory in that region after WWI was followed, in 1918, by murderous pogroms that drove thousands of Jews to Vienna as refugees. Horowitz, still in his teens, was already a leading figure in Hashomer Hatzair ("youth guard"), a Galician Jewish youth movement. Secular and socialist, influenced by Marx and Freud as well as romantic nationalism, Hashomer Hatzair articulated a Zionism of rebirth in the land, manual labor, and intense communal fellowship (Margalit 1969). Horowitz joined other members in emigrating to Palestine in

1919 and taking up the hard life of a rural communard. By the early 1930s, however, Horowitz began to entertain doubts about the agrarian project.

Rapid development

In 1935 David Ben-Gurion became chair of the executive committee of the Jewish Agency, and Horowitz, now his associate, was appointed director of the Agency's economic department. In 1935 Horowitz published a controversial attack that

> denigrated the social, moral, and symbolic assumptions of the agrarian ethos. His article was considered so radical and controversial that the editor of the *Bulletin* inserted a disclaimer stating that, "This article by D. Horowitz, which presents a new approach concerning one of the basic questions of the Jewish economy, expresses the views of the author alone." The article refuted the claim implicit in the agrarian school that Jewish nation-building required a productivization of the nation, at least in the sense "productivization" was defined within the agrarian ethos. The agrarian ethos defined productivization as a transformation of the occupational structure of Jewish immigrants from urban occupations to agriculture.
>
> (Krampf 2010, p. 88)

The political rationale was clear. There were limits to the economic dynamism of agriculture, and buying land was a tediously piecemeal process. Possibly, too, extended experience of back-breaking rural labor had belied Ruppin's claims for its spiritually uplifting qualities. In any case, if Zionists wanted to attract and find work for large flows of new Jewish immigrants, especially those beginning to flee Germany, there was a strong argument for coming to terms with capitalism and urban life. A related context was the ongoing struggle with the British authorities over levels of immigration. The British justified restrictions on Jewish immigration by claiming that the local economy had a limited capacity to "absorb" new immigrants. It was hard to meet that argument if your vision of Jewish economy was primarily rural. So by 1935 Horowitz, now in the employ of the Jewish Agency, developed an argument for the potential dynamism of a multi-sector Jewish economy. Horowitz contended that new immigrants should be understood not as additional mouths to feed and people to employ, but as bearers of demand for goods and services, whose addition to the local economy would make it grow enough to "absorb" them. Today this argument reads as precociously Keynesian, though it was theorized by a different route.[4]

Horowitz did not persuade everyone. Ruppin's disciple A. L. Gaathon (1898–1982) riposted that "there is no doubt that the enormous size of the commercial sector ... is a sociological inheritance from the Diaspora." In his view this justified "as deep a transition as possible from secondary to primary employment, and above all to agriculture. Not because we consider these [secondary] occupations 'parasitical', but because they are an inorganic relic of the social structure of the Diaspora."[5]

Horowitz's side of the argument was fleshed out in a remarkable 1938 publication of the Jewish Agency's Economic Research Institute, the *Economic Survey of Palestine*, which he co-authored with Rita Hinden.[6] The study takes the "Palestine" it studies as self-evidently Jewish. Chapters on population, agriculture, industry, housing, and so forth carefully separate data about Jewish and non-Jewish activity, down to the level of splitting Jewish and "Arab" production of wheat, milk, eggs, chickens, and vegetables. *Economic Survey of Palestine* is thus a rhetorical exercise to limn a coherent, bounded Jewish economy within the territory of Palestine.[7] It is also an exercise in stepping away from the agrarian ethos toward the idea of an integrated multi-sector economy.

Let us pause a moment to consider the challenges. Someone writing from Ruppin's romantic nationalism had no trouble founding a Jewish economy on an ideology of renewal through sweat and soil. But what happens when agriculture is no longer the material and symbolic core of the economy, and just one more kind of business? What glues together this new economic ensemble? What makes that ensemble distinct from other ensembles in the same geographical space? The standard move if you have an already-existing nation is to assume that *national markets* do the coordinating.[8] But that was not so easy in this case, because *existing* markets in Palestine crossed communities: anyone could buy or sell in them. At several points the text acknowledges that goods or labor stray across the conceptual barriers between these two economies, which after all occupied the same space. For example, on food production, the authors write that

> The greatest difficulty has been felt in vegetable production. There is little difference in quality and the vegetables from the modern farm sector appear on the market simultaneously with the produce of the indigenous cultivator, who is able, through his cheaper production costs, to offer his output at a lower price. Price variations are also accentuated by different marketing methods – the highly organised co-operative methods of the modern cultivator, clashing with the primitive salesmanship of the villagers.
>
> (Horowitz and Hinden 1938, p. 58)

Jewish organizations in Palestine worked hard to encourage Jews to buy from each other and employ each other (Shoham 2013). The anxiety about buying "indigenous" vegetables in the above-quoted paragraph reflects concrete efforts to discourage this kind of commerce.

So given that markets were unreliable engines of national integration, Horowitz and Hinden drew on alternative rhetorics to make the idea of a distinct and unified Jewish economy plausible. One is a classical Marxist historical materialism: non-Jewish Palestinians were portrayed as feudal, that is as pre-capitalist in economic organization and mentality. Jews, by contrast, were poised somewhere between capitalism and socialism. A second rhetoric is an appeal to Europeanness and colonialism: the text likens Jewish settlers in Palestine to

European immigrants to the U.S., Canada, Australia, and New Zealand …
The Jewish immigrants are the bearers of a Western civilisation closely
resembling the civilisation which was carried to these other immigration
lands, and are establishing in Palestine a similar type of economic life.

(Horowitz and Hinden 1938, p. 19)

A third rhetoric grounds difference in bodies. A striking feature of the Horowitz and Hinden text is its limited willingness to make direct comparisons across
Jews and non-Jews. In some areas, the authors show no hesitation using a single
abstract framework to measure and discuss both communities. For example there
is a comparative discussion of agriculture that examines the greater use of capital
on Jewish farms, using the concept of capital intensity to directly compare the
two communities.

But at other moments the authors refuse comparison. In the chapter on population, they assert that "it is most important to divide Palestine's population in to
Jews and non-Jews, as in each sector of the community an entirely different state
of affairs is prevailing" (Horowitz and Hinden 1938, p. 23). Though both Arab
and Jewish birth rates were then above global averages, the Arab rate, they say,
"must be explained by the fact that the Arabs of Palestine are still, in the main, a
primitive people, who have not yet been educated in contraceptive practices"
(p. 26). But for high Jewish fertility, "the only acceptable explanation of this
high specific fertility has been put forward by Prof. Carr-Saunders." Carr-
Saunders, a British eugenic sociologist, is quoted to the effect that "The Palestinian Jews are co-operating in an endeavor which gives them hope and confidence;
moreover, their aim is to re-people their former home." In other words, Horowitz
and Hinden refuse the idea of any parallel examination into, say, contraceptive
use in both communities, or the possibility that an ideology of re-peopling might
exist among non-Jews in Palestine.

Analogously, a chapter on workers discusses differences between Jewish and
Arab wages and discusses how Jewish workers spend their incomes, but refuses to
do the same for Arab workers.[9] "It is well-nigh impossible," says the text (p. 200)
to make such a comparison, because of an absence of data, because food markets
"are, in the main, segregated," and because "the diet of the Arab worker differs so
greatly from that of any European, that such comparisons are meaningless." What
can "meaningless" mean here? As other chapters of the survey show, Jew and non-
Jew alike ate bread, eggs, chicken, and vegetables. Though on average less poor
than other communities, most Jews in 1930s Palestine led relatively frugal lives.
Basic dietary concepts like caloric intake were well understood in the 1930s. So
there is something about human bodies, whether present as wombs or stomachs,
that makes the authors unwilling to compare them directly, to share concepts
across communities.[10] This impression is reinforced by a passage in Horowitz's
1953 memoir when, stopping over in Cairo, he reflects that its

incredible destitution, its filth, vice, pauperism, and disease on one hand,
and the fabulous luxuries and wealth on the other, typifies with painful

clarity the complexity of the tragic Middle Eastern social problems. The Egyptian fellahin and the urban working-class, underprivileged, illiterate, and impoverished, are so thoroughly submissive and listless as a result of hereditary illness and debility that they lack the slightest will to change their way of life by reform or rebellion.

(Horowitz 1953, p. 9)

At these moments identification with "Western civilization" is emphatic, and difference inheres in bodies.

Gaathon's accounts

While Horowitz and Hinden's volume is rich in data and careful reasoning from data, it does not estimate national income. That distinction is reserved for *National Income and Outlay in Palestine 1936*, written between 1937 and 1939 and published in 1941 by the above-mentioned A. L. Gaathon, under the direction of Arthur Ruppin.[11] In a 1978 reprint, Gaathon added a preface on the circumstances of the study:

In the spring of 1936, the Arab terror attacks on Jewish settlements and lines of communication known as the Disturbances prompted the Executive of the Jewish Agency to discuss the danger that the supply of vital commodities to the Jewish urban communities (Tel Aviv, Haifa, Jerusalem, and their suburbs) might be cut off by the Arabs.

(Gaathon 1978, p. xiii)

Ruppin organized the data-gathering, and then

I compiled physical supply-demand accounts for 22 commodities or commodity groups adding such information as how far wheat and rye were ground in Jewish or Arab flour mills...
    This study was never published, at first for security reasons, and later because it no longer seemed of practical interest.
    Several years later I realized that the approach of these supply-demand balances was very similar to that used in the Soviet Union by the planning authority, Gosplan, with respect to basic materials like steel and cement ... [the Soviets encountered] a complex of economic planning problems of similar character to that confronting the Jewish community in Palestine in the 1930s because of mass immigration from Europe and the Arab countries.

(Gaathon 1978, p. xiv)

Although this pioneering[12] exercise in national income accounting was published after Horowitz and Hinden's study, and is a much more austerely technical document, it reflects the romantic/agrarian sympathies of Gaathon and Ruppin.

Gaathon makes agriculture central, building his model of a national economy by tracking flows between it and other sectors. Unlike Horowitz and Hinden, Gaathon showed no rhetorical difficulty justifying the separation of Jewish and non-Jewish activity in his figures, and no anxiety putting data for Jew alongside data for non-Jew. He took integral Jewish nationhood for granted, an assumption reinforced by the military origins of the study.

Gaathon addressed the analytical and practical task of carving out a Jewish economy by developing a double-entry framework, producing a "detailed input-output matrix for a two-community economy (Arab and Jewish)." While he offers no direct criticism of Horowitz and Hinden, he provides the tools for such criticism by theorizing the Jewish economy's interlinkages more rigorously than they do. For example, in his introductory material on method, Gaathon discusses the relation of capital inflows to growth, and writes that "such investments mean creation of permanent employment, i.e., room for new immigration." Horowitz had advocated such investment.

> But it fails in its purpose if such opportunities are seized by others than Jews. It is therefore necessary to examine the relations of the Jewish and non-Jewish sector with regard to the exchange not only of consumption goods, but also of production goods and labour, as well as services such as commerce and transport.
>
> (Gaathon 1978, p. 4)

A mathematically rigorous thinker, Gaathon recognized that arguments about the dynamism of a multi-sector economy made strong assumptions about the way those sectors were linked to each other and their capacities for growth. Without attention to these links, one risked bottlenecks and unwanted spillovers. There is a conceptual link here to Dudley Seers and the "structuralist" position discussed in Chapter 5.

Writing in 1943, South African economists Herbert Frankel and Hans Herzfeld praised Gaathon's system of accounts as "original," and described them carefully on the assumption that they would be novel to readers. Their assessment is worth quoting at length:

> Apart, however, from all practical considerations about the usefulness of the method, there is a certain aesthetical satisfaction in it, as it is a statistical counterpart to the theoretical contention that every economic process has two aspects.
>
> Palestine is a country that, in spite of its smallness, is interesting to the economist in more ways than one. Here we have a rapidly expanding community, whose European population is recruited from Jews all over Europe, people who with European training and experience have set in motion a vast new economic expansion.... There is, however, another aspect of this matter. "Here we have to deal with not one but two national incomes, that of the Jews and of the non-Jews" (p. 3.) Therefore the statistics in this book are

"based on the assumption of a complete separation between the two sectors".... *It is in this separation of the two groups that the neatness of the statistics which the double entry book-keeping system makes possible is most pleasing.*

(Frankel and Herzfeld 1943b, pp. 64–65, emphasis added)

Frankel and Herzfeld were at that time pioneering estimates for the national income of South Africa that segregated people of European origin (Frankel and Herzfeld 1943a). Frankel later become a prominent critic of the application of the concept of national income to African economies, on the grounds that they were too culturally different from Europeans to make the accounts meaningful (see Chapter 5).

Gaathon's work figured in yet another context. Robert Nathan (1894–1985) was a student of Simon Kuznets and his deputy at the Commerce Department. In 1943, Nathan was asked by a U.S. Zionist foundation to prepare a study on the "potential of Palestine" (Durr 2013, p. 58) and recruited several colleagues to produce a large study published in 1946 (Nathan *et al.* 1946). By this point Nathan and his co-authors had absorbed Keynes' theory and national accounting practice. They recognized Gaathon's parallel invention of national income accounting, and drew on his study.

Nathan and his collaborators felt the need to justify the Jewish versus non-Jewish difference on more than simply national difference. Their chapter on "National Income" begins:

It is as misleading to refer to the Palestinian economy as it is to refer to the Palestinian population. The economic differences between the two communities are as great as the cultural differences described in the preceding chapter. Palestine comprises two distinct communities – with inter-relations, whether on the social or economic level – held at a minimum.

(Nathan *et al.* 1946, p. 147)

Please note "held." They write that

the Zionist is in principle a pioneer and innovator, with Western cultural and economic standards.... He has, in a measure, absorbed the American slogan, "Time is money." The Arab ... is generally a firm believer in the most typical proverb of the Middle East, "All hurry comes from the Devil."

(Nathan *et al.* 1946, p. 146)

The wording is important in the context of economic theory, because it is an argument that Jews in Palestine are deliberate, rational economic actors (and thus qualified to compose an economy) while Arabs are not. Socialist, romantic, and spiritual strains of Zionism are muted. The discussion of time and money bears comparison to the way Rao and Gilbert wrote housework out of economy (Chapter 1).

Horowitz and Crossman

In 1945, Horowitz was asked by his Jewish Agency employers to assist in presenting the Zionist case to the newly formed Anglo-American Committee of Inquiry. The Committee emerged from immediate postwar tensions over Jewish migration from Europe to Palestine, something which, broadly, the U.S. government favored and the British government opposed.[13] It was probably intended to play for time and paper over differences between allies. But its work provides a glimpse into the role of ideas about economy in the construction of a nation.

Rather than being a group of experts, the Anglo-American Committee was a sort of jury, composed of six middling-prominent men from each country, none of whom had prior knowledge of the region. The British Prime Minister decided to appoint "no women or Jews or Arabs" (Podet 1986, p. 82); none of the U.S. appointees fell into those categories either. Zionist organizations took the opportunity of its hearings not just to argue for immigration, but also to make the case for rapid movement to an independent Jewish state in Palestine.

Horowitz attended the Committee's hearings in Washington DC. There he met informally with British committee member Richard Crossman (1907–1974). Crossman, a former academic and a Marxist, had entered the House of Commons in 1945 with Labour's postwar victory. Horowitz describes the Washington meeting as a conversation between two socialist intellectuals, and a breakthrough. Crossman reproached him for wanting different wages for Arab and Jewish workers, but warmed to his description of Zionism as a progressive force:

> I went on to describe, from the dialectical standpoint, the influence wielded by Jewish settlement in the Middle East ... I alluded to the social revolution brought about by Zionism in the Jewish world, the metamorphosis of the social and class structure, and the impulses stirring the movement. He showed rapt interest.
>
> (Horowitz 1953, p. 45)

> He asked me about my own past, and I told him of my years as a road-laborer and settler in a *kibbutz* in the early period of Emek Jezreel settlement, when I also took a hand in swamp reclamation.
>
> (Horowitz 1953, p. 47)

Horowitz's arguments, though tailored to Crossman's politics, were hardly opportunistic: he was describing his experience as a young Hashomer Hatzair militant, converting himself into a manual worker (he was the son of a prosperous businessman). He drew on the classical Marxian historical-materialist framework that was evident in the 1938 book, noted above.

In Crossman's memoir of the Anglo-American Committee, it is those nationalist themes that resonate. Here is his description of the Washington encounter with Horowitz and a colleague.[14]

I cannot remember much of that conversation except that it lasted for over three hours and I went to bed happy and excited for the first time in Washington. These two Palestinians, I discovered, belong to a completely different world from that of the American Zionist. Palestine for them was not a cause which they had taken up, a gigantic piece of organized philanthropy or a stick with which to beat the British. Palestine was their native country.... I felt I could trust these two and poured out to them all the repressed resentment of ten days. They listened patiently and then Horowitz said, "Your dislike of the American Zionists is the best argument for Zionism. You trust us and treat us as normal people because in the national home we have been freed from all the Jewish qualities you dislike, the shrillness, the irresponsibility, the ersatz-Zionism ..."

Had they ceased to be Jews in our sense of the word – foreign elements in other nations – and become the nucleus of ... the new Hebrew nation?

(Crossman 1946, pp. 40–41)

This is of course Crossman's account of the conversation. Nonetheless the views he ascribes to Horowitz are consistent with Hashomer Hatzair's ideology of a Jewish rebirth through land and labor, and more broadly with the "agrarian ethos" described earlier in the chapter: the idea that there was something false and artificial about a diasporic existence that could be fixed by returning to the *land* of Palestine. It was the nationalism that resonated with Crossman, redeeming Horowitz and his colleague ("their native country") as opposed to the American Zionists who had aroused Crossman's anti-Semitism.[15] Although Crossman does not mention anyone by name, prominent among those American Zionist witnesses had been the economist Robert Nathan, whose work was noted earlier in this chapter.

In Crossman's account of the Committee's subsequent visit to Palestine, it is again the national and civilizational themes that dominate. Horowitz set up meetings for Crossman with Zionist socialists and labor leaders, and Crossman describes those encounters warmly. In one passage describing a session at the Jewish Confederation of Labor, he writes that

if I shut my eyes, I might have believed I was present not at the meeting of the executive of a Palestinian Labor organization, but at a session of the Socialist international. Russian socialists with flowing white beards, who had fled from the Bolsheviks, Polish socialists, leading members of the old German Social Democrats, men from the American trades-unions, Bulgarians, Italians, now totally uninterested in Europe, and fanatically building what they believe will be the only free Socialist society in the world.

(Crossman 1946, p. 162)

These are his people, European socialists in a new Arcadia. In Crossman's descriptions of visits to Jewish sites, he warmly recounts the hospitality he receives. By contrast Muslim Palestinians, though attracting his sympathy for their political and material weakness, repulse him. The repulsion condenses around bodies and food:

> Arab conditions are abominable. We inspected a show village today at Sulfit.... Many of the boys had ringworm and looked undernourished. When I asked the top form what they were going to be, one said a doctor, four or five teachers, and all the rest said, "work on the land." They cling to the soil, even with education...
>
> The mayor's lavatory was one of those standing affairs. I washed my hands in his dining room just behind the table, despite the fact that he is one of the wealthiest men in Palestine. He gave us a staggering meal with all the notables...
>
> This is still a people of clans and blood feuds, of feudal courtesy and poverty, charm and misery...
>
> No. it is no good. These two people just don't mix, and the more you mix them, whatever the material benefits to the Arab, the more they hate each other and each other's way of life.
>
> (Crossman 1946, pp. 137–138)

Palestinian Jews occupy the slot of full modernity, in contrast to the impoverished and soon-to-be-dispossessed *fellahin*.

In Horowitz's mind and remarkable career are united many of the themes explored in this book. He was an expert who produced persuasive documents and presentations with scientific dispassion, an economist who helped summon a national economy into existence. He was a proto-Keynesian in his theory of capitalist growth. He was a leading theorist *and* a leading critic of romantic Zionism.

This is also an exemplary story about who pays the cost for good numbers. Horowitz's project had no counterpart among non-Jewish Palestinians, who had no similar British-recognized institutions (Seikaly 2015). He recounts with satisfaction that, in testimony to the Anglo-American Committee when it visited Palestine, "the Arab case was weak and ill-prepared." He recounts an overheard telephone conversation in which an activist working on that case asked "aren't we able to find an expert of our own too, a *real* expert with diagrams and figures and facts?" (Horowitz 1953, p. 70). At the same time, the record does not demonstrate that beyond his impressive *performance* of "diagrams and figures and facts," Horowitz's arguments had great influence on the Committee (Horowitz 1953, p. 74). Crossman's memoir does not discuss the substance of his economic arguments; neither does the other published memoir by a Committee member, that of Bartley Crum.[16]

Over the course of the mid-twentieth century, economic rationality became the dominant way of differentiating the deserving from the undeserving, the haves from the have-nots. Poverty became *evidence* of some more fundamental lack, a lack to be addressed with discipline and dispossession (Ravela 2013). This was an early example.

Notes

1 Gaathon (1978), Horowitz and Hinden (1938), Nathan *et al.* (1946).
2 For other discussions of the politics of describing economy in this context, see Owen (1982) and Kamen (1991, pp. 66–70). Metzer (1998) makes a careful institutional case for the dual-economies approach. See also Krampf (2010), Hewett *et al.* (2015), and Shamir (2013), in particular pages 134–137, on the carving out of a separate Jewish economy.
3 The terms "agrarian ethos" and "ethos of rapid development" are drawn from Krampf (2010).
4 Krampf (2010, p. 91). On the absorption argument see e.g., Horowitz (1953, p. 39) on Notestein's evidence, and p. 65, on the British administration's "effort to prove the limited economic absorptivity of the country."
5 Gaathon (then Grünbaum), quoted in Krampf (2010, p. 90).
6 On the book's favorable reception as a "dispassionate account" see Krampf (2010, pp. 97–98).
7 See also Leibler (2008, pp. 128–130; 2004) and Leibler and Breslau (2005).
8 Even if such national markets *do not exist*: this point will return in Chapter 5, when British economists studying British African colonies combined estimates of total agricultural output for a colony and multiplied it by available price data, even when very little of that output actually passed through a market to which that price corresponded. Figured was not so much the actual economy as the *imagined* national economy.
9 The authors argue that Palestine's Jewish proletariat has been formed by immigrants formerly "engaged in small trade or liberal professions" (p. 185) who have faced an "occupational transformation" (p. 186) to manual labor; while the "Arab proletariat … has been created as a direct result of the impact of capitalism on the primitive rural economy which characterized Palestine until a generation back" (p. 188). The chapter notes that

> the strong Trade Union activities of Jewish labour were, in part, brought about by the presence of a cheap and unorganised Arab labour force, raising before the Jewish worker the threat of being reduced to the primitive standard of life to which the Arab has been accustomed for centuries.
>
> (Horowitz and Hinden 1938, p. 193)

10 The refusal to compare parallels the work of Alfred Sauvy on population, discussed in Danby (2012). Alfred Sauvy's 1952 "Trois mondes, une planète" article is now remembered for its invention of the term "third world"; what is less remembered is that he defined three worlds in order to insist on their incommensurable separateness, including their ethical alienation from each other.
11 Gaathon wrote as Ludwig Grünbaum in 1941; the 1978 reissue by the Bank of Israel updated the name.
12 Rosen (1979) terms this "unique" work "a genuine pioneering effort" in national income accounting. Richard Stone said in his 1984 Nobel Prize Lecture:

> In 1941, estimates of British national income and expenditure, which James Meade and I had worked out as civil servants in the War Cabinet Offices, were published at the instigation of Keynes … In the same year Gruenbaum (Gaathon) published his National Income and Outlay in Palestine, 1936, which was also set in an accounting framework, and van Cleeff in Holland published two papers on a system of national bookkeeping. Thus, as so often happens, the idea was in the air and made its appearance in several guises at the same time.
>
> (Stone 1986, p. 11)

The words "set in an accounting framework" are significant because the framework is the innovation for which Stone received the prize. Gilbert and Stone (1954, p. 2) also credit Gaathon and van Cleeff as pioneers. Szereszewski (1968) provides an insightful discussion of the structure of Gaathon's accounts.

13 See Tufan (2015), Podet (1986), and Tamari (2008).

14 In Horowitz's recollection the colleague, an international activist engaged in aiding clandestine Jewish immigration into Palestine, is present only at the end of the conversation. In Crossman's recollection she is there from the beginning.

15 Crossman was, to be fair, reflective about this: "Jewish argumentation was stimulating the anti-Semitic bacilli which breed in every Gentile's unconscious" (Crossman 1946, p. 39). Horowitz (1953, p. 47) notes this reflection.

16 Crum (1996). Even the *Jewish Telegraph Agency*, which normally covered the Anglo-American Committee's hearings with keen attention, gave Horowitz's testimony only one dry sentence: "David Horowitz, appearing for the Jewish Agency, gave the members of the committee a comprehensive lecture with illustrated maps, charts and graphs on Jewish immigration, employment, Moslem child mortality and other aspects of Palestine life" (*Jewish Telegraphic Agency* 1946).

3 Body of the nation

Intuiting economy

In a biographical essay on Isaac Newton, whose papers he collected, John Maynard Keynes wrote that Newton "was not the first of the age of reason" but "the last of the magicians."[1] Keynes was pointing to Newton's alchemical and esoteric investigations, but also to his method:

> I believe that Newton could hold a problem in his mind for hours and days and weeks until it surrendered to him its secret. Then being a supreme mathematical technician he could dress it up, how you will, for purposes of exposition, but it was his intuition which was pre-eminently extraordinary...
>
> His experiments were always, I suspect, a means, not of discovery, but always of verifying what he knew already.
>
> (Keynes 1971b, pp. 365–366)

Keynes (1883–1946) was concerned throughout his career with a small set of linked problems: inflation, depression, wartime finance, unemployment. Understanding these things required not just new theory, but new concepts from which to build theory. Only once those concepts were stabilized could one imagine measuring them. The coincidence of WWII with the height of Keynes' prestige enlisted the British government in estimating Keynes' categories and giving them an official stamp.

In other words it would have been impossible to develop Keynesian macroeconomics – his theoretical framework for addressing inflation, depression, wartime finance, and unemployment – by pure induction, that is from the study of existing data. At the time of WWI there were some price series available, and limited production data for major industries. Trade was reasonably well documented because of customs and tariff systems. But what we now think of as national aggregates were simply not there, barely *conceived of* let alone measured and reported on any regular basis (T. Mitchell 1998, 2005). In broadly analogous fashion Newton had to invent a concept of force, and stabilize linked concepts of mass, velocity, and acceleration, in order to build classical mechanics.

Keynes, then, had to imagine an "economy" as a thing that generated phenomena like inflation and unemployment, as a machine with interlocking parts. This required close interest in available data *and* constant effort to see beyond those data. Stone writes that his "capacity for observing and assimilating facts was remarkable, and facts for him included numbers. He liked to get a sense of the order of magnitude of the problems with which he was dealing..." (Stone 1978, p. 64).[2] His contemporaries did not always trust his intuitions. Roy Harrod, his colleague and first biographer, writes with a slight edge that Keynes "was always ready to guess a figure in order to illustrate a point."[3] Richard Stone tells this story from the early 1940s:

> He did more than anyone else I have known to break down the Cult of the Zeros, by which I mean the practice then common among statisticians of writing down zero when what they meant was that no reliable information was available. I shall give a typical example. At an early stage in a discussion on estimates of the balance of payments we were presented with a table containing the usual zeros against a number of items. "Look," said Keynes, "you know as well as I do that the change in Commonwealth balances cannot have been zero last year: what do you think it was?" "We don't really know," was the reply, "but probably between three and four hundred million." "Then put it down as £350 million" said Keynes "and try to get some accurate information in the future, for by your own admission it is very important."
>
> (Stone 1978, pp. 71–72)

Keynes' first job was a 1906–1908 stint as a civil servant in the India Office. There he learned to conceptualize the Indian economy as a unit to be managed, figuring out institutional linkages within a colony he never visited.[4] Like IMF officials a few decades later, Keynes the colonial administrator was a critical consumer of statistics. He lamented their patchiness and joined public controversies about the size of aggregates like the value of British investments in India (Chandavarkar 1990, p. 17). In a 1909 review for the *Economist* he lamented the poor quality of Indian statistics both for routine business uses and for political arguments: "The apologist of our Indian administration still asks in vain for the simple statistical data which would upset the statistical fiction of an India declining under British rule" (Keynes 1971d, p. 36). The benefits of British rule were intuitively obvious to Keynes; data lagged.

When Keynes resigned from the British Treasury in 1919 to protest the terms of the Versailles treaty and wrote *The Economic Consequences of the Peace* (1919) attacking it, he used rough magnitudes throughout. The book's argument that the reparations payments demanded of Germany were impossible rested both on estimates of German productive capacity and a global argument that Germany could only achieve such payments via trade surpluses that its main trading partners would not accept.[5] Here is an example of what the IMF now calls "bilateral surveillance" – the comprehensive view of a *national* economy by a technocrat – *and* an example of what the IMF now calls "multilateral surveillance" – the global technocrat's ability to pull multiple countries and national policies into a single analytical frame and point out incoherences between national policies. This will be pursued in Chapter 6.

In the mid-1930s, as he developed the framework sketched below and the policy arguments of the *General Theory of Employment, Interest, and Money* (1936) that depended on that framework, Keynes looked for data to flesh out his concepts.[6] As WWII approached he returned to the problems of wartime finance he had wrestled with as a junior official during WWI, and published *How to Pay for the War* in 1940 (Keynes 1940a). That pamphlet worked out how to shift production from civilian to military purposes, and maximize military output, without that wartime inflation that was likely when workers tried to spend their incomes on the smaller output of civilian goods. When Keynes returned to government employment later in 1940, he used his position to gather data to clothe his framework. He arranged for the hiring of James Meade (1907–1993), who had been until recently an economist at the League of Nations, and Richard Stone (1913–1991), a 1936 graduate of Keynes' Cambridge department. Keynes put them to work on the technical elaboration of his system, and gathering data to fill it (Mitra-Kahn 2011).[7] I will tell that story in Chapter 4. But for now, anticipating that the underlying ideas may be unfamiliar to some readers, I turn to a slightly more detailed exposition of how the standard Keynesian "national economy" emerged in the early decades of the twentieth century, and some of the choices it entailed.

Circular flows

In Chapter 1, we watched economists sort a messy social world into two bins called "households" and "businesses." "Economy" was defined as everything going on in the business sphere, and measured via the business sphere's *interactions* with the household sphere. This produced a simple national model (Figure 3.1) with matching circular flows of goods/services and payments for them.

Given the assumptions on which the model is built, the monetary flows top and bottom must equal each other over any span of time: all payments to the business sector produce incomes for somebody, and all incomes are spent on output. If we measure the bottom flows, we are tracking the incomes that businesses pay households. This flow can be split into the different types of incomes paid to owners for the use of different "factors of production" (also called "factor services"). In classical Economics the factors were land (which received rents), labor (which received wages), and capital (which received profits). Up top, it is customary to specify *two* ways of looking at the same flow of output from businesses to households: as *expenditure* on output, from the household point of view, and as *production* of output, from the business point of view. These are two ways of looking at the same flow, but take advantage of different sources of data: household consumption surveys on the one hand; figures from producers on the other.

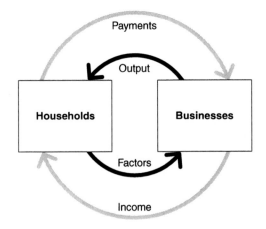

Figure 3.1 The simple national economy.

Before the twentieth century most efforts at estimating national income (almost all private and sporadic) took one of these three concepts (income, expenditure, and output) and tried to measure it; in the early twentieth century a number of people in different places came to the obvious conclusion that it would be better to try and measure all three, at least in order to check them against each other.[8]

What "counts" as national income/output? We have already seem (Chapter 1) how "domestic" production of goods/services like childcare and cooked meals – the things that happened inside the household sector, were excluded and tucked inside the "households" bin. But this does not exhaust the questions to be settled. Out of the numerous conceptual and technical issues I will discuss just two major ones: how to deal with capital goods, and how to deal with government.

Capital goods are long-lasting goods like hammers and houses that we use to make other goods, or to provide services. It is clarifying to consider what national income would look like *without* them. Irving Fisher (1867–1947), one of the most prominent U.S. economists of the early decades of the twentieth century, proposed in 1906 the concept of "national dividend" to measure national income. Fisher's national dividend included goods actually used up during a year (like food) plus the services *for that year* provided by longer-lasting goods. He preferred:

> to regard uniformly as income the service of a dwelling to its owner (shelter or money rental), the service of a piano (music), and the service of food (nourishment); and … to exclude alike from the category of income the dwelling, the piano, and even the food. These are capital, not income; and the instant we include any such concrete wealth under the head of income, that instant we begin to confuse capital and income. The newly purchased or

newly constructed house is not an element of income, but of capital. The income appears afterward in the services the house yields its owner, the shelter it affords through subsequent years or the bringing in of a money rent to its owner. In like manner the newly acquired piano and loaf of bread are not income, but capital. Their income follows later in the form of piano music and nourishment.

(Fisher 1906, p. 106)

There is an admirable conceptual simplicity to this: Fisher wants to count only the actual enjoyment, or use, of goods. If my overcoat lasts 5 years, I need to count, in a given year, only the *use* I get from that overcoat during that year, essentially by amortizing its purchase price over 5 years. Fisher's "national dividend" concept is *closer* to being a measure of welfare, or well-being, than the concepts discussed below, because it tries to isolate *the direct benefits people receive.* It would be a plausible concept for studying poverty. Fisher and Simon Kuznets (Chapters 1 and 4) started from a "welfarist" orientation to national income data, because this was the kind of question they thought national income should answer (Desrosières 2003, pp. 558, 561).

But while there have been occasional efforts to compute Fisherian national dividends, this concept has not been adopted by governments, and standard "consumption" figures include the *entire* value of your piano in the year that you bought it, rather than trying to work out the value you receive from playing it in a given year. This choice can be attributed partly to the difficulties in estimating flows of services from long-lived purchases (clothing, furniture, appliances, etc.) and mostly to the Keynesian system's interest in actual *spending* in a given year. Output and employment in the piano industry depends more on purchases of new pianos than on people's enjoyment of old pianos. "Consumption" as it is now used just means "final sales to households," with zero interest in what households do next. The national accounts do not ask whether you buy a piano in order to play it, put a vase of flowers on top of it, or set it on fire in the back yard.

This focus on spending extends to capital spending by businesses, which is what "investment" means in the simple Keynesian framework. A business purchase of a long-lived good, like a drill press, "counts" as part of national output just like a consumer's purchase of a drill press for hobby purposes. There is an obvious objection to doing this. The drill press bought by a business will have a useful life of, say, 10 years. It has no *direct* benefit to me as a consumer – I can't stroll into their factory and use it. Over its life all of its value, so to speak, will pass into the goods the business produces. So why not just ignore business purchases of capital goods, and count only the actual, ultimate flows of goods and services to consumers? Even if capital investment is an excellent thing and promises higher future productivity and growth, why not wait for those benefits to actually arrive, and count them only when they do? (It is surprising that critics of GDP have not made more of this given the distributional implications: business capital assets are the property of business owners, who are on average relatively wealthy.) The answer, again, is that the set of questions that *Keynesian national income accounting* is aimed at answering concern aggregate *spending* and current output, not household well-being.

This gives us the germ of the Keynesian system, the identities he put forward in the 1936 *General Theory of Employment, Income, and Money*. Take Figure 3.1, remove the goods/services flows (for graphical simplicity, but also because this is an analysis that privileges spending), and divide the spending flow into consumption and saving. This will generate Figure 3.2.

You could imagine a simple economy in which all businesses were small sole-proprietorships, and so "saving" happened when a business owner (who is a member of a household) used current income to buy another building or machine for that business. There would be no intermediating financial sector. In Figure 3.2 we add a financial sector that makes loans to businesses to finance the purchase of capital goods on the one side, and that accepts household savings (as, say, bank deposits), on the other side. This may seem a simple point, but it was vital to Keynes' ultimate analysis that business decisions to borrow to finance new capital, and household decisions to save, are made by different people and for different reasons.

Figure 3.2 can be expressed as simple equations (or more formally "identities," because they are true by definition): output (Y) equals consumption plus investment ($Y = C + I$), and output equals consumption plus saving ($Y = C + S$).

There is no government visible in Figure 3.2. Keynes theorized in 1936 on the basis of a consumer-and-enterprise economy, and offered no explicit treatment of

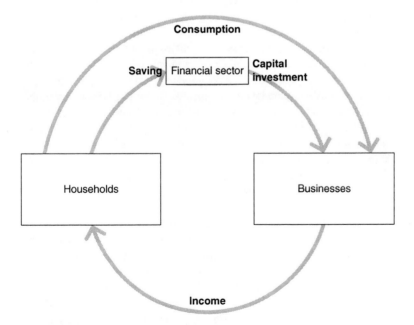

Figure 3.2 National income with consumption and investment.

government.[9] When, in later chapters of the *General Theory*, he made the famous case for counter-recessionary government spending, he simply treated government like a consumer or like a business undertaking capital investment. He did not recast the framework. This is consistent with the national income literature of the 1920s and 1930s, which showed absolutely no consensus on how to treat government. Simon Kuznets (see Chapter 1) treated government as part of the business sector. He treated taxes paid by households as payments for government services. However involuntary those payments are, he treated them as the result of a collective political decision by households to buy roads, courts, national defense, and so forth.

The full Keynesian system, worked out during WWII, pulled *all* of government out of the business sector, and gave it its own compartment.[10] Government could finance itself either by taxes or by borrowing from the financial sector (it could also, in periods of budget surplus, make net transfers *to* the financial sector). The remaining business sector is essentially the "private sector," and government purchases *from* private business are now pulled out and put on a par with household purchases from private business. This gets us the core Keynesian national income anatomy in Figure 3.3. From this we get the standard textbook identities, $Y = C + I + G$ and $Y = C + S + T$. Figure 3.3 summarizes.

The anatomy presented in Figure 3.3 is designed for grappling with the difficulties of wartime finance in a market economy. In wartime – especially a war of the scale and duration of WWII – a government wants the private sector to produce as much military goods as possible. Those goods will flow from "business" to "government" in exchange for the "government purchases" flow of spending. But as businesses (a) hire more workers to produce more military goods, and (b) shift their output from civilian to military goods, you have a problem. Total civilian *money* incomes rise, but total production of civilian goods, the goods on which those incomes can be spent, falls. The result will be disruptive inflation in the prices of civilian goods if nothing else is done. To avoid inflation the simplest remedies are to throttle down the flow of spending from civilian earnings. You can do that by raising taxes (thereby taking wages away before they can be spent) or by persuading wage-earners to lend some of their incomes to government (e.g., buying war bonds) instead of spending it. Both measures divert wages from consumption spending. This is a simple insight, but it was essentially unavailable to wartime policymakers before Keynes, because they lacked the framework to see it and to work out the relevant magnitudes.

Keynes was deeply concerned throughout his life with avoiding disruptive inflation. His 1924 *Tract on Monetary Reform* (Keynes 1971a) is still one of the clearest expositions of inflationary mechanisms and the social and political dangers of inflation. These were concerns taken seriously by any observer of European events during the 1920s and 1930s. It is *this* concern that is the central legacy of Keynes to the contemporary IMF (Chapter 6). Keynesian national income accounting shines an especially bright light on what governments do – it brightly illuminates government's taxing and spending and borrowing, and it

1.
Take the simple circular-flow diagram (Figure 1.2) and simplify to show only
money and income payments.

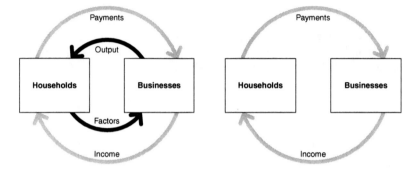

2.
Split payments into three parts, adding a government and a financial sector.

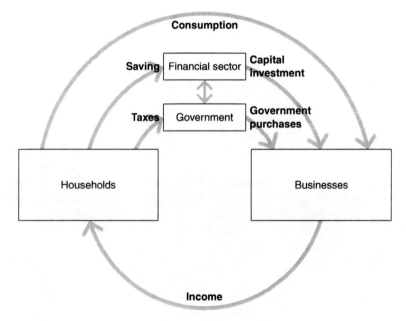

Figure 3.3 From the simple circular flow to the Keynesian system.

provides a useful basis for assessing government influence over a nation's financial sector.[11]

Now, there is a frequently-made argument that goes like this: (a) Keynesian
national income accounting overplays government, (b) bureaucrats like big government, and so (c) bureaucrats adopted Keynesian accounting to advance the

cause of big government (Seers 1952; Waring 1988; Rothbard 1993; Waring 1999; Dequech 2003; Cochran 2014). This is given plausible coloration by the contemporary conflation of "Keynesian" with expansionary fiscal and monetary policy. In my view, this argument grabs the wrong end of the stick. We need to ask exactly what bureaucratic purposes were being pursued. Hence my argument, developed in Chapters 5 and 6, that the relevant bureaucrats responsible for the standardization and spread of Keynesian national income accounting were not *national* bureaucrats, but *international* bureaucrats interested in establishing a perch as disinterested technocrats with special insight into the malfeasance of *national* governments.

The body visible

J. M. Keynes imagined a new thing, a national economy linked by flows of money and guided by financial markets. But his 1936 *General Theory*, which described this mental object, was not an easy book. So a number of younger economists set to work making this newly-imagined thing, this strangely-behaving monetary national economy, more clearly visible to themselves and others. The most famous effort was the two-equation "IS-LM" model developed by John Hicks in 1939, still a teaching standby and handy tool for policy analysis. Economists like mathematical models because they are tiny oases of clarity, with everything unambiguously defined and all connections specified. A model like IS-LM does not capture all that Keynes "really meant," but it is a more easily-shared representation.

This section discusses a physical analogue of the IS-LM model, a hydraulic computer developed in 1949 to model a national economy along Keynesian lines. This physical model was the result of collaboration between a graduate student, William Phillips (1914–1975), and his tutor, Walter Newlyn (1915–2002). Phillips, like many students, found the early Keynesian literature difficult and frustratingly vague on certain assumptions. But Phillips was an unusual student: he had a previous career as an electrical engineer, and wide experience fixing and improvising electrical and mechanical machines. He persuaded Newlyn that Keynesian macroeconomics could be modeled, and thus clarified, hydraulically. Newlyn got funding and the two built a prototype. An engineering firm was then enlisted to make a more durable version (Figure 3.4), of which about a dozen were ultimately manufactured.[12]

To get a sense of the Newlyn-Phillips machine, it is useful to start from a physical description of a control mechanism.

At the center of Figure 3.5 is a tank of water.[13] Water flows into the tank through a pipe above and drains out through a pipe below. There are three moving parts. Each flow, top and bottom, is controlled by a valve (A and B). Each valve is a bar that can move horizontally. When the bar moves left, it reduces the flow of water; when it moves right, it lets the flow of water increase. The two valves are controlled by the third moving part, which is free to move only vertically. That part consists of a float (C) which moves up and down with

Figure 3.4 Newlyn-Phillips machine and Phillips.[1]

Note
1 From LSE Library's collections, IMAGELIBRARY/6, reproduced by permission.

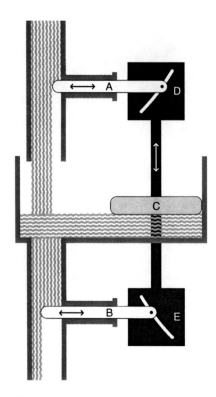

Figure 3.5 Control mechanism.

the level of the water. The float is attached to a vertical bar. At the top of the vertical bar is a square plate (D) with a slanted slot cut into it. At the bottom is another such plate (E). Each slot engages a pin at the right-hand end of a valve bar, so that when the float/plates assembly rises or falls, the valves are opened or closed.

In the position depicted in Figure 3.5, the upper flow exceeds the lower flow.[14] In that case the level of water in the tank must rise. As the float rises atop the rising water, it moves both plates upward. The rising upper plate will move the top valve to the left, reducing the upper flow. The rising lower plate will move the lower valve right, increasing that flow. Thus if the upper flow exceeds the lower flow, the level of water in the tank rises, reducing the upper flow and increasing the lower flow. If on the other hand the lower flow exceeds the upper flow, the level of water in the tank falls, causing the float-and-plate assembly to drop, opening up the upper flow and reducing the lower flow. I appeal to your plumbing intuition that, given a little time, this mechanism will equalize the upper and lower flows.

We can now give this physical system an economic interpretation. The top flow in Figure 3.5 represents the flow of production of a good. The tank represents the total unsold stock of that good in shops. The lower flow represents consumer purchases of that good. A rise in unsold stocks causes merchants to reduce the market price; if stocks fall merchants raise the market price. Each of the square plates in Figure 3.5 can be read as a little graph showing quantity (horizontally) as a function of price (vertically). The top graph is the supply function. The place where the horizontal valve/bar meets the curved plate shows the current market price. Thus as the plate *rises* against the bar, the pin at the end of the valve bar engages the plate at a *lower* part of the plate, indicating a lower price. (This is a bit counter-intuitive because the frame rises as price falls, but think of yourself as a tiny observer riding on the float/plates assembly and just watching the pin.) So, up top we have the supply function: once producers perceive a lower price, they reduce the quantity they produce. Below we have the demand function: as the price falls, consumers increase the quantity they buy.

This is a *model*: a physical analogue of a social institution. It is a model of how a competitive market in a single good might function, with a single market price equilibrating two flows.[15]

The idea for a "micro" (just one market) model of this kind was not original to Newlyn and Phillips. Their originality was in recognizing that you could construct a "macro" (national economy) model incorporating multiple adjustment mechanisms of this kind within a larger circular flow. The interest rate, for example, could be shown as a function of the available stock of investment funds in the banking system. Other relations hypothesized in Keynesian theory, such as the idea that consumption spending was a stable function of income, could be turned into physical connections between flows. You could set the machine up to simulate a particular set of theoretical assumptions plus policy variables, turn it on, and let it "solve" the system: when it did this it was essentially computing multiple simultaneous differential equations. Plotters could be added to graph both prices and flow quantities, giving the experimenter a through-time picture of how a national economy responded to changes. It would require many more pages to provide a thorough description, but Figure 3.6 sketches the core flows, omitting control mechanisms, in a way that roughly corresponds to the photograph in Figure 3.4.

You can see that this is just a rearranged version of Figure 3.3, with imports and exports added in. In the machine, the income earned by households is pumped to the top. Some of it is sluiced away in taxes. The after-tax income either spent (consumption) or saved. Savings flows into a financial system from which businesses borrow to fund capital investment spending; government spends tax revenue and may also borrow from the financial sector. Thus the total flow of domestic spending is the C + I + G that converges in the middle of the figure. The machine adds imports and exports at the bottom right. (On foreign flows, please see Chapter 4.) After adjusting for trade, total purchases of domestically-produced goods and services flow into the "businesses" box. Businesses pay household incomes (wages, profits, etc).[16] Those incomes cascade to the bottom to be pumped up top again.

The "classical" system (or "Treasury view") that Keynes argued against can be thought of as a machine in which *all* markets self-equilibrate: the labor

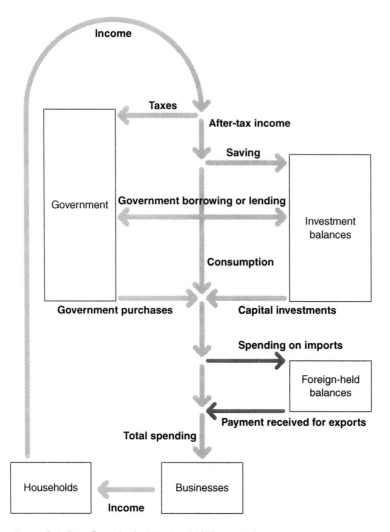

Figure 3.6 Core flows in the Newlyn-Phillips machine.

market, the market in loanable funds, and all markets in goods and services. Under those assumptions, government intervention cannot fix unemployment. Keynes had argued that a national economy was hooked up differently – that it had a different internal anatomy, that it was internally self-regulated differently. The Newlyn-Phillips machine was a way of demonstrating those different internal connections and working out how a national economy would behave under Keynesian assumptions.[17]

So we come full circle, or perhaps more than full circle. At the start of this chapter Keynes described Newton's ability to assemble classical mechanics in his head, imagining a core set of relations that made up a powerful new model of the physical world. Newton helped us understand physical systems as coherent, law-governed things. Students typically learn classical mechanics through experiments that let them see on the lab bench what the equations describe. An acquaintance with Newtonian mechanics helps us approach the Newlyn-Phillips machine *itself* as a law-governed system, and further learned habits of analogy help us "see" this little law-abiding physical system as a representation of a national economy.

Haunting the physics is just a little of the old Newtonian alchemy, because the machine is also readable as a living thing, a struggling organism with its own will.[18] Numerous observers have commented on its body-like qualities. Phillips dyed the water red for visibility, and the machine resembles a stylized model of a body's circulatory system.[19] More interestingly it did not behave like a simple machine – say, a kitchen appliance – in which changes to controls cause direct changes in the machine's behavior. Rather, you changed a control and then watched a series of adjustments, over 5 or 10 minutes, as the machine gurgled its way toward a new equilibrium. Such adjustments are called *homeostatic* in biology: an example is your body's ability to regulate its internal temperature.[20]

The circular flow is a powerful metaphor. It is founded, let us remember, on the sentimental household/business split traced in Chapter 1, mapping the inter-action between these two spheres and signifying their complementarity. It is elaborated by Keynes to highlight capital investment, government, and the finan-cial sector, producing a circulatory anatomy useful for certain policy questions. But it had an aesthetic extension, producing visual confirmation of the integrity of the nation, its beating heart and coursing arteries and veins.[21] The national economy became a body with organs.[22]

A romantic Keynes?

Keynes thought globally in the 1910s and 1920s. As an India Office official he helped administer an empire, and as a dissenter from the Versailles accords he worked out the international repercussions of reparations. His 1920s arguments against the gold standard show deep awareness of the structure of the inter-national financial system and the different positions of different countries in it. His *Treatise on Money*, published in 1930, theorized an open economy, with trade and international investment built into the theory from the beginning.

Keynes thought nationally in the 1930s. The 1936 *General Theory* theor-ized a closed economy, paying scant attention to foreign flows. There are plenty of good explanations for this shift. The Great Depression, plus protec-tionist responses to it, caused a collapse in foreign trade. Foreign lending fell. Thus a closed economy was a more defensible simplifying assumption in the 1930s than it had been earlier. The kinds of anti-depression policies Keynes began advocating were also more effective in a relatively closed economy. The prospect of another war, looming from the mid-1930s, raised the salience of the national unit.

But whatever the causes of Keynes' national turn, it had a cultural dimension. Keynes was a Bloomsbury figure and arts patron. In essays in 1932 and 1933 that closely track Mill's assessment of Coleridge, Keynes wrote of protectionists as economic idiots who had nonetheless grasped something important:

> The protectionist has often used bad economic arguments, but he has some-times had a truer sense of the complicated balances and harmonies and qual-ities of a sound national economic life, and of the wisdom of not unduly sacrificing any part even to the whole. The virtues of variety and universal-ity, the opportunity for the use of every gift and every aptitude, the ameni-ties of life, the old established traditions of a countryside – all those things, of which there are many, even in the material life of a country, which money cannot buy, need to be considered.
>
> (Keynes 1971c, Vol. XXI, pp. 206–207)

As Mill had done, Keynes cast the orthodox free-trade position as idealistically cosmopolitan and freedom-loving, but neglecting culture and national feeling. He echoed Coleridge when he wrote that

> we have until recently conceived it a moral duty to ruin the tillers of the soil and destroy the age-long human traditions attendant on husbandry, if we could get a loaf of bread thereby a tenth of a penny cheaper.... To-day we suffer disillusion, not because we are poorer than we were–on the contrary ... but because other values seem to have been sacrificed.
>
> (Keynes 1971c, pp. 206–207)

In this essay he made the further argument that direct foreign investment, though well-founded in orthodox theory that capital should seek the highest return, caused social and political tension because "in times of stress," owners of a firm in one country were set at odds with managers of the firm in another – the bonds of sympathy and shared knowledge that should unite owner and manager failed. The same argument could be made about foreign lending. Keynes repeated argu-ments for the virtues of a shared national culture in 1930s writings advocating civic pageants and state support for the arts. As Esty (2009) shows, in this shift he followed Bloomsbury colleagues who also rediscovered the virtues of shared Englishness in the 1930s.

Keynes' romantic turn should be interpreted cautiously.[23] He enjoyed paradox, relished surprising his readers, and was not above rhetorical opportun-ism. Moreover in the essays I quote from above the romantic elements are always discursively contained, allowed to run briefly and then reined back. But regardless of his underlying views, it is remarkable how much of the positive romantic doctrine of economy (see Chapter 7) shows up in Keynes' mid-1930s writings: economy is a matter of communication and shared knowledge; national economy can create national sympathy and solidarity; the nation is the appropri-ate unit for shared knowledge and common culture; these virtues exist at a wider level than individual freedom and initiative and in certain balances outweigh them. As with the contemporaneous development of a Jewish economy in Palestine discussed in Chapter 2, romantic ideas of the nation breathed life and purpose into mathematical abstractions. In these moments romanticism was not the antagonist of rationalism, but its complement.

Conclusion

Before we move to the story of how Keynesian national income accounting conquered the world, it may be useful to summarize the main choices it embodied.

First, it was an elaboration of a basic circular flow conception that rested on a split between household and business, which was in turn an expression of modernist ideology. In other words, the assumption that the productive activity of a society can be sorted into two categories, and sorted by the state of mind of the people doing that activity, is foundational.

Second, the Keynesian version of the basic circular flow stresses *monetary* spending. This is because it is concerned with inflation, a monetary problem, and more broadly with the command over goods and services achieved by the distinct flows of spending by consumers, businesses, and government.[24] The theoretical rift is easily overlooked because there are two quite different ways to *read* these diagrams – like one of those trick pictures that is either a rabbit or a duck. One way is to interpret the money merely as a unit, that is as a convenient way of putting a single number to flows of disparate "real" goods and services. The other way, Keynes' way, is to treat money as important *in itself*, as a financial asset with its own properties. Keynes did not ignore "real" flows of goods and services, but did not treat economy as *reducible* to real flows of goods and services. He argued that the kind of economy that developed in Britain in the late nineteenth century – with a large financial system generating short- and long-term credit, and in which most of the money used for transactions is bank deposits that can be generated by new lending – is a quite different beast from an idealized barter economy in which real goods and services are swapped for each other. So while it is certainly possible to use money as a mere unit, just like an inch or an ounce are mere units, in key respects a dollar is *not* like an inch or an ounce. You can hold dollars, spend dollars, or find yourself short of dollars; you cannot hold, spend, or find yourself short of inches or ounces.

The monetary/real question points to an immense field of theoretical controversy. There is a large tradition of orthodox economic theory, before and after Keynes, which believes that economy should be understood and theorized in "real" terms, and that money is simply a "veil" over a real economy. Thinkers in this tradition have tended to resist government policy to remedy unemployment or ease recessions. But some radical critics of globalization (Chapters 9 and 10) *also* postulate a "real" economy, *also* believe money is most properly a unit of account, and *also* find it spooky and alarming when money and finance take on any life of their own. For those critics money *ought* to be a transparent coding of the real, and something has gone wrong with the world if the coding takes on its own life.

We can highlight the differences by pointing to two alternatives to Keynesian national income accounting, both of them real rather than monetary. One alternative was the "input-output" analysis developed by Wassily Leontief (Leontief 1953). Input-output analysis divided production into multiple compartments, like mining, metals, textiles, machinery, and agriculture, and traced the flows between them. It is attuned to bottlenecks: if demand for food increases, and farmers order more tractors, can tractor output keep pace? The Keynesian system, which is "very condensed" as Vanoli puts it, cannot see this kind of problem (Vanoli 2010, p. 3). Another not-chosen path was the welfare approach developed by Simon Kuznets (Chapter 1), which sought to measure the flow of life-improving benefits to households. The Keynesian system was neither designed nor intended to address welfare (i.e., well-being) questions.

We turn next to what happens when you build a world economy out of these national units.

Notes

1 The essay was written in 1943 (Skidelsky 2001, pp. 164–165).
2 See also Dostaler (2007, pp. 68–70).
3 Harrod (1951, p. 507). See also Patinkin (1982, p. 238 and *passim*) on this theme. Stone (1978), though characterstically emollient, is insightful. Among the merits of Patinkin's article, published in *Econometrica* in 1976 before republication in expanded form in 1982, is that its sharp criticism of Keynes provoked Stone to greater clarity on Keynes' attitudes toward data and theory (Tily 2009).
4 See also T. Mitchell (2002, pp. 6–7).
5 See also T. Mitchell (2005) on the role that debates over German productive capacity played in generating conceptions of a national economy.
6 Hans Singer (interviewed by Keith Tribe (1997, p. 59)) described the work he and fellow-student V. K. R. V Rao (see Chapter 1) did under Colin Clark (1905–1989) and adds:

    So we worked ... you might say, as a team under Colin Clark, inspired by this then-new idea of national income, and of course very much encouraged by Keynes. Because Keynes wanted a statistical equivalent of his concept of aggregate demand for the *General Theory*.

    See also (Clark 1985, p. 62). Patinkin (1976, pp. 1111–1118) critiques this story, arguing that Keynes' 1930s support for Clark's work was lukewarm, and noting the criticisms Clark's work attracted during that decade. Clark, perhaps feeling unappreciated, left in 1937 for a high-profile career in his native Australia (Maddison 2004, pp. 8–10). When Keynes became engaged with the subject around the end of the 1930s, he turned to a junior statistician, Erwin Rothbarth, to help him develop data and concepts and shift away from the elements of Clark's work he found troublesome (Keynes 1940b; Suzuki 2003, pp. 479–481; Tily 2009; Mitra-Kahn 2011, pp. 211–215).
7 Comim (2001). See also Moggridge (1992, p. 645), Mitra-Kahn (2011, pp. 210–225) and Harrod (1951, p. 503): "Three or four times each week Mr. Stone visited Keynes, who took a meticulous interest in every detail."
8 Mitra-Kahn (2011); Studenski (1958). I will say more in Chapter 5 about estimation, but it should be emphasized that even in the wealthiest nations with the most capable statistical bureaus, nobody has anything like complete information on any of these flows. The work of making national income accounting *persuasive* was twofold: its audience had to be convinced both that the theoretical frame made sense, *and* that the

numbers attached to it were good enough for useful work. There is a danger in expounding only the theory, as I am doing in this chapter. The danger is that it is easy to assume that the theory's formal elegance and pleasing interlockings were persuasive on their own. They were not. An informed critic could see the interlockings as mere jiggery-pokery, an effort to make a small body of data look more impressive than it was.

9 See discussion in E. O'Brien (1989).

10 Treatment of government as a *separate* productive sector is clear in Rothbarth and Keynes (1939); Keynes (1940a, 1940b), Great Britain, Treasury (1941), Stone *et al.* (1942), and Gilbert (1942).

11 Along these lines see Singer (1987) and Toye (2006). I am largely bracketing off the larger story of the development and spread of Keynesian macroeconomic theory. A starting point is M. S. Morgan (2003, p. 293), who shows that Keynes had developed a much simpler theory than competing economists in the 1930s, and that his work inspired younger economists to do further formalization, model-building, and exposition.

12 On the Newlyn-Phillips collaboration see M. S. Morgan (2012) and Newlyn (2011), on Phillips' career see Bollard (2016), on the physical properties and difficulties of the machine Ryder (2009) is wonderfully illuminating. The video demonstration by McRobie (2016) is highly recommended to get a sense of a working machine; other essential literature includes Phillips (1950), Barr (1988, 2000), Hayes (2011), Bollard (2011), and M. S. Morgan and Boumans (2004).

13 This is adapted and simplified from Phillips (1950, p. 285). I follow his exposition fairly closely.

14 In physical reality the flow is not just a function of the width of the pipe left open by the valve, but also of the head of water above it. Phillips employed ingenious hydraulic mechanisms to get around this problem and keep heads constant; I omit them for the sake of simplicity. See Ryder (2009) on the difficulties making a physical system do what Phillips needed.

15 Its most interesting feature is that the level of a *stock* controls the rates of two *flows*. If you take a microeconomics course, you will learn an algebraic version of this model: supply and demand curves are linear functions solved for the equilibrium (P,Q) pair – the flow equilibrium. This physical model dramatizes the process of *finding* equilibrium: the plumbing apparatus will not instantly find the equilibrium price but will only gradually converge on it, with some overshooting and undershooting and general sloshing about. Further, as long as the functions represented by the slots are continuous and have the right overall slope (the supply curve slopes up and the demand curve slopes down), they do not need to be linear, nor need they have *any* simple algebraic expression: as long as you can cut the shape, the machine will solve for equilibrium (Phillips 1950, p. 287).

16 I am simplifying here and omitting the transactions balances tank at the bottom, and skirting a certain ambiguity in Phillips' (1950) formulation about at what point water/ income at the bottom should be interpreted as flowing from businesses to households. For more complete diagrams please see Phillips (1950) and Barr (1988); Barr's diagrams inspired Figure 3.6.

17 The machine could be set up to model different theoretical assumptions including the "classical" view.

18 Part of the experience of teaching macroeconomics is struggling with this metaphorical thicket: students are primed to think of the nation as an organism possessing its own spirit and will, thriving or languishing, and competing with like organisms.

19 See Stevenson (2011, p. 153):

What is most striking about the machine is that it gives 'the national economy' – that invisible yet omnipresent being – a physical body. The hitherto unseeable multitude of social processes and restless circulatory activity that we call the economy and recognise only via its abstractions can, with this model, be viewed in its entirety, in the round ... beyond these economic capabilities it is also an undeniable sculptural presence.

20 There is a rich literature on homeostasis and cybernetic feedback models in social sciences e.g., Giddens (1977, pp. 96–129) and Mirowski (2001).

21 On the visuality of national income accounting see also Fuerst (1950), Vanoli (2005), Klein (2001), Thompson (1998), Speich Chassé (2008), and Hirschman (2015).

22 As Comim (2001, p. 220) describes Stone's accounts: "The basic forms of economic activity when put together would provide a display of the basic structure ... The main message conveyed by the measurement framework of an accounting structure was of mutual interdependence among definitionally separate parts." On bodies see Thompson (1998, p. 299). Writes Desrosières (2003, p. 560): "What was most crucially new in the Keynesian perspective was the presentation of the economy as a whole, developing through several macroeconomic flows that could be measured and joined together within theoretically coherent and exhaustive tables of accounts."

23 See Esty (2009), Skidelsky (1992, p. xix), and Karl (2010).

24 T. Mitchell (2005). The difference is also a core theme of the Post Keynesian literature e.g., Davidson (1994).

4 Shape of the world

WWII marks a watershed in economic representation. It is not just that abstract economic measures and frameworks were standardized globally, but that data began pouring in to fill them, and the resulting figures were published. The postwar period saw a radical shift in the scope, consistency, and availability of information about global production, trade, and finance. This was largely the work of a set of new international institutions. The key early players were the Organisation for European Economic Cooperation (OEEC) and United Nations; the IMF and World Bank also came to play important roles in the standardization and publication of data. This chapter spotlights national income, but the new visibility extended to a much wider range of data, including statistics on health and population.

A new global system of international institutions could compel the production of data according to their standards, and supervise national governments through it. The postwar period saw the creation of a three-level governmentality with national governments in the middle: sovereigns of their populations, but subjects of international organizations. Governments were collectors of data and newly visible through data. As argued in Chapter 3, the spotlight that Keynesian national accounting shines on government does not necessarily *favor* government.

The postwar system featured rapid decolonization, a shift from a world of empires to a world of formally equivalent sovereign nations (McNeely 1995). The new international organizations structured nationhood: one did not just become independent, one became independent *into* a particular order of nations. At the largest structural level, what happened was a transformation that constrained and channeled the governments of newly independent countries, imposing watchful disciplines on them and their populations.

This broad argument is not novel, and the basic problematic was set in T. Mitchell (2005), who is particularly clear about the link between the development of Keynesian monetary economics and the new emphasis on the bounded national economy. What I aim to contribute in this first part of the book is that the concepts imported with national income accounting had significant content, globally normalizing ideologies about household, market, and rationality, ideologies about which people are the deserving subjects of modernity, and which are the appropriate objects of tutelary discipline.

This chapter contains three sections at rising levels of abstraction. The first is the people-and-institutions story, because some specifics of the unfolding of the globalization of Keynesian national income accounting matter. I then want to pin down a central analytical point: that when national accounting figured the nation as a discrete and self-sufficient organism, that was *also* a theory about how the international economy worked. National income accounting not only overplayed the influence of national governments, but also screened from view the structural properties of the world economy. Finally, I return to the three-level governmentality noted above, and the paradoxical position of the state within it.

Gilbert and Stone conquer the world

The first chapter examined how economists split economy from household in the early twentieth century. The third chapter discussed Keynes' *particular* reassembly of the hived-off "economic" bits into a single integrated national economy, a framework that could be filled with data. But Keynes was hardly the only academic economist in the late 1930s with opinions on these matters. We have mentioned the very different views of U.S. economists like Fisher and Kuznets. There were also long-standing, and arguably more sophisticated, traditions of national accounting in France, Germany, and the Scandinavian countries. How and why did Keynes' particular vision prevail? The key moments in the institutional story:

> *Wartime Britain*: Keynes persuaded the British government in 1940 to hire James Meade and Richard Stone to estimate data using his framework as an aid to wartime planning. He got their estimates officially published.

> *Wartime U.S.*: Government planners, most notably Milton Gilbert, adopted Keynes' framework, displacing Simon Kuznets' approach. British and U.S. Keynesians established close collaborative relations during the war.

> *Postwar U.S. and OEEC*: Gilbert assured the defeat of Kuznetsian accounting in the U.S. and then moved to the Organization for European Economic Cooperation, which was in a position to require Keynesian accounting by U.S.-aided countries in Western Europe.

> *OEEC and UN*: Gilbert's ally Richard Stone became the chief technical expert engaged in developing the OEEC system, the leader of UN national accounts standardization, and the director of a research unit at Cambridge that did essential early research in national accounting

In a nutshell, a set of international organizations emerged right after WWII that needed standardized nation-level concepts. Richard Stone and Milton Gilbert had forged a common Anglo-American position during the war on national income accounting. They found influential roles in those organizations after the war, and dominated the postwar discussion into the 1950s. There was no serious competitor. No alternative system of national accounting had such well-placed advocates or was as well poised to claim global applicability.

Let us trace the story a little more fully. Keynes served in the British Treasury during WWI, but resigned in protest during the Versailles talks and held an academic post at Cambridge University during the 1920s and 1930s. He remained well-connected to official circles, though not universally popular in them.[1] In 1939 he began circulating drafts of what became the 1940 pamphlet *How to Pay for the War* (1940a), which marks the first formal appearance of the $Y = C + I + G$ framework, as described in the previous chapter. Even before he returned to the British Treasury in an advisory role in 1940, he persuaded friends in the Cabinet Office (circumventing the Treasury) to hire two economists to begin estimating the elements of that framework (Pesaran and Harcourt 2000, p. 148). The British government up to that point had no equivalent of Simon Kuznets' unit at the U.S. Commerce Department; no official interest in measuring national income or output with *any* methodology. Austin Robinson (1897–1993) had been a close colleague of Keynes at Cambridge in the 1930s and worked for the British Cabinet Office during the war. In a 1985 reminiscence he tells the story:

> At the beginning of the war, as everyone will remember, Keynes published his pamphlet "How to Pay for the War." I had heard him give this as a lecture in Cambridge. It was obvious that the proper management of a war economy necessitated the regular preparation of a national income estimate. I reported this to Francis Hemming, my boss in the small group of economists then late in 1939 working in the Cabinet Office. He took me to explain it to Sir Edward Bridges, Secretary of the Cabinet, and we were given authority to recruit two persons to tackle the work. We invited James Meade and Richard Stone.
>
> (Robinson 1987, p. 144)

Meade (1907–1995) had been an economist at the League of Nations; Stone (1913–1991) was a 1936 graduate of Keynes' Cambridge department. Under Keynes' guidance, they worked on the technical elaboration of his system and gathered data.[2] In 1940 and early 1941 this remained a marginal effort, which might easily have produced only obscure internal memos. Meade, Stone, and Keynes faced highly informed criticism from British Treasury officials over the sketchiness and thin evidentiary basis of Stone and Meade's estimates (Suzuki 2003, pp. 496–498). The fact that the Keynesian system rested on identities like $Y = C + I + G$ made it possible to estimate some totals not directly, but simply by subtraction from other more easily estimated totals. Keynes and his colleagues carried on a contentious exchange of memos with Hubert Henderson (1890–1952), an Oxford Economist serving as Economic Advisor to the Treasury, over this point. British Treasury officials regarded it as a public trust to publish only figures that could be derived from "ascertained facts"; Keynes was proposing to publish precise-*looking* numbers that rested on meager evidence and rough-and-ready guesswork. In the background was a policy tension: the Keynesian system that these numbers would flesh out was an effort to overturn the "Treasury view" about the ineffectiveness of public spending as an anti-recession measure. This explains why Keynes (after considering various expedients) turned to his cabinet-office friends to publish Stone and Meade's estimates as an appendix to an April 1941 working paper on wartime finance, circumventing Treasury. Stone wrote: "It was a great day. We drank champagne that night and felt we had accomplished something."[3]

Even more important changes were afoot across the Atlantic. As noted in Chapter 1, Simon Kuznets was hired by the U.S. Department of Commerce in 1932 to estimate U.S. national income. His concept of national income emphasized the well-being of households. Kuznets ignored government purchases from businesses. But a new locus of economic investigation opened up in 1941, when Franklin Roosevelt established the Office of Price Administration and Civilian Supply (OPACS), part of the new and war-related Office for Emergency Management. Though best known for developing wartime price controls, OPACS economists quickly took on the tasks of quantitative planning, and for this they adopted Keynes' framework, *not Kuznets'*.[4] The central figure was Milton Gilbert (1909–1979), a student of Kuznets who had worked in the Commerce Department unit that Kuznets had established before joining OPACS. Gilbert and his colleagues drew up national accounts on Keynesian lines as early as June 1941, and consulted with Keynes himself in June and July 1941 during one of Keynes' U.S. visits (Mitra-Kahn 2011, p. 251).[5] Keynes' 1936 *General Theory of Employment, Interest, and Money* had already been widely read and absorbed by younger U.S. economists (Hall 1989; Rauchway 2015). Canadian technocrats, notably George Luxton (1914–1945) also adopted Keynesian national income accounting during the war (McDowall 2008, pp. 84–93). This meant that as the war ended, leading technical experts in the United States, Britain, and Canada were already in close theoretical and technical alignment.[6] Keynes died in 1946, but people he had trained and influenced were early in their careers, energetic, confident, bureaucratically experienced, and in communication with each other.

After the war, Gilbert consolidated the victory of Keynesian national income accounting in the United States, ensuring that there would be no peacetime reversion to Kuznets' system.[7] This was a moment of some drama. In 1947 the National Income Division of the Commerce Department, now directed by Gilbert, published *National Income and Product Statistics of the United States 1929–46* which pointedly redid all the estimates Kuznets had produced in the 1930s, using Keynesian concepts, and signaled that the Keynesian framework would be used going forward. Kuznets attacked the new figures in a 1948 article. Among other points he criticized the use of the term "accounting," a word he had never used, as providing an impression of spurious coherence, drawing unwarranted authority from business accounting. He charged that the new system may allow the investigator to rest too comfortably on the monetary surface of economic circulation, without forcing him to examine closely the real flow of commodities and services beneath the surface – a danger which, as the discussion below suggests, the report does not avoid.

(Kuznets 1948, p. 154)

This is as clear an example as you could want of an advocate of "real" analysis attacking monetary analysis as superficial. As shown in the previous chapter, Keynesian analysis emphasizes flows of spending *for their own sake*, not as proxies for something else, and integrates them into a *monetary* macroeconomic theory. By contrast for Kuznets, the central purpose of national income, moral as well as analytical, was to measure the flow of real benefits to households: good meals, warm houses, decent clothes.

Kuznets observed that the Commerce Department "classifies all goods purchased by governments as final products." He argued that this could be justified in one of two ways. One way would assume that "all government activities are devoted to providing goods to ultimate consumers." He dismisses this possibility. In his view military spending

is not a direct service to consumers: it is rather an antecedent and indispensable cost of maintaining society at large – a condition of economic production rather than an activity directly yielding final economic goods. And in times of war the proportion of government activity, the share of goods it purchases, that is devoted to services to consumers, is minor indeed.

(Kuznets 1948, p. 156)

Kuznets was hardly a pacifist. He had only a few years earlier been closely engaged, at the highest levels, in the planning of U.S. military production during the war – work that won him the awed respect of his colleagues.[8] But his prior commitment to the direct measurement of material benefits flowing to households meant that he was not prepared to include military spending among those benefits. Having disposed of this possibility, he then argued that the only other possibility was that the Commerce Department now

conceived [government] as an ultimate consumer itself, given a corporeal entity the satisfaction of whose needs is raised to the same status of finality as the satisfaction of the needs of the men and women who comprise the community.

(Kuznets 1948, p. 156)

Which was, he charged, "fetishism, with dangerous implications that should be obvious."

In their published reply, Gilbert and his team took advantage of Kuznets' earlier musing, quoted in Chapter 1, that

> All the gigantic outlays on our urban civilization, subways, expensive housing, etc., which in our usual estimates we include at the value of the net product they yield on the market, do not really represent net services to individuals comprising the nation but are, from their viewpoint, an evil necessary in order to be able to make a living.
>
> (Kuznets 1937, p. 37)

And riposted:

> Wherever Professor Kuznets may mean to draw the line between final and intermediate products by the few hints in his review, it is apparent that he is painting with a wide brush in blacking out goods and services that are commonly regarded as part of total production.
>
> (Gilbert *et al.* 1948, p. 189)

They zeroed in on the difficulty of distinguishing between "a condition of economic production" and "an activity directly yielding final economic goods," and argued that even with Kuznets' desired exclusions, national income would be a poor measure of welfare.[9] They stoutly defended the inclusion of armaments production in national output. They concluded that section:

> The moralistic flavor he wishes to inject into national income measurement might be in the tradition of Ruskin – it is not in the tradition of quantitative economics.
>
> (Gilbert *et al.* 1948, p. 189)

This was a harsh rebuke for Gilbert's teacher, and for the greatest quantitative economist of the mid-twentieth century.[10] For the purposes of this book it is noteworthy that Gilbert and associates reached for John Ruskin, the nineteenth-century romantic thinker, in order to name the despised opposite of quantitative Economics.

Gilbert moved from the Commerce Department to the OEEC in 1951 as head of its Department of Economics and Statistics. This was a significant post. The OEEC was formed in 1948 at Washington's behest. It was a nominally European organization, designed to compel the recipients of Marshall Plan aid to coordinate their requests for assistance. The OEEC's task was not merely to divide up the aid, but to propose national development plans that cohered with each other. Its work thus represented a pioneering example of what the IMF today terms "multilateral surveillance," the gathering of national strategies into a larger analytical frame. Such a frame required common concepts. Gilbert thus played a pivotal role standardizing and imposing Keynesian national accounting on Western Europe. His work has been overshadowed by his more famous friend and ally Richard Stone, the recipient of the 1984 Nobel Memorial Prize in Economics. Gilbert published relatively little and died of a heart attack in 1979. Although the UN has gotten more attention in the literature, I suggest that it was

Gilbert's OEEC that played the essential role in worldwide national accounting standardization.[11]

Still, there can be no doubt of Stone's vigor and ubiquity. He convened the key 1944 meeting among British, U.S., and Canadian government economists that reached a "tripartite agreement" to adopt Keynesian national income accounting. In 1945 Stone obtained an invitation from Alexander Loveday, the British Director of Intelligence of the League of Nations (and former employer of Stone's wartime colleague James Meade) to write a paper on national income.[12] Stone's League of Nations paper was adopted by the United Nations, the League's successor, in 1947. The United Nations became a prominent international standardizer of national income accounting and provided technical assistance to governments in building these accounts.[13] Stone also ran the OEEC's National Accounts Research Unit from its establishment in 1949 (in Cambridge) until 1951, when it was handed off to Milton Gilbert and transferred to OEEC offices in Paris (Pesaran and Harcourt 2000, p. 94). Vanoli writes of the "period of standardization in the framework of the OEEC" that

> On Richard Ruggles's instigation, at the time staff member of the Marshall's administration, a national accounts research unit is created at Cambridge, from 1949 to 1951, under Stone's direction, to prepare a normalized system of accounts. Stone's position then becomes dominant in the genesis of the first generation of standardized systems [of the OEEC and UN] ... Within the OEEC framework, where Milton Gilbert has become the Statistics and National Accounts director, the discussions are limited to Europe. Stone is surely arbitrating most of the discussions ... The United Nations is mostly useful in order to "globalize" the OEEC system.
>
> (Vanoli 2005, p. 132)

Vanoli directs us to Norwegian economist Odd Aukrust's recollection that

> Together with, among others, Jean Marczewski from France, I worked as an assistant to Stone at the "OEEC national accounts unit" in Cambridge, England, during the autumn months of 1949 when the "OEEC simplified system" was drafted. None of us had the slightest influence on the outcome. Attempts by Ingvar Ohlsson, Kjeld Bjerke and myself to influence the system in 1951 when a later version of it came up for discussion by OEEC member countries were equally unsuccessful. The standardized system of the United Nations from 1953 was agreed without contribution by Scandinavian experts.
>
> (Aukrust 1994, p. 59)

Stone's Department of Applied Economics at Cambridge *also* sponsored pioneering research on British colonial accounts, which will be explored in Chapter 5.[14] Thus in the decade after the war Stone was a central player in all three major institutions involved in globalizing Keynesian national income accounting: the UN, OEEC, and Department of Applied Economics at Cambridge. He could sponsor technical research and shape careers.[15] Some of that research is discussed in the next chapter. This is an extraordinary achievement for a technocrat who was still in his thirties. But his ability to play this role must be at least partly explained by the larger structural shift that created the need for standardized data.

Closed and open

The Keynesian national accounting framework, as we saw in Chapter 3, conceives the nation as a discrete body with linked organs.[16] Those organs include a government capable of taxing incomes, a central bank that regulates a domestic financial system, a business sector that borrows from that financial system, and savers who save by buying domestic financial assets. In classroom pedagogy, one first models a "closed economy" walled off from the rest of the world, with a government, financial system, firms, and consumers theorized as part of a self-sufficient, fully enclosed system.[17] Only once the student has mastered this closed model, and learned to think of the national economy as a discrete, self-sufficient system with interconnected parts, is the model then "opened," and flows of goods and finance permitted to trickle across its borders.[18] But when we do that, none of the *national* institutions are rethought. I will leave the formal expansion of the accounting framework laid out in Chapter 3 to an endnote.[19] For our purposes, the central point is that these accounts *begin* by imagining a self-sustaining, self-contained national economy, and add the foreign flows only later. The Newlyn-Phillips machine (Chapter 3) is a wonderful representation of this, built (as a teaching tool) to operate on its own, a visual and mechanical metaphor for the self-containedness, the institutional self-sufficiency, of this national economy.

Why worry about this? Let us start with an extreme example. In a well-known critique of this approach to the world, James Ferguson (1990), examined Lesotho in the early 1980s. Lesotho is entirely surrounded by South Africa. Though nominally independent, it was essentially a labor reserve for South Africa, not unlike the "homelands" or Bantustans that South Africa used in the apartheid era as legal fictions for the disenfranchisement of its black population. Most of Lesotho's paid labor force migrated to work in South Africa; almost all the goods available for purchase in Lesotho came from South Africa. There was almost no formal financial system. Yet if you consult the IMF's *International Financial Statistics*, you will find that Lesotho boasts a full set of "national" accounts. Ferguson shows that international organizations and aid agencies required the confection of a measured "national economy" for Lesotho, plus the attendant fictions that its government carried out national policy.[20] He argued that this approach obliterated history and headed off the obvious conclusion that most problems identifiable within the boundaries of Lesotho were due to the South African state.

In other words two assumptions are not only built into globally-applied national income accounting, but actively advertised and promoted by the published data: that every country is in the same way integral and complete with similar internal institutions, and that the relations between national economies are relatively thin and inconsequential.[21] The fact about Lesotho that Ferguson emphasizes, its highly dependent relation to South Africa, is nowhere to be seen in its national accounting data – there is simply no data concept to which that fact of dependence corresponds. Lesotho, like South Africa and every other country in the world, *appears* through these numbers as a discrete national economy connected only to an abstract global space of goods and financial flows, without power or politics, without alliances, antagonisms, or spheres of influence. And it appears in the numbers as though it had the same internal institutional structure as, say, France.

Take a less extreme example. About 30 percent of Canada's output is exported; about two-thirds of that to the United States. What does it mean to say there is a "Canadian" economy? One of the most interesting features of Duncan McDowall's *The Sum of the Satisfactions* (McDowall 2008), a lucid and insightful history of Canadian national accounting, is that it is *also* a nationalist text. "By observing the GDP's barometric ups and downs," writes McDowall, "Canadians had learned to calibrate their economic citizenship ... [i]t provided illumination where only two generations ago in the 1930s economic darkness prevailed" (McDowall 2008, p. 248). The accounts hold up a mirror in which Canadians can see themselves as a discrete nation. McDowall reaches a high note in his discussion of the role of national income data in resolving vexed questions of the distribution of federal spending among provinces, questions that had threatened national integrity. He presents national accounting as a story of increasing Canadian self-knowledge, a practice that permitted Canadians for the first time to see the *whole* of Canada reflected in the data, and embrace the interconnection of its fractious parts.

For an image of what the *international* economy looks like after we assume discrete and self-sufficient national economies, consider Figure 4.1, which depicts two linked Newlyn-Phillips machines (Chapter 3) in one of James Meade's early 1950s classes in International Economics at the London School of Economics. Each machine represents a complete national economy. A single machine could be run as a lone "closed economy," or opened up with a foreign sector in a "spare tank" (Barr 1988). But to model an *international* economy, two mirror-image machines were built, linked so that the exports of one were the imports of the other. Writes Barr: "the two machines formed a two-country world economy; it was possible to show the effect on the UK of, say, a budget deficit in the USA; and it was possible to show the effects of a trade war" (Barr 1988, p. 329).

Meade's students are looking at a world economy. In the picture are not only two self-contained national economies, but also an interstitial space connecting them, a "space of flows."[22] That near-empty space through which Meade strides is the space of the international economy, the space the IMF would later invest with its own spirit. His students can examine one or the other national economy (what the IMF will term bilateral surveillance), or they can examine the connected ensemble (what the IMF will term multilateral surveillance). Barr provides examples of both:

Figure 4.1 James Meade demonstrates an international economy with linked Newlyn-Phillips machines.[1]

Note
1 From LSE Library's collections, MEADE/16/1, reproduced by permission.

Meade ... would make one student Chancellor of the Exchequer, with instructions to manipulate taxation and government spending so as to achieve a target level of national income; he would then make another student Governor of the Bank of England with instructions to use monetary policy to similar ends. Each student was instructed to ignore the other, to show how counter-cyclical fiscal and monetary policy, if unco-ordinated, can end up making matters worse. With the two machines connected, he would add the US Secretary of the Treasury and the Chairman of the Federal Reserve, and the four students, each acting independently of the others, would show how destabilising policy in one country can readily be transmitted to another and how, in the extreme, an interlinked international economy can be even more unstable than a domestic economy. Richard Cooper, subsequently US Assistant Secretary of the Treasury and Professor of Economics at Yale, said at the time that it was the Phillips machine which first showed him how much one thing depended on another.

(Barr 1988, pp. 329–330)

The most important element of the photograph in Figure 4.1 is the gaze of the assembled students, a gaze the photograph invites us to join from the back of the classroom. They, and we, are being trained to see the *world* economy.

For a more purely mathematical example, consider the pioneering 1954 monograph by IMF theoretician Jacques Polak, titled simply *An International Economic System* (Polak 1954).[23] Polak starts by constructing a detailed single-country model. Each country has its own *self-contained* set of "autonomous factors" which influence national income and imports. Polak requires three chapters to build the standard national model. Once that work is done, he needs *less than a page* to build a world model: he simply reduces the national model to a single equation showing imports as a function of exports, imagines one such equation for each country, and sums them all up to produce a world equation.[24] This is how the world is made! Each national economy is treated like any other national economy *in its internal structure*. Each interacts not with other particular economies, but with a composite entity called "world trade" (Polak 1954, p. 16). The "autonomous factors" that affect a country's income and import behavior are *internal to that country only*; no re-specification of the isolated national model is made once the country is imagined as part of a world. This is a world without international power, and without any institution aside from "world trade" that spans multiple nations – no transmigrants or families resident in multiple countries, no transnational unions or transnational businesses or border-crossing financial systems. The specific relations between South Africa and Lesotho, or between the United States and Canada, are illegible. The close relations between any particular export sector and particular foreign buyers are illegible. There is no category – no conceptual category, no measurable thing – in which the structure of the international financial system might appear.

In this way the *international* market is conceptualized as a space of pure flows, a space without people or institutions, who are all tucked away inside national economies. This effect is strengthened by the way orthodox economists like to model markets, as efficient, anonymous, smoothly adjusting mechanisms to facilitate flows of goods and services and exchanges of assets.

Discipline

Collection of data according to standardized categories eased its publication. Almanacs of data published by international organizations like the United Nations or IMF represent the imposition of a standardized grid of surveillance across the world. The world appears within the pages of these publications sliced into separate national compartments, each described by the same grid of data concepts, each with the same regular progression of time. The grid has an *individuating* effect in the way each national economy is conceptualized as a discrete whole, its condition traceable to the policy successes and failures of its national government.[25] This was quite different from the world that appeared in maps and almanacs before WWII, which was a world of sprawling, geographically-discontinuous empires, a world in which international power was much more obvious.

This fit the panoptic quality of official post-WWII international organizations, dividing the world's population into national cells and spotlighting their condition by means of statistics-gathering. The brightly lit UN General Assembly is a visual metaphor for this observed world, each formally identical nation named and fixed in space. While the fit with Foucault's (1977) discussion of Bentham's prison is not precise – the observed nation is not a person – the larger points about representation and the generation of knowledge hold, as does Foucault's characteristic emphasis on mundane institutional practice – while the theoretical innovations of figures like Polak are important, they must be seen against a background of hard, constant, self-effacing technical work to fill categories with persuasive data. The weight that statistical almanacs carry depends on their capacity to fill space and time with numbers, or, perhaps, to generate attractive representations of time and space, of history and scale, *via data*.

Foucault's later work on "governmentality" is helpful for thinking about the power relations linked to this kind of knowledge. Governmentality is sometimes glossed as "the conduct of conduct" and approaches government not simply as restrictive, but as *productive* of subjects who learn to govern themselves.[26] Most of the literature on this concept treats it as an "art of government" developed in various self-contained (generally Western European) nation-states, so that there are just the two levels of government and governed. Here it may be more useful to think in terms of a three-layered governmentality. At the bottom are households and firms, conceived of as tiny self-governing units, but also subject to criticism and regulation if they fail to produce people (households) or goods (firms) properly. At the next level up is the national government, responsible for the surveillance of its households and firms but always with the knowledge that the top layer, international organizations, is staring over its shoulder.

National income accounts let us look at nations through the eyes of international organizations like the IMF. Thus governments gained new powers of knowledge and persuasion via national accounting, but those powers came, as in a fairy tale, with a curse.[27] Government *itself* became more visible and vulnerable, more exposed. If we put this in the context of Foucault's argument that "the market" became "a site of veridiction of for government practice" in the eighteenth century (Foucault 2008, p. 33), national income accounting extends the idea of the "economy" as something that is not only outside government, but whose "performance" could be used to judge whether a government governs properly.

From one side of WWII to the other, there was a shift in the way powerful governments and international organizations categorized and represented the world. Before the war global-scale difference was understood racially and civilizationally, which often amounted to the same thing. After the war official rhetoric and representation shifted quickly. Every nation got its own seat in the key multilateral organizations; every nation was awarded its own economy. Explicit, talked-about difference shifted from race to ordered and developed versus disordered and underdeveloped economies and societies. A rhetoric of discipline and punishment – for disordered people, families, and nations – structured the emerging world and international institutions. In other words, difference worked differently: on the one hand rigorously standardized categories of nation, government, household, business, and citizen promised formal equality; on the other hand the world could be divided into those who lived up to and enacted these categories, and those who fell short and therefore required tutelage and discipline.[28]

This is an exemplary "scale-making project," in Tsing's language, a complex of representational and discursive work to make a scale thinkable and effective. It built on Keynes' modular notion of "national economy," a notion that traveled (Speich Chassé 2008). As we will see in the next chapter, Keynes intended this portability from the beginning.

Notes

1 On Keynes' fraught relations with Treasury see Skidelsky (2001, pp. 69–71) and Patinkin (1982, p. 254 footnote 53). Aside from his 1919 resignation-in-protest, Keynes' academic and policy work from the mid-1920s onward was an extended attack on the "Treasury view" about the ineffectiveness of government policy in countering recession. See one instance in Moggridge (1992, pp. 491–495).
2 See Comim (2001), Mitra-Kahn (2011, pp. 210–225), Harrod (1951, p. 503), Moggridge (1992, p. 645), Stone (1951).
3 The fullest account of this conflict is in Suzuki (2003). The quote is from (Stone 1951, p. 85). See also Seers (1976) and Mitra-Kahn (2011).
4 Worked out by Mitra-Kahn (2011) with great care; see also McDowall (2008), Suzuki (2003), Patinkin (1976), Tily (2009) Comim (2001) and Kendrick (1970). Note the interaction between Stone and Gilbert's 1943 papers, and their shared critique of Kuznets. See also Stone (1978, pp. 68–72).
5 Özgöde (2015, pp. 118–152) provides a fascinating and context-rich exploration of Gilbert's U.S. work.
6 See also Alway (2009, pp. 84–98).
7 Mitra-Kahn (2011) Kuznets (1948), Kane (2012), Perlman and Marietta (2005). The extent of Gilbert's renovation, and the subsequent controversy with Kuznets, is described fully in Duncan and Shelton (1978, pp. 84–95) and explored in Kane (2012, pp. 17–20), which demonstrates how Gilbert's thinking developed during the war. Perlman (1996) shows how and why the Kuznets-Gilbert difference developed and provides a sympathetic discussion of Kuznets' point of view; I am much indebted to Perlman and his collaborators. Note the prior skirmish in Gilbert *et al.* (1944) and Gilbert's 1942 and 1943 papers.
8 Galbraith (1980, pp. 77), Perlman (1996, p. 217), Fogel (2000), and Lacey (2011).
9 The irony is that this (entirely reasonable) point is deployed here to fend off Kuznets: if you're interested in welfare, Gilbert says in effect, go and develop appropriate indicators. Compare this to the Sarkozy story in the Introduction, in which the failure to measure welfare becomes a *critique* of national income.
10 Kuznets went on, in the 1950s and 1960s, to do the seminal work in economic growth that earned him the 1971 Nobel Memorial Prize. He returned to the controversy over government in Kuznets (1951).
11 The necessity of a common frame, and the work to build it, is presented clearly in Gilbert and Stone (1954). Key OEEC products are Gilbert and Kravis (1954) and Gilbert (1958), which was prepared by OEEC staff under Gilbert's direction (Tribe 1997, p. 170). The handoff from the OEEC to UN is discussed in Vanoli (2005) and summarized in Maddison (2003, p. 24) and Kendrick (1972, p. 19). On the UN's work

please see Ward (2004, pp. 45–103). A representative contemporary assessment is Cooper and Crawford (1953, pp. 222). Remarkably little research on OEEC history has appeared given how central this organization was, especially in the 1950s and 1960s, to international economic policy and frameworks for understanding it. See also Malaguerra (2003) and Alway (2009, p. 303).

12 Stone's account in Pesaran and Harcourt (2000, p. 94) describes this as almost accidental, but Stone tended to play down the bureaucratic side of his work. See also Stone (1951, pp. 97–100).

13 For early UN work see United Nations Statistical Office (1947, 1948), United Nations (1953, 1955) Accounts include McNeely (1995) and Ward (2004). On the subsequent development of national accounting standardization see in particular Vanoli (2005, 2010) On this period see also Korzeniewicz *et al.* (2004).

14 Breit (2013): "Following the war, Stone returned to Cambridge where, at Keynes's urging, the Department of Applied Economics had been founded. With Keynes's strong backing, Stone was appointed its first director." See Stone (1978, pp. 86–87), Epstein (2014, pp. 142–143), McNeely (1995, p. 77) and Kendrick (1970, p. 310) on the UN's role in standardization.

15 Stone described the series of events in Pesaran and Harcourt (2000, p. 94).

16 Bergeron (2004, p. 8) See Buck-Morss (1995) on the larger history of the figuration of the "social body." Also Gibson-Graham (1990, pp. 95–119).

17 Danby (2000, 2004b) further specifies what can be called an *openness-invariant* understanding of a national economy. On accounting Yanovsky (1965, p. 14) writes:

> A social accounting system is admissible as long as it has a coherently determined plan for the analytical presentation of economic aggregates, so that there is some interdependence between them. It is *the interdependence and not the comprehensiveness* that determines whether the set of accounts constitute a system or not.
>
> (Emphasis added)

See also Cameron (2003) and Hirst *et al.* (2009). See Thompson (1998, p. 312) on the balance of payments. Seers (1952, 1976) provides a cogent critique of the assumptions that the unit under discussion is whole, homogeneous, and independent. Radice (1984) is a pioneering critique along these lines.

18 This "opening" of the model typically happens much later in the textbook, or in a different course.

19 A simple version: part of domestic output is bought by foreigners (exports or "X") and part of total domestic demand is met by foreigners (imports or "M"). Hence the trade balance (X – M = Net exports). Some foreigners purchase domestic financial assets. Call that gross foreign saving. Some domestic residents purchase foreign financial assets. Call that gross foreign investment. *Net* foreign investment (NFI) is therefore gross foreign investment minus gross foreign savings. This yields a compact balance of payments:

$$X - M = NFI.$$

We add this to

$$C + I + G = Y = C + S + T$$

And get

$$C + I + G + (X - M) = Y = C + S + T + NFI$$

20 See also T. Mitchell (2002) and Bergeron (2004). This section, and indeed a large part of this book, follows trails blazed by Bergeron's study of development Economics, and her critique of the use of the national unit is much more fully worked out.

21 See also Alway (2009, pp. 152, 186, and *passim*) and Escobar (1995).

22 The precise hydraulic, mechanical, and/or electrical linkages Meade was using to model flows between the two machines/countries are not documented in the published literature. Phillips (1950) suggests simply hooking the export hose of one country to the import hose of another and assuming a fixed exchange rate, but Meade (Barr 1988) appears to have used an apparatus that allowed modeling both fixed and float- ing rates, and Barr, in a personal e-mail, writes that the linkage in Figure 4.1 was mechanical rather than hydraulic. The machine is also a creature of its time (see Chapter 6) in that it did not model foreign capital flows.

23 Polak was also an early enthusiast of the Newlyn-Phillips machine (Dorrance 2011, p. 117).

24 Equation 51.4, for the nation:

$$m_i = \rho_i \sigma' x_w + a_i$$

(m_i and x_w are national imports and world exports; see p. 42 of Polak 1954 for the def- inition of ρ, p. 49 for the definition of σ', and 54 for the definition of a_i).

   Equation 51.5, for the world:

$$\sum_i m_i = x_w \sum_i \rho_i \sigma' + \sum_i a_i$$

from which he generates a world multiplier, given that $\sum_i m_i = x_w$.

25 Similar programs of surveillance can be seen in the other Bretton Woods institutions e.g., Cammack (2002) on the World Bank.

26 Burchell *et al.* (1991), Dean (1999), Bratich *et al.* (2003), Foucault (2008, 2009, 2011).

27 Desrosières (2003, p. 561): "Here again, state and statistics were co-constructed. As the state gained this new responsibility to preserve macroeconomic equilibrium without sacrificing the market economy, there arose a new mode of description and analysis – national accounting and macroeconometric modeling..."

28 This becomes clearer if we set literature on economy alongside contemporary liter- ature on population (Connelly 2010). See McCann (2016) and Danby (2012). Note also the tendency in some economic models to blow up the "the household" to the national scale via a "representative household" that stands for an entire country (Bergeron 2004, pp. 106–108). In all these examples the trace of race remained, espe- cially in ideas of disordered reproduction.

5   Discovering economies in British Africa

Why colonial accounts mattered

It is sometimes argued that national income accounting is a narrowly Anglo-American system that was heedlessly exported to the rest of the world. This was not quite the case. For one thing, Keynesian national income accounting was far from a simple or obvious expression of the British or U.S. "economies." We have seen already (Chapter 4) that leading experts in both countries (Simon Kuznets in the United States and Hubert Henderson in Britain) found those accounts misleading or worse. But more interestingly, Keynesian national income accounting was developed from the beginning with the aim of broad application. Experimental national income estimates in British colonies in the 1940s and 1950s paved the way for the global expansion of national income accounting.

In 1941, only a few months after finagling to get his British accounts officially published (Chapter 4), Keynes organized an effort to build similar accounts for three British colonies. In addition to demonstrating the broad applicability of Keynesian national accounting, these early exercises expanded the technical capacities of national income accountants at a time when there were only a handful of people in the world who could be so described. Was national income accounting a portable technique? It was one thing, for example, for Simon Kuznets and his 1930s Commerce Department colleagues to develop, over years, a deep institutional understanding of U.S. industry, agriculture, and commerce, and a "feel" for the reliability of different data sources: such knowledge was not transferable to other countries. Could a technician parachute into an unfamiliar country and produce a respectable set of accounts in a few months?

Addressing the technical questions that arose in colonial accounts forced renewed attention to what counted as production, and where to draw the boundary between household and economy, issues that were more settled (or at least, less debated) in Britain and the United States. Aside from working from exceptionally scant data, the most interesting technical challenge was how to measure production that did not pass through markets. As we saw in Chapter 1, Marshall and his successors assumed that Britain and the United States were "modern" societies characterized by a sharp distinction between love and money. But what did it mean to take these ideas about economy and apply them to Africans, one of modernity's longest-serving others? We will see a variety of responses to this challenge, but the upshot was the statistical construction of African modernity.

Alternatives to that view were simply read out of economic practice. This chapter will discuss two discarded alternatives. Herbert Frankel's romantic view that Africans had a fundamentally different notion of economy from Europeans was forced out of Economics and, for better or worse, into Anthropology. Dudley Seers' preference for country-specific analyses sensitive to linkages to the outside world fell on deaf ears not because his arguments were unsound, but because they denied easily replicable statistical practice.

Thus in the end, the fundamental binary we saw in Mill and Marshall (Chapter 1) prevailed. "Economy" was business, rationality, and the herald of full modernity; "household" was a sphere of loving domesticity excluded from economy. Measuring economy made it real as a distinct sector.

I will focus in this chapter on early national income accounting in British Africa. But one other stream of postwar research bears mention. There got underway in the early 1950s a United Nations effort to provide technical assistance in national accounting to a range of countries, many recently independent. This produced some outstanding work.[1] But those studies bear the hallmarks of the consultant working for an international bureaucracy and writing for an independent government: they tend to be cautious, non-controversial, and limited in the data they could access.[2] What made the African colonial studies featured in this chapter interesting was their freedom to experiment and pursue controversy, and their authors' relatively privileged access to official data.

National accounting as bricolage

It is time for the promised words on estimation. An accountant working for a business normally expects to build up accounts from records generated by actual transactions. Figures are in principle accurate to the penny. You could imagine an ideal (or nightmare, depending on your point of view) national economy that generated documentation of similar exactness. Every transaction would be reported instantly to authorities by every transactor, giving them the complete view, and multiple cross-checks, that an accountant working in a business might expect.

No national statistical authority, anywhere, has anything like that. All published national income figures are estimates. Many are crude estimates. Moreover, while the interlocking structure developed during the war by Meade and Stone has the virtue that totals can be checked against each other, it has the corresponding vice of making it easy to estimate missing figures as residuals. In other words, if according to my accounting framework $A + B = C$, I would ideally arrive at estimates of all three and use them to check each other. But if I have no clue about B, I can just plug in $C - A$ and the numbers will *look* good.

This was one of the objections raised in the British Treasury to what their experts considered the thinly grounded estimates of Richard Stone and James Meade (Suzuki 2003, pp. 496–497). Saving, for example, is routinely estimated as a residual in national accounts because of the scarcity of useful data. I do not mean to imply there is anything underhanded about this: the technical literature is luminously clear on these limitations, and Stone, to pick only the most prominent figure, devoted great effort to developing statistical techniques that would take the best possible advantage of sketchy data, and to advocating the collection of better data to address gaps.[3]

But if we understand the challenges she faces, the art of the national income accountant becomes clearer, an art best demonstrated against the scantiest data. National income accountants draw on disparate data from different sources, data compiled for different reasons and with different methods, to construct a plausible integrated picture.[4] Some numbers, like, say, the output of individual large firms, might be available with a fair degree of precision. On the other hand, consumption (purchases of goods and services by households) might be estimated by multiplying household survey results by an estimate of the total population.[5] Agricultural output can be estimated by multiplying plot estimates by estimates of total land under cultivation. National income accounts are "statistical" in both senses of the word: they are state-produced figures (the original German sense of *Statistik*) and they routinely rely on statistical inference from surveyed samples.[6]

So national income accountants became expert scavengers, turning up a production series here, a household survey there, some tax records over there – data that could be cobbled together, with a few informed guesses, into a coherent estimate. This opportunistic quality unites early private estimators like Colin Clark with early official figures like Stone and Meade, who were, though government employees in 1940, still junior, barely-tolerated figures who had to scrounge data and equipment (Patinkin 1982, p. 253). Later technicians with more official support still faced daunting obstacles getting the simplest figures.

But what mattered *most* was keeping the larger framework in mind. Lury writes, in a review of early African accounts:

> A national accounts calculation cannot be started in a vacuum, although many statisticians must have felt that this was what they were doing! But once a minimum amount of information is available, more will probably be gained by fitting it together crudely to provide some over-all picture of the economy than by improvements in the coverage of any particular sector.
>
> (Lury 1964, p. 104)

A pioneer bricoleur was Australian economist Frederic Benham (1900–1962). From 1942 to 1945 Benham served as economic adviser to the Comptroller for Development and Welfare in the West Indies, and while there calculated, apparently on his own initiative, accounts for Jamaica, St. Vincent, Barbados, Grenada, and British Guiana. He went on to prepare accounts for Malaysia (1951) and Singapore (1959) after his appointment as commissioner-general for the United Kingdom in South-east Asia, still as an unofficial sideline. Ernest Doblin wrote in a 1945 review of Benham's Jamaica study that:

> Not very often in the history of national income estimates have economists owed to an author so much information from so little statistical raw material.
>
> (Doblin 1945, p. 224)

Studenski, who surveyed the entire corpus of early estimates, wrote appreciatively:

> These estimates are distinguished by the application of modern national income concepts and estimating techniques to underdeveloped countries possessing only the scantiest statistics. The various short cuts employed by Benham are suggestive of what may be done under such circumstances by skilled technicians.
>
> (Studenski 1958, p. 443)

Estimation matters in the story of national income accounting for several reasons. First, as noted in Chapter 4, early acceptance of Keynesian national income accounting by technically astute policymakers was impeded by the obvious sketchiness of the estimates produced. Why pay attention to lightly grounded guesses about eccentrically defined aggregates, much less base serious policy decisions on them? The labor of figures like Stone and Gilbert was simultaneously a technical effort to improve the estimates and a rhetorical effort to win the respect of other technocrats.

Second, a routine rhetorical maneuver of advocates of Keynesian national income accounting was to recast any and all critiques of their work, no matter how fundamental, as technical quibbles about the quality of estimates. If the problem was just the quality of estimates, then the obvious answer was more data-gathering to make them better. We will see examples of this maneuver later in this chapter.

Third and relatedly, as origins are forgotten and traditions of collecting data harden, effects become confused with causes. An example is unpaid household labor. Given an adequate system of household surveys, estimating unpaid household labor is easy – or at least, no harder than estimating many things currently included in standard measures of national output. But because it is excluded, uniform standards are lacking, and there is little official support for household surveys. After seven decades it becomes easy to attribute the exclusion to the poor quality of available data, but the causality is the other way around.[7] This chapter should fill in a little more about the politics of estimation.

Into Africa

Benham's workmanlike pamphlets inspired other estimators, but they were relatively terse documents. By contrast research on British Africa by a cadre of junior economists, some barely out of their twenties, took a much deeper interest in theory and method, and showed greater appetite for theoretical controversy. Significant figures include:

*   Phyllis Deane (1918–2012) on **Northern Rhodesia** (now Zambia) and **Nyasaland** (now Malawi), 1948 and 1953.
*   Dudley Seers (1920–1983) and C. Richard Ross (1924–1996) on the **Gold Coast** (now Ghana), 1952.
*   Alan Prest (1919–1984) and Ian Stewart (1923–) on **Nigeria**, 1953.
*   Alan Peacock (1922–2014) and Douglas Dosser (1927–) on **Tanganyika** (now part of Tanzania), 1958.

Deane is the pioneer among this group, and the one anointed by Keynes. In Chapter 3, I quoted Austin Robinson's 1985 reminiscence of hiring Meade and Stone in mid-1940 to build British national accounts. Immediately after telling that story, Robinson moved on to describe his role hiring Phyllis Deane in late 1941 to build colonial accounts:

> At that time there were hardly any statistics for a colonial territory. I had worked with Lord Hailey on the economic chapters of his vast African Survey…. I talked to Richard Stone about the possibility that … one might possibly be able to check the guesses that one would have to make of some of the elements and arrive at the order of magnitude of the national income of some of these territories … We were lucky enough to recruit Phyllis Deane to do the work.
>
> (Robinson 1987, p. 145)[8]

Deane recalled in a 1993 interview:

> I was invited to go down to join the National Institute of Economic and Social Research in London, where I was asked to do a project inspired by Keynes and by Richard Stone and James Meade, who had just set up a system of social accounts for the UK national income accounting. And what they wanted to do was to apply it – what *Keynes* wanted to happen – was to apply this particular system to a completely different economy than the UK and they thought they would apply it to colonial territories. So I sat in London for most of the war using the Colonial Office library and other such sources trying to work out a national income for Northern Rhodesia and Jamaica to see whether I could put that into a UK system of social accounts and what I had to do about it.
>
> (Deane and Crafts 1993)[9]

It is relevant to this story that Keynes himself had worked in the India Office as an economist from 1906 to 1908 (Chapter 3), and therefore understood the task of visualizing a distant "economy" through the scraps of data the archive yielded.

The timing is also significant: while the military situation in late 1941 was not nearly as dire as it had been a year earlier, the war's outcome at that point was far from certain. It shows an interesting level of confidence and long-term vision that Keynes and his close colleagues thought it worth devoting time and resources, *at that moment*, to launching Deane's project.

Deane's wartime work in the archives produced a book published in 1948, *The Measurement of Colonial National Incomes: An Experiment.*[10] She prepared accounts for the year 1938 for Northern Rhodesia (now Zambia) and Nyasaland (now Malawi), and for 1929–1938 for Jamaica. She concluded that "for Jamaica no very serious problems arose" in producing accounts on the British model (Deane 1948, p. 152). But for Northern Rhodesia and Nyasaland, "it soon became clear that a more comprehensive and direct knowledge of the social and economic structure of Central African peoples was essential if a satisfactory framework was to be evolved" (Deane 1948, p. 152). She specified "evaluating untraded output" and drawing the production boundary as key problems, noting in particular the dilemmas of how to treat "the whole range of women's activities, from tilling the ground to collecting firewood to preparing meals" (Deane 1948, p. 153).

One feature Deane's African studies shared with the work on Palestine discussed in Chapter 2 was an explicit racial division.[11] Data for income, output, and expenditure were split between European, Asiatic (traders of South Asian desent), and African sectors. Deane made no division of that kind for Jamaica. This reflected British colonial policy that aimed to keep, or make, Africans rural and tribal (Mamdani 1996).

After the war Deane, supervised by Stone, pursued the question of "evaluating untraded output" in Northern Rhodesia and Nyasaland (M. Morgan 2011). In 1946 she joined a cohort of young British social anthropologists working in Nyasaland and Northern Rhodesia, under the aegis of the Rhodes-Livingstone Institute in Northern Rhodesia.[12] Deane relied on her anthropologist colleagues to help administer her surveys at their field sites. The book that emerged, her 1953 monograph *Colonial Social Accounting*, can be read as a record of an economist's dialog with anthropologists.

The 1953 book's key contribution is its extensive elaboration of survey methodology for rural Central Africa. Deane wrote eloquently about the difficulties of estimating agricultural output when the range of crops planted was large and harvests were continuous. She also acknowledged the difficulties of valuation, in cases in which there was only a very limited local market that could be consulted for the prices by which quantities of production could be turned into money-measured output. But she regarded these as data-gathering challenges rather than conceptual conundrums.

Much more troubling to Deane were the problems of drawing the production boundary between economy and household, and sorting out households from each other. Households were fluid: "the sleeping household, the eating household, the income household, the producing household, and the spending household all represented different combinations and permutations within one wide family group" (Deane 1953, p. 148). Children circulated between households.[13]

As we saw in Chapter 1, the tradition exemplified by Marshall, Kuznets, and Rao generated "the economy" by splitting it off from household and family. Economy and family were opposed mentalities.[14] But when Deane visited her anthropologist colleagues' field sites, family filled the social horizon. "All a man's neighbors in the village may be related to him and to argue by analogy with a European-type family may be highly misleading" (1953, p. 126). Families were neither discrete nor bounded.[15] There were large polygamous groups, and young bachelors with ties to multiple households.

One logical solution would have been to treat these villages as large households, and simply exclude them from the measured national economy. National income accounting in Britain and the United States largely ignored activities that did not use money. But Deane, even in her archival 1948 study, had argued that non-marketed African agriculture was transitional: "[I]n studying economies which are at an early stage of development it is necessary to lay particular emphasis on activities of a kind that would be treated as exceptional, or relatively unimportant, in advanced countries."[16] In other words her argument was that a national income statistician in 1940 could safely ignore non-marketed parts of the British rural economy on the grounds that they were small and stable, but that non-marketed familial or communal output in Central Africa should be treated as poised to enter the market sphere.[17] For this reason policymakers needed data on it. But Deane was *also* deeply aware of the distinction underlined in Chapter 1: what differentiated economic from non-economic activity was not the activity, but what was in the mind of the person doing it. She brooded on the difficulty:

> The jargon of the market place seems remote, on the face of it, from the problems of an African village where most individuals spend the greater part of their lives in satisfying *their own or their families'* needs and desires, and where money and trade play a subordinate role in *motivating* productive activity.
>
> (Deane 1953, pp. 115–116, emphases added)

> [If] a man helps a neighbor to pay his tax in the definite expectation of getting a return ... the money is not gifted. Where, however, a man helps in the payment of another's tax because it is an obligation of kinship ... then this could fairly be described as a transfer payment between members of the same family. In practice, the difficulty is one of establishing the existence of a claim or expectation, however indirect it may be, or of defining the limits of the family ... Time and again in answer to the question "And what did you give in return for such-and-such a good or service?" comes the reply "Nothing. He did it to help me."
>
> (Deane 1953, p. 126)

The subaltern answer "he did it to help me" was no help to Deane. The surveyed African refused to make the economy/family split, and refused the invitation to put the neighbor either in or out of his family. Deane returned throughout the book to the problem of imputing motivation:

> we have still to establish any firm conclusions of the *mainsprings of economic behaviour* in African rural communities, on the *motives* for work or leisure.
>
> (Deane 1953, p. 10, emphases added)

> [M]oney does not have the same *power of inspiration* in the semi-subsistence economy. Social and psychological considerations frequently outweigh the money factor as a determinant of activity ... *they often do not even try to make profits* from either production or exchange.
>
> (Deane 1953, pp. 129–130, emphases added)

Deane thus anticipated the romantic view, soon to be elaborated by Herbert Frankel, that African economic activity aimed not just to produce goods but to produce society: "It has often been remarked that among primitive communities exchange itself has a social rather than an economic significance."[18] She added that much the same might be said of "more developed" economies – people may choose their jobs based partly on social characteristics, or choose where to shop partly for social or ideological reasons. Deane writes that "what is different for the primitive community is merely the degree to which social and psychological conditions determine economic activity." But despite "merely the degree," she was not ready to simply align primitive and advanced communities, because she found Africans inscrutable:

> the accounting problem is not simply that of the acute scarcity of quantitative data ... It is also a qualitative problem which brings into question the fundamental validity for primitive communities of the social accounting concepts themselves.
>
> (Deane 1953, p. 115)

> Without a more thorough knowledge of the motives for economic behaviour in the semi-subsistence economy and of the fundamental theories of value which colour the African outlook on economic matters it would not be profitable to do more than recognize the qualification and accept the limitations on the possible economic analysis. Certainly our knowledge of *the African economic outlook* is not sufficient to permit a more precise analysis.
>
> (Deane 1953, p. 228)

Let us remember that Deane did not do the village surveys on her own, but with the help of a cohort of British social anthropologists whose field sites she visited. We are thus reading the results of a three-way conversation between Deane, the anthropologists, and the surveyed Africans. We can read this as collaboration, but we can also read it as negotiating the terms of separation between Economics and Anthropology.[19] Deane's African work lets us trace a direct line from Marshall's definition of economy (itself influenced by nineteenth-century Anthropology) and Keynes' accounting framework through to the "formalist-substantivist" debate among anthropologists in the 1960s. "Substantivist" anthropologists carved out a position in opposition to mainstream Economics on relativist grounds: that theirs was a study of social wholes, each different from others and graspable only in its wholeness. This opposition is already present in Deane's work.

Deane addresses her readers as fellow members of "a highly developed community" (1953, p. 130) who fully understand our own "motives for economic behaviour" while finding Africans puzzling. Opacity and backwardness in one place stand in relation to clarity and progress in another. If we readers choose to accept the implied compliment that we are "highly developed," we accept the proposition that we share a common economic outlook that makes us understandable to each other.[20] This is the basic modernist move described in the introduction to this book, and there are visible in Deane elements of both the rationalist view – that the modern is progressive clarity and the traditional is backward opacity – and of the romantic doctrine that societies are discrete, bounded, self-enclosed systems of understanding.

The obvious postcolonial point is that the presumed self-clarity of the European economy was *itself* a fabrication: remember Alfred Marshall's story (Chapter 1) about the modern family versus the market sphere, and Kuznets' insistence that family *must* be excluded from economy in order to make sense of "economy." This myth of a society whose members all share a common rational economic motivation which makes them comprehensible *to each other* has been central to conceptions of the "modern" economy.[21]

Deane was a skilled bricoleur, and at the same time deeply reflective about the theoretical armature to which data were being attached. She remained active in national income accounting through the 1960s, doing additional survey work in the British Caribbean and reviewing others' work in this burgeoning field. She joined the Cambridge Department of Applied Economics chaired by Richard Stone. Her next major project was constructing British national accounts going back to 1688, extending expertise on the distant present of Africa to the distant past of Britain.[22]

The scandal of Prest and Stewart

One logical solution to the problem of untangling household from business in the rural African communities Deane studied was to regard them as very large households, with no "business" at all, thus excluding rural villages from the measured economy entirely. Deane rejected that. There is also the opposite extreme solution to this problem: treat them as all business, with no "household." This is what Alan Prest and Ian Stewart did a few years later in Nigeria (Prest and Stewart 1953). Unable to untangle the complex kinship systems and skeins of obligation that had so worried Deane, they instead drew the boundary of "the household" around each Nigerian *individual*, and pushed into their measured "economy" *every* good or service received by an individual from anyone else, no matter how close. Notoriously, they used bride-prices to estimate the value of wives' services to husbands. Nigeria was *all* business, in the eyes of Prest and Stewart.[23]

The unanimous condemnation is instructive. Phyllis Deane in a 1954 review discussed "the strange reasoning whereby they embrace such activities as child-bearing, child-minding, and the like in total production, and measure a year's supply of non-agricultural, non-trading activities of women in terms of the bride payments in a given year."[24] Herbert Frankel, whose work will be discussed more fully below, termed these assumptions "farcical." Milton Gilbert scolded:

> I violently disagree, as I have argued elsewhere, that housewives' general services of cooking, cleaning, child bearing, child minding and the like should be considered economic activity-or that their value should be measured by the annual sums paid over in bridal prices.
>
> (Gilbert 1955, p. 322)

Peacock and Dosser's study of Tanganyika, published in 1958, called Prest and Stewart's assumptions about households "far-fetched." A 1964 discussion termed Prest and Stewart's study "notorious" (Lury 1964, p. 101).

Prest and Stewart provoked equally strong responses from Nigerian economists. Pius Okigbo (1924–2000),[25] in the course of introducing his own estimates, accepted that subsistence output should be included in total production, and then framed his difference with Prest and Stewart:

> However, they proceed to argue that including subsistence output involves including *all* subsistence *activity:* thus we would be obliged to value not only all identifiable output but all services as well. On Prest's argument the reason why all intra-household activity (including services) should be treated as a part of the gross domestic product of countries like Nigeria is that the relationship between the members of the family is closer to a commercial one in Nigeria than that to which we are accustomed in the West. This led him to the dubious but amusing exercise of estimating services by reference to the number of wives and the average bride price. It is doubtful whether this would have made sense to a Nigerian in 1950; it certainly does not make sense today.
>
> (Okigbo 1962, p. 14, emphases in original)

I. I. U. Eke wrote:

> Prest seems to have included the output of practically all agents or factors whose activities are remotely economic. He included activities which are considered illegal, imputed value to intra-household services, and placed monetary value on child bearing. This excursion by Prest could easily be dismissed as ludicrous, but it is much more serious than that. Prest seems to have gone into all this needless trouble not just because of his stated reason (that family life is more commercialized in Nigeria than in the West which

of course is an illusion) but also because of his stated objective. He wanted to measure the level of economic welfare. He seemed to have failed to realize that no matter how widely he may define his output the omission of services and products which affect people's welfare is unavoidable.

(Eke 1966, p. 334)

This is a fascinating moment, which looks back to Marshall's delineation of economy in opposition to households, and forward, perhaps, to Gary Becker's theorization of *all* family relations as commercial just a few decades later (Becker 1981). There was nothing *logically* wrong with what Prest and Stewart did. Nor was their use of bride-prices to estimate wives' services, however outlandish it can be made to appear, outside the practice of *bricolage* described earlier in this chapter, that is to say opportunistically using any available data to estimate different sectors of an economy. What made it "strange," "farcical," "ludicrous," "dubious," and "notorious" was its taboo-breaking challenge to the foundational assumptions about "economy" as Marshall had framed it. Marshall's argument, discussed in Chapter 1, was that a modern distinction between love and commerce allowed each to flourish in its own sphere; the modern society was thus superior in both respects to the traditional society in which these things were mingled.[26]

Okigbo's and Eze's rebukes to Prest and Stewart can be set alongside V. K. R. V. Rao's defense of the separateness and non-economic nature of Indian households, discussed in Chapter 1. All these authors recognized the implicit insult of regarding the domestic arrangements of their native countries as commercial and calculating, as falling short of fully self-sacrificing love. In the overarching modernist context, the only way to rescue love was to adopt the same conventions British national income accountants followed. But what is interesting is not just that Rao, Okigbo, and Eke disputed the idea that their native countries were deficient in love, but that British and U.S. economists *led the charge*. An economist like Milton Gilbert probably had little interest in Nigerian family life as such, but he had a large stake in the universal applicability of standardized national accounting. Okigbo and Eke spoke his language and supported his project; Prest and Stewart challenged it.

Herbert Frankel's dissent

Herbert Frankel (1903–1996) has already appeared in Chapter 2 as an appreciative reviewer of Gaathon's accounts for Palestine. Frankel was a South African of German Jewish descent with a distinguished career as an empirical economist and as a theorist. His early work on state-administered railway pricing made him a laissez-faire liberal and critic of government intervention in market processes. Frankel was on liberal grounds an opponent of apartheid; the postwar rise of the National Party was one reason pushing him to leave for a professorship in Oxford in 1946 (Toye 2009). He also believed that Africans were fundamentally culturally different from Europeans, and on that basis became a leading critic of the extension of national income accounting to Africa.

Frankel began working on national income accounting in South Africa in the 1940s. He started, like Kuznets, from the "welfare approach" to national income: that is, he thought national income accounting's project should be to measure the sum of good things flowing to people. He never abandoned that view. That meant that, like Kuznets, he had to address ethical questions of what counted as good. In Frankel's view, what Africans considered good was fundamentally different from what Europeans considered good. As he developed that argument, its underlying romanticism became clearer. Just as German or British romantics described the ideal village economy as a rich, society-making process whose purpose was as much to maintain dense social interactions as to produce goods, Frankel argued that Africans did what they did for complex traditional reasons: they hunted not because they wanted meat but because they liked hunting; they made large work parties for farming not because it was efficient but because it was social.[27]

> The income-creating process is itself part and parcel of the income it yields, and the results of the process cannot be abstracted from the process itself. It is inadmissible to "evaluate" the activity of hunting merely by the number of animals caught, and still more fallacious to compare the figure so obtained with, say, the "value" of meat obtained by another society from the slaughter of domestic beasts. The activity and the income are inseparable and are both embedded together in the customs and ways of thought which mould the social life of the community as a whole.
>
> To endeavour to assess and compare "welfare" merely by comparing national income aggregates for societies with different laws, rules, conventions, hopes, and ideals is as fallacious as to try to assess the pleasure which a pair of players derive from playing dominoes, and then compare it with that yielded to another pair engaged in playing chess, by comparing the points scored by the players in each game.
>
> (Frankel 1952, p. 6)

Frankel, therefore, would have left all African activity outside national income accounting on the grounds that any estimates of its value were vacuous.[28]

Frankel took little interest in the Keynesian project or in monetary analysis, and lacked sympathy for the underlying theoretical armature on which Phyllis Deane and others were building.[29] He had even less sympathy for programs of rapid modernization, in particular efforts to make "traditional" agriculture commercial. Frankel also had deep experience working with concrete data in South Africa and Rhodesia.[30] In this respect he is like Kuznets on the United States. So it is not surprising to find in his work a certain impatience with young British economists who parachuted into a colony for a few months to compute national income figures.

If we think in terms of the logical choices presented by the Marshallian definitions, which are to regard African economies as falling entirely under the sphere of household, entirely under the sphere of business, or somewhere in between, we could slot Frankel into the "all household" camp, Prest and Stewart into the "all business" camp, and Deane somewhere in between. This explains the difference between Frankel's polite skepticism toward Deane and open hostility toward Prest and Stewart. Frankel also dissented from Deane's view that non-marketed African activity was poised to enter the market, and should. He was hostile to "development" Economics as it gathered steam after WWII, assailing "dualist" models like that of Arthur Lewis that foresaw the rapid modernization of the "traditional" sector of a nation's economy.

Though Frankel found few sympathetic ears among economists after the 1950s, his dissent registered in the 1960s formalist-substantivist controversy in Anthropology. In a key early statement of the substantivist position, anthropologist George Dalton (1926–1991) approvingly quoted Phyllis Deane's doubts about applying economic analysis to African settings, and then moved to Frankel's view, quoted above, that in those settings "the income-generating process is itself part and parcel of the income it yields, and the results of the process cannot be abstracted from the process itself." Dalton followed with his own credo:

> If the categories we use to describe output disposition are to be analytically revealing they must be derived from the special characteristics of indigenous African economies. We follow therefore the African emphasis on the social obligations to pay and to give, and the rights to receive goods and services, built into social situations.
>
> (Dalton 1962, p. 71)

Significantly, Dalton followed Deane in assuming that mainstream academic Economics *is the appropriate self-understanding of the developed West*. Here we see again that statements about Africans are also statements about Europeans. Dalton simply positions *himself* as the defending the different self-understanding of the non-West.[31] This argument closely follows the romantic trope of the cultural unit that must be understood on its own terms and according to its own categories, not by an alien and universal logic.[32]

The confrontation is an example of the *productive* nature of the rationalist/ romantic split: productive in the sense of providing discursive grooves that allowed rationalists and romantics to establish their positions, roles, and authority by pushing off against each other.[33] Introducing a 1964 conference volume, anthropologist Melville Herskovits (1885–1963) noted "the need for what amounted to a cross-disciplinary attack on the problems of economic growth" and segued into a lament about differences between "academic disciplines," finishing:

> The difficulty in communication was brought out clearly in an earlier conference which attempted to assess the problems of the study of economically underdeveloped areas on a multidisciplinary basis ... yet those who attended these sessions are not likely to forget the failure in communication that characterized the discussion of points raised by participants who

belonged to different disciplines. One recalls how difficult it was for economists to see the importance of taking aboriginal economic patterns or total
cultural context into account ... and how the anthropologists had equal difficulty in grasping the relevance of concepts employed by the economists
because their applicability was restricted to the industrialized countries of
Europe and America.

(Herskovits 1964, p. 6)

Once again, an anthropologist allows economists to speak unproblematically for
and about "the industrialized countries of Europe and America" *in order* to
justify a separate place and role for Anthropology as the interpreter of Africans.
Herskovits' "not likely to forget" functions as gate-keeping and boundary-
drawing, a founding trauma and warning to other anthropologists to steer clear
of economists. Neither Dalton nor Herskovits asks whether "social obligations to
pay and to give" or "total cultural context" might also matter in "industrialized
countries." Thus their argument, while functioning as gate-keeping for Anthropology, also gives economists a free pass to ignore culture.

Within the Economics literature, what we can call the "strong" anti-
comparability view articulated by Frankel has a small and heterogeneous following, in which we might include Austrians like Pater Bauer, many contemporary
institutionalists, and left relativists (e.g., Apffel Marglin and Marglin 1990). The
mainstream view in Economics (e.g., Rao 1953) has been to concede multiple
technical challenges to making comparisons, but insist on the validity and necessity of making them. Advocates of that position often argue that given the existence of an international data-gathering apparatus, we must simply do our best to
make good data.[34] It is perhaps for this reason that Frankel, after a few fertile
years following his 1946 move to Oxford, largely dropped out of the debate
(Toye 2009). His combination of Smithian liberalism and romanticism did not fit
the times, aligning neither with technocratic mainstream Economics nor with the
moral hostility to markets and capitalism of substantivist thinkers like Dalton
and Karl Polanyi.

Dudley Seers' dissent

In 1952 Dudley Seers, then a Lecturer in Economic Statistics at Oxford University, published two significant works: a study (jointly with Richard Ross) on the
Gold Coast (now Ghana), and an article titled "The Role of National Income
Estimates in the Statistical Policy of an Underdeveloped Area." The article combined a highly informed critique of the sketchiness of current national income
accounting in Africa with an argument for an alternative approach to colonial
economies. Seers saw in the Gold Coast not a homogeneous national economy
but a fragile assembly of distinct sectors.[35] In particular, Seers was interested in
the linkages between the export sector (the colony produced about half the
world's cocoa), the domestic agricultural sector, and various kinds of non-
agricultural production. Seers was impressed by the degree to which this colonial

economy was buffeted by changes in international prices over which it had no control, and the weakness of integration of the different parts of the "national" economy. Seers' critique was thus broadly in line with James Ferguson's critique of accounts for Lesotho quoted in Chapter 4.

The 1952 article is a measured and insightful critique of national income accounting and an argument for placing greater stress on other kinds of data. Seers shows that "the statistical material is so thin for parts of all underdeveloped economies that estimates of the national income, on any definition, are subject to large and varying errors" and argues against the usefulness of these estimates either for comparisons across countries or even for the same country in different years. He shows how economists are lured into building models that reproduce the assumption that the modeled country is an internally coherent, stable creature for which we have only to work out the nature of its coherence, just as you might take apart a mechanical clock to figure out how its parts are linked. Seers argues that this freezes a changing institutional structure. Moreover:

> We run some danger of overlooking this central weakness because of the words we use: we need the help of metaphors when we think about an economy, and in carrying over a metaphor from the economies of developed economies we may tacitly be carrying over a description. The very words "mechanism" or "model" convey the mental picture of a great piece of machinery. It is not at all certain whether this is the most useful mental picture even for a developed economy; it suggests a misleading stability of structure.... Such "models" are in any case hardly needed to explain economic developments.
>
> (Seers 1952, pp. 161–162)

He then pivots to the structure of the world economy:

> The explanation of the trade cycles of primary producers is usually obvious enough: fluctuations in the markets of the main customers, generally the United States and Western Europe, supplemented by internal inventory fluctuations. The economic history of a primary producer, whether trends or cycles are being studied, can generally be explained in terms of the history of the main commodities: do we need a single summary indicator of activity, as we do for a diverse economy.
>
> (Seers 1952, p. 162)

Thus Seers moves from the argument that national income estimates overstate the stability and coherence of the national economy to the contention that external factors like world commodity prices are much simpler and more obvious explanations for what is going on economically in a place like the Gold Coast. Seers goes on to suggest an alternative approach which places far greater emphasis on foreign transactions:

This approach implies that as a first priority, instead of trying to fill the gaps in the "national income," statistical resources should be devoted to strengthening and extending foreign trade statistics – particularly to improving valuation and classification. Since an underdeveloped country *ipso facto* relies on the proceeds of exports for much of her income, and on imports for most consumer goods (other than food) and for nearly all capital goods, the trade returns supply much of the information which has to be taken elsewhere from tax statistics (on sources of income), from censuses of production and distribution, or the statistics collected by trade associations and retailers (on supplies to the home market).

(Seers 1952, p. 163)

This is a lucid précis of the argument presented in Chapter 4: that Keynesian national income accounting starts by assuming a coherent and self-sufficient closed economy with a complete set of institutions, and then only grudgingly opens the borders to allow goods and finance to trickle across them – but without reimagining the institutions that structure the national economy. Seers is calling on us to *start* with the international linkages, and then build our picture of the "national economy" out of those.[36]

Seers' critique provoked a sharp retort from Alan Prest, who had just finished the estimate of national income in Nigeria discussed above. Apart from a brief argument (1957, p. 225) that Seers overstates the reliance of underdeveloped countries on exports, and apart from an irritated exaggeration of Seers' critique of modeling (he summarized the above-quoted critique as "model building is a mirage"), Prest evaded Seers' main arguments and focused on minor points of estimation. Prest never questioned the existence, coherence, or stability of the thing he was measuring, and *read* Seers only as a series of quibbles over *how* it was to be measured. These are the same tactics that were used against Frankel: translate all fundamental critiques into technical quibbles, and then argue that the technical quibbles are resolvable with more technical work.

A similar dialog of the deaf happened in the 1960s in the Latin American "structuralist-monetarist" debate, in which Seers was also a participant. The structuralist side, which included even more radical figures like Celso Furtado and Juan Noyola, understood Latin American economies as theaters of political/economic conflict between different groups, not all of them national (Danby 2005). Depending on the country in question, those groups might include agricultural exporters whose interests and economic lives were much more closely tied up with foreign markets and finance than with domestic institutions. I will return to these figures in Chapter 11. A standardized Economics that understood national economies as bounded, uniform organisms had no place for these insights.

Conclusions

Estimates for British colonies were important for the global development of national income accounting because they were a sandbox in which controversies

could be fought out, and in which economists could develop a replicable technical practice. In the controversies discussed in this chapter we can trace the development of a more or less hegemonic discourse, evident by the early 1960s. Two
points of discursive consensus emerged.

1   National economies must be treated as *national* economies, not as overlap-
pings of foreign influences.
2   National economies must be modeled as though they are modern in the Marshallian sense, with distinct household and business sectors. Problems of
making the distinction will be treated as merely technical.

On the first point, Seers' critique was simply ignored. On the second point, two
challenges had been dismissed. On the one hand Prest and Stewart's effort to
understand Nigeria as hyper-modern, as all business and no love, had been universally rejected. The separate and distinct household was too ideologically
important. On the other side Herbert Frankel's romantic effort to understand
African economy as premodern got no traction in Economics, although it was
welcome in Anthropology.

From time to time, scholars argue that the extension of national income
accounting to places like Africa was Eurocentric or that it constitutes an ethno-
centric projection of "West's" self-understanding onto the non-West.[37] Such critiques assume (1) that there exists a bounded and coherent place called the
"West" and (2) that this "West" has a good self-understanding, expressed in its
social science, and errs only when it tries to extend this understanding to places
that are not like it. I deny both propositions (1) and (2) and my denial of (2) does
not depend on my denial of (1): I see no good reason to believe that everyday
material life in places like Western Europe or the United States of America is
deeply comprehended by any Economics, orthodox or heterodox. What is going
on is not the exporting of an autochthonous "European" perspective, but the fabrication of a European self-imagination.

Imagine a Nigerian social scientist arriving in mid-twentieth-century
Britain and trying to puzzle out its economy by direct observation: how to
understand formal and informal employment, factories and backyard gardens,
kinship obligations, Godparents, inheritance and marriage practices, trade
unions, religious congregations, civic festivals, private charities? Where does
this economy begin and end? What are the *motives* for these people's behavior? How to interpret their contradictory ideological stew of feudal class hier-
archy, New Testament radicalism, and *laissez faire*? European economies
were and are far from self-evident things. The way economists from Marshall
onward imagined families – as small nuclear units in which a working man
had a wife who raised children – was an ideological project rather than the
result of inductive social science. Kinship, rather than being a large system or
rubric connecting many people, was reduced to tiny nuclear units attached to
individual, independent men. This was hardly an accurate representation of
the real world in Europe or anywhere else, but it was via this conceptual

maneuver that kinship was written out of economy, and economy was made to look modern.

Notes

1 E.g., Rijken van Olst (1953), Ady (1952), Abraham (1952). See Averch *et al.* (2015, p. 184) on Abraham's authorship of the Philippines study, which is credited to "an Expert" in the published version.
2 Creamer and Creamer (1948) on Puerto Rico might also be included in the genre of colonial national accounts. Daniel Creamer was also a collaborator in Nathan *et al.* (1946), discussed in Chapter 2.
3 Comim (2001, p. 228), Stone *et al.* (1942), Stone (1951, 1994), Oshima (1957). Pyatt and Roe (1977), with an introduction by Stone, is an excellent later example of how integrated accounts can be built from data of varying reliability.
4 M. Morgan (2011) is especially compelling on this theme.
5 See Desrosières (2003, p. 561) and Lury (1964, p. 103). Jerven (2013) examines the history of African national income statistics. Oshima (1957) is powerfully illuminating on the method of assembling national income figures from scant and disparate data.
6 One of the underlying shifts is the increasing respectability of data that are not directly observed but drawn from statistical inference. See Ward (2004, p. 40) on the specific question and Hacking (1990) on the larger arc.
7 On household surveys see Esquivel (2013), Wood (2003), Elson (1995). On arguments about its exclusion see Hawrylyshyn (1976), Jaszi (1986), Hirschman (2015, pp. 138–157).
8 See Robinson's foreword to Deane (1948), which also mentions Benham. Clark (1985, p. 62) also notes Robinson's experience in India in the 1920s. Clark writes of his supervision of Rao's thesis on Indian national income that "We saw nothing incongruous about embarking on such a study in Cambridge, where much of the reference material was found to be available, supplemented by a few postal questionnaires on some technical points" (Clark 1985, p. 62). The empire is most visible from the metropole's archives.
9 This is my transcription from the videorecording.
10 See also M. Morgan (2011) on Deane.
11 Other racially divided accounts include Irvine (1955) on Northern Rhodesia (now Zambia) and Frankel and Herzfeld (1943a) on South Africa. See also Frankel (1940).
12 Schumaker (2001). See also Asad (1993, pp. 318–320) on the Rhodes-Livingstone Institute.
13 See Guyer (1981) for further discussion of these questions, especially pages 98–99.
14 A minor controversy illustrates the moral stakes. In her 1948 study Deane wrote:

> It is usual in the United Kingdom calculations of social income, to exclude the income of prostitutes. This is so not only because it would be difficult to find the evidence for an estimate, but also because it does not represent a return for "productive activity," at least according to the prevailing social code in the United Kingdom. In Northern Rhodesia, however, the organisation of the mining industry on the basis of migrant labour has made prostitution an integral part of the economy.
>
> (Deane 1948, pp. 24–25)

(More or less the same argument, but without mentioning prostitutes, appears on page 116 of Deane's 1953 book.) What Deane did in the 1948 study was extremely simple: she made an overall estimate for all "women workers in the towns, such as beer-brewers, nurses etc., and prostitutes" (p. 31). In their 1966 textbook Van Arkadie and

Frank write dismissively, under the heading of "illegal, immoral, and blackmarket operations" that

> It is amusing to note in this connection, how involved with these conceptual niceties some estimators have become. Miss Phyllis Deane, in her first estimates of the Northern Rhodesian accounts, prepared during WWII, advocated the inclusion of prostitutes on the basis of a rather lengthy argument to the effect that the organization of mining communities in that country made them an integral part of the economy.
>
> (Van Arkadie and Frank 1966, p. 221)

But Deane's cogent 1948 argument was no more "lengthy" than what is quoted above, and Van Arkadie and Frank offer no counter-argument to the "integral" point. It is clear that they are simply expressing moral discomfort. Prostitution, combining the intimate and the commercial, disrupts the household/commerce divide.

15 Along these lines see the critique of Arthur Lewis in Wood (2003).
16 Deane (1948, p. 2). See also Deane (1953, pp. 10 and 116).
17 The conceptual boundary she uses is essentially the same as that used by Kuznets (1941), who includes in his definition of output "products retained by producers for their own consumption (especially important for farmers)" while excluding domestic services (Kuznets 1941, p. 9). Compare Deane (1948, p. 24). Another way to put it is that the "line of difference between economic and non-economic areas existing in real life" (Kuznets 1933, p. 209) is no longer a parameter to be respected ("shifting") but something to be *shifted* via colonial modernization.
18 Deane (1953, p. 126). Frankel, reviewing Deane's 1948 study, praised her scruple: "No author could be at greater pains to warn the reader of a tentative conclusion, or a suspected margin of error." But he wondered

> why it should ever have been expected that a technique which suits a highly developed and large-scale national economy such as the United Kingdom should, even if it could, be applied to small so-called "national" units which are only just entering the world economy through the development of one or two specialised products in them. The whole procedure looks like an experiment to discover whether the system of accounting applicable to General Motors can throw light on the operations of a wayside petrol station run by a man whose main livelihood is obtained with the assistance of his wife and children from an agricultural allotment ... Are these aggregates a practical tool, or are they the symbols of fashionable concepts transferred from very highly developed economic regions to hide our ignorance of economically backward ones?
>
> (Frankel 1949, pp. 594–595)

19 It seems clear (Schumaker 2001) that personal and working relations between Deane and her anthropologist colleagues were fine. But the evidence suggests that *intellectual* commonalities were thin and contact made them no thicker. Schumaker rightly notes (2001, p. 104) that Deane's

> economic approach ... shared some basic features with [Max] Gluckman's style of social anthropology. Her postwar Keynesian approach treated national economies as coherent wholes that could be understood and controlled through planned intervention, a view similar to that of the view of society accepted by functionalism in anthropology. The approach of both disciplines shared political roots in R. H. Tawney's earlier vision of the functional society.

But she also writes:

> Despite these very general commonalities, however, the two disciplines' intellectual differences in terms of theory may have been highlighted by Deane's presence in

the field – at least for Gluckman, who thought that national incomes was an "arid topic," and for [Fred] Barnes, who had already become "disenchanted with economics" in 1936 while contemplating a switch from mathematics to economics as an undergraduate at Cambridge.

(Schumaker 2001, p. 104)

Schumaker's assessment is supported by Gluckman (1955), which indeed makes the theoretical point that "each society exists as a system of regularities" (p. 651) but fails to connect it to Deane, who appears only in a brief, polite mention at the end of the article:

> Investigation of the links which build up the region's politico-economic framework is only partially anthropological. Miss Phyllis Deane has published an analysis of the national income of Northern Rhodesia and Nyasaland for two selected years, and there are of course numerous government economic reports. But we need analysis of the whole problem of how Africans get to work: Niddrie has made a beginning on this point.

The "but" speaks volumes. See also Schumaker (2001, p. 657) on the Anthropology-Economics gap. The failure to connect is all the more striking because Gluckman published extensively on economic activity in the societies he studied. Frankenberg (2005, p. 175) traces the difference to Gluckman's grounding in Marxian Economics, by contrast with which the categories measured by Deane might indeed seem arid.

20 See Huxley and Deane (1944) for more use of this colonial "we." This corresponds to what Zein-Elabdin (2004, p. 22) terms the "non-economic core" of Economics.
21 Historical change is also phrased in terms of household and gender:

> In effect, therefore, while the man is the spearhead of change the woman is the principal worker and the guardian of the traditional processes. Now, when change is largely a function of the link with the money economy, this means that the woman is the chief earner in the field of subsistence production and the man in the field of production for sale.

(Deane 1953, p. 221)

European colonial efforts to develop African economies tended to emphasize drawing men into cash-crop production; it was male household-heads whom the British taxed to compel labor. Woman is to man, as rural is to urban, as traditional is to modern. See also Bergeron (2004, pp. 57–59) and Ferguson (1999). This links to the larger literature on colonial governmentality (D. Scott 1995; Kalpagam 2000).
22 See Fabian (1983) on the modernist alignment between historical and spatial difference.
23 M. Morgan (2011, pp. 314–319) and Speich Chassé (2011, pp. 14–15) provide fascinating readings of this study.
24 Deane (1954, p. 275). Deane and Richard Stone had been part of the advisory committee for Prest and Stuart's work, which was a project of Stone's Department of Applied Economics at Cambridge (M. Morgan 2011, pp. 306–307). Another critical reviewer was Wrigley (1954). I have found no defenses of Prest and Stewart on this point in the published literature.
25 Dosser's review (1963, p. 331) also welcomed Okigbo's riposte to Prest and Stewart. There are a few more reflections on method in Okigbo (1963).
26 Prest did not defend his treatment of households in subsequent writings. Prest (1957, pp. 19–20) swipes only at Frankel's hardline position. His rather clenched review (1963) of Okigbo's book avoids the issue entirely.
27 This theme is developed eloquently in Frankel (1953); Benham's comments (pp. 169–177) printed after that paper are useful to get a sense of the debate at that moment. That 1953 volume, which includes Rao (1953), marks a decisive moment in

the comparability debate. Frankel's cultural relativism was consistent throughout his career. See his 1943 praise for Gaathon (Frankel and Herzfeld 1943b), his apprecia-tive (1940) review of Furnivall's monograph on economic dualism in the Dutch Indies, and his comments on Elazari-Volcani's *The Fellah's Farm* (1992, p. 126). He was clearly aware of resonances with romantic thought later in his career: his last works undertook an Austrian exposition of Simmel (Frankel 1978, 1980). Was this so earlier? The suggestion of Malinowski and Thurnwald as Frankel's intellectual sources by Speich Chassé (2014) is intriguing but difficult to demonstrate; an equally plausible source might simply be the common colonialist's view that natives are incorrigibly native.

28   Peacock and Dosser's (1958, pp. 15–17) study of national income in Tanganyika con-tains a riposte to Frankel, arguing that that no matter what the ceremonial importance of it as a commodity, if its production incurs an opportunity cost it can be brought under the view of national accounting. Theirs is a particularly clear example of the argument that valuing non-marketed output is a "technical problem" (p. 16) but never a conceptual problem.

29   See his extended critique of Keynes' approach to money in Frankel (1978).

30   Frankel's father was a grain merchant in South Africa, and his brother took on that business at his father's death, with considerable success.

31   Please see also Mirowski (1994).

32   See also Dalton's comments in Frank *et al.* (1971). When Dalton writes that "Frank is incredulous because he has a Universal Model in his head: a single worldwide capital-ist system having reached into and destroyed all traditional tribal and peasant soci-eties" he precisely reproduces the modernist romantic/rationalist split.

33   Charusheela (2001) describes the same structure of argument in contemporary debates around choice and relativism.

34   Another way of posing the question is: what explains the shift from the relatively crit-ical – indeed, bordering on hostile – response to Colin Clark's 1930s comparative estimates (Speich Chassé 2011), to the normalization of a standard framework by the late 1950s? The marginalizations of Frankel and Seers suggest that one requirement for being a mainstream economist in the postwar period was accepting comparability, which meant accepting the underlying theoretical armature. See also Speich Chassé (2016).

35   Frimpong-Ansah (1991), Seers (1952). See also Speich Chassé (2011, pp. 16–17).

36   These arguments are further developed, along with a useful review of the relevant history, in Seers (1976).

37   E.g., Mehmet (1999), Apffel Marglin and Marglin (1990). Frankel (1949, p. 595) made the charge of Eurocentrism, *avant la lettre*, when he wrote: "Are these aggreg-ates a practical tool, or are they the symbols of fashionable concepts transferred from very highly developed economic regions to hide our ignorance of economically back-ward ones?"

6   The IMF makes the world

Previous chapters showed how universalized national income accounting had the conceptual and representational effect of tucking all production into standardized national compartments. This thinned out the international economy, turning it into a space of pure flows. This thin interstitial space was hardly an obvious place to speak *from*, much less with authority. So how did the IMF do it? This chapter traces the conversion of the IMF from a narrowly focused organization with an obscure mandate into the leading producer of knowledge about the international economy.[1]

Most of the postwar international bodies – the IMF and World Bank, UN organizations, OEEC – combined data-gathering and assessment functions with publicity functions, which is to say that they not only took in information, but used it to produce authoritative representations of the world for public consumption. Among this group the IMF did its part, publishing an annual report, the monthly *International Financial Statistics*, and staff working papers. But these were technical publications aimed at specialists. If you had asked yourself in 1950 which international organization would be most successful at bringing the world economy into public view, you would probably have picked the United Nations, whose agencies had picked up the work of the League of Nations with new resources and political support, and which publicized itself vigorously. The IMF kept a low profile (Dawson and Enoch 2009, pp. 149–151) and lent little. It may be widely known today as a condition-imposing lender, but its resources in the initial decades were scant and its total lending was much lower than the levels attained starting in the 1980s.

The IMF we know today is the result of a remarkable transformation in the late 1970s and early 1980s. I am most interested in its emergence as a maker of knowledge, in the way it moved from data to analysis to policy advocacy to warning and finally to actively ventriloquizing the world economy. But this story is also about the transformation of its operational role.

The IMF's history falls into two parts, which can be roughly divided pre- and post-1976, the year "surveillance" became part of its official mandate.[2] Broadly: from 1944 to the early1970s, the IMF understood itself as the guardian of a system of fixed exchange rates. During most of this period private international capital flows were relatively low, the IMF itself did relatively little lending, and

Table 6.1 First and second IMFs

	First IMF 1944–1971	Second IMF 1978–present
Exchange rates	Fixed; IMF to be consulted on changes	Floating
Private financial flows	Minimal; capital controls widespread	Rising levels of short- and long-term flows; few capital controls
IMF lending	Relatively scant	Increasing and often large-scale
Collaboration with private banks	Minimal	Closer
Bilateral surveillance	Occasional and unsystematic	Annual for all members, highly systematized, and increasingly public
Multilateral surveillance	Occasional and without publicity	Regular and aggressively publicized

its staff did not engage in regular consultation with most member governments. Its multilateral consultations were private.[3] The collapse of that system of exchange rates might have ended the IMF. But a second IMF emerged in the late 1970s that embraced and began to speak *for* the private international capital flows that had undermined the fixed exchange rate regime. Table 6.1 summarizes the transformation.

The first IMF

The IMF that emerged from Bretton Woods was the institutional embodiment of a monetary disarmament treaty. Signatories agreed to yield a measure of sovereignty over exchange rate policy to an international organization. The specifics were designed to support a return to free trade (but not free capital mobility), something U.S. policymakers thought politically and economically desirable. Signatories agreed to peg (fix) their currencies to the U.S. dollar, and to alter those pegs only in consultation with the Fund, which would have nominal authority to approve such adjustments; it was hoped this would prevent unilateral efforts to gain advantage over other countries by competitive devaluations. A fixed exchange rate means that a nation's central bank stands ready to buy or sell foreign currency at that fixed rate, or "peg." But this was limited: Bretton Woods signatories agreed to such "convertibility" of their currencies for purposes of trade, but not necessarily for purposes of capital mobility. So for example the Central Bank of France would have to sell a French importer dollars (that is, exchange dollars for the importer's francs) for the purpose of importing automobiles from a U.S. manufacturer, but it could refuse to sell dollars to a French investor who wanted to buy shares in a foreign firm. Most Bretton Woods signatories retained capital controls, and for good reason. Pegged exchange rates are vulnerable to rapid flows of private capital. A rapid outflow of capital, which can happen for many reasons, becomes effectively a run on the central bank's foreign reserves. Once the reserves are exhausted, the peg breaks. It therefore seemed highly prudent to keep capital controls in place. Capital controls also gave national governments room to conduct domestic policy in ways that might be punished by mobile capital (Eichengreen 1996).

Before going any further we must observe the unlikelihood of even this narrowly focused project. However inevitable it may seem today, the Bretton Woods consensus depended on fragile circumstances, among them the emergence of support for its goals in U.S. official circles before and during the war, the meeting of minds between John Maynard Keynes and Harry Dexter White that provided technical and theoretical underpinnings, and the political skills and planning capacities of the Roosevelt and Truman administrations. Had these plans not been ready to go right as the war ended, their political support might well have evaporated.[4] The unlikelihood and fragility of this project has been apparent to IMF figures.[5]

International organizations are vulnerable to dissension among members and abuse by powerful members. A key to the IMF's story is the efforts of staff, helped at key moments by Executive Directors, to develop and preserve a measure of independence. The official IMF histories are detailed and reflective chronicles of the process and perils of carving out bureaucratic independence. IMF critics routinely highlight the fact that voting by its Executive Directors is weighted by the contributions of the nations they represent to IMF capital, and sometimes conclude that the IMF is a mere tool of U.S. policy, or of a few wealthy nations. This is much too simple. Though their success has been incomplete, IMF staff have worked strenuously since 1948 to avoid being pawns of U.S. or other national interests. Their efforts to achieve bureaucratic independence explain a great deal about what the IMF has actually done and the role it now plays in the world.

One generator of IMF orthodoxy is the defensive solidarity of the professional staff of any organization ruled by a potentially fractious board. Given a board whose members represent contending national interests, staff strive to speak in a unified and consistent voice. Were they to present conclusions to the board that were open-ended or pluralist, they could play into national rivalries and become vulnerable to those rivalries. If they did not have a standardized methodology, theory, and grid of data, they could be accused of playing favorites. In other words, the practices of uniform assessment and analysis and studiously even policy discourse arise from the *tension between* an international bureaucracy and its most powerful member governments, not from a smooth alignment of interests.[6]

In terms of legal doctrine, the IMF is a treaty organization whose staff speak for the treaty and its goals rather than for individual members. This requires even-handedness, at least formally (Pauly 2008, p. 195). Joseph Gold (1912–2000), the IMF's leading legal theorist, argued for example that the inability of less-wealthy countries during the 1944 Bretton Woods negotiations to carve out an exception for themselves was a key moment in the formation of an organization built around strict even-handedness (Gold 1975). Applying a single technical framework to every economy is useful because it makes such equivalence *visible*.

Given the IMF's initial purpose, though, the scope for its staff's voice might seem tediously narrow: the technical matter of exchange rate policy. For example an arms-limitation treaty might include verification and assessment of compliance by a technical staff, but such verification and assessment would not extend beyond the particular weapons named in the treaty.

Enter national income accounting, and the theory that could be built atop it. Once you have a frame describing how the parts of a national economy fit together, an exchange rate reveals itself as part of a tightly-linked mechanism.[7] Hence any evaluation of the exchange rate must take into account domestic credit-creation, fiscal policy, and a range of other factors not specifically named in the original treaty: "the intricate interconnection between external and internal balance" (Guitián 1992, p. 49). Legal interpretation of the treaty, argued Gold (1967, p. 294), required "recognition that the Articles were drafted by lawyers and economists acting in concert, that the language of the Articles is permeated by economic terminology, and that the Articles regulate economic affairs." In his view the terminology carries with it "simple" economic concepts that are true for all nations.[8] In other words the fact that exchange rates had broader implications, something that had been evident long before national income accounting, was not enough. Nor would it have worked to generate a range of different frameworks for different nations, because that would have left open the question of which framework applied where. Only a highly standardized national framework could support the argument that staff were merely pursuing the implications of a universal economic logic.

The outstanding facts about the IMF in its first three decades are (1) the achievement of a certain (albeit circumscribed and periodically threatened) bureaucratic independence to assess exchange rate policy and (2) the expansion of that writ to a wider economic policy gamut than was explicitly named in the original treaty. Achieving (2) required a standard national framework atop which standard national models could be built.

The second IMF

Our second act begins with a crisis that threatened the IMF's existence: the collapse of the fixed exchange rate system because the United States, producer of the key currency around which the original system was built, refused to play by its rules and floated the dollar in 1971. Efforts to re-establish fixed parities over the next few years failed. Given that the IMF was set up as the guardian of a fixed exchange rate system, and as the assessor of whether national exchange rate policy was appropriate to that larger context, you could have made a plausible argument at that point for winding the organization up.

The fixed exchange rate system was undermined by the growth of private international financial markets.[9] These markets became by the early 1970s

capable of moving enough money, quickly, that they could undermine or cir-
cumvent existing capital controls. Leading governments probably *could* have
constrained these flows, but did not.[10] The re-emergence of a private global financial system not only made fixed exchange rates too difficult to hang on to, but
also meant that the resources that the IMF could lend were dwarfed by potential
private flows. The IMF's rebirth in the 1980s reflects a decision, taken as much
by its staff and managing directors as by its member governments, to embrace
the international capital flows that had undermined the first IMF.[11]

The post-1970s IMF is a combination of:

- A revised doctrine of *bilateral* surveillance, within which the older apparatus of assessing national economic policy in terms of fixed exchange rates
  was rebuilt. This was supported by a newly routinized and intensified practice of nation-level assessment, built around annual visits ("missions") to
  each country by staff teams that audited data and discussed policy, back-
  stopped by rigorous critique of each team's work by a distinct internal division.
- An expanded doctrine of *multilateral* surveillance, linked to publication of
  the results.
- Expanded lending with conditionality, plus direct engagement with private
  lenders.
- A large-scale public relations effort, by which the Fund sought to manage
  its public profile and disseminate its views.

Bilateral surveillance

Bilateral surveillance entails routinized annual *assessment* of every IMF
member, something that was not done during the Fund's first three decades. The
process is formalized. At the beginning of the annual cycle for a country, the
country desk officer, along with others in the regional division, prepares a brief-
ing paper specifying informational and policy concerns. The paper must then
pass a central "Strategy, Policy, Review" (SPR) department which can demand
changes. The SPR's role is to discipline country-specific and region-specific
staffers, who are considered vulnerable to becoming too close to the governments they monitor, and ensures adherence to a single core model.[12] A team then
visits the country for a "mission" of a couple of weeks to gather data, meet with
officials, and communicate areas of IMF concern. On its return it drafts a document that must pass the SPR before being submitted to the IMF's Executive
Board. The key output is the IMF Executive Director's "summing up" of the
mission's results, after board discussion (Harper 1998). While the mission's
document and Director's "summing up" can be kept private at the request of the
national government under scrutiny, many governments opt to make them
public. The very regularity of the process creates pressures to conform and to
display one's conformity. A revealing episode happened in the early 1980s
when, swamped by the pressure of carrying out so many annual missions and

processing so many reports, staff and board proposed that some less-significant countries might be reviewed only every other year. But in the end no national government was ready to admit that it was too unimportant to qualify for annual review. Surveillance generates a need to be surveilled.

The scope of bilateral surveillance has enlarged over the years. At its core are efforts to pin down actual government spending, taxation, borrowing, and lending, a task that is more difficult than it might seem. Real-world governments are not simple things. Many are loose aggregates of disparate institutions that may be working at cross purposes, some with their own sources of income and borrowing. There is often a penumbra of parastatal bodies that may or may not be considered part of government. Differences in internal accounting practices make aggregating hard. There may be intra-governmental arguments over data. This is not to say public finance is an illusion, but it is to say that tracking and aggregating the actual spending and taxing and borrowing of an actual government is far from trivial. In Harper's ethnographic account, a considerable part of the time and effort of an IMF "mission" during its 2 weeks in the country under review is making the rounds of ministries and pulling together data.[13] The IMF creates the single nation-level panoptic eye which we may *imagine* national governments possess by definition, but which in fact they often lack. One of the purposes of meetings with senior government officials at the end of a mission is to persuade them to formally accept the figures assembled by the IMF mission, or at least to commit to *one* set of figures.[14] A second purpose of the annual mission is a ritualized discussion of national policy. The 1999 *External evaluation of IMF surveillance: Report by a Group of Independent Experts* (International Monetary Fund 1999) relays common criticisms of the process:

> [A] lack of flexibility in the Fund's analysis … failure to appreciate adequately the political environment in which decisions are taken, and/or to allow for it in policy advice … missions came into countries with a preconceived template of ideas, based on a theoretical or textbook model, housed in Washington, into which they fed country information.

The authors counter:

> It should also be noted, however, that this apparent rigidity may still have a positive impact, especially in the core macroeconomic areas, as the following revealing quotation from an Asian official shows: "Strangely, it is worthwhile to go through the Article IV consultations that dispense this very standard, undifferentiated advice. It is like a confessional – the government sits on one side of the booth and the IMF is on the other side. Each knows what the other is going to say, but by repeating the lessons of an introductory course in macroeconomics to the sinning government, the IMF priest does help limit temptations to deviate too far from the orthodoxy." This view of the Fund as a useful reality check was not uncommon.
>
> (International Monetary Fund 1999, p. 36)

The most current figures are estimated rather than strictly measured. When you look at data for, say, U.S. GDP for the most recent quarter, you might think you are looking at data about past facts. But you are really looking at a *projection* based on data for earlier quarters. Thus the process of bringing together a "current" set of numbers is itself contentious and reflects not only ascertainable historical facts but also views about the likely future.[15]

Multilateral surveillance

In bilateral surveillance, staff occupying a space of technical neutrality carries out serial routinized assessments of individual members. Multilateral surveillance moves the observing eye up one level, and examining how policies of different members interact in the world.

There are many precedents. As noted in Chapter 3, John Maynard Keynes' *Economic Consequences of the Peace*, in which he showed that the trade surplus that Germany would have to run to pay its reparations was inconsistent with the unwillingness of the other major Versailles signatories to run trade deficits with Germany, is exemplary multilateral surveillance: it pointed up a fundamental incongruity that was not evident if you looked country by country (Keynes 1919). During the 1950s the OEEC practiced multilateral surveillance to be sure that U.S. aid to Western Europe was not being used at cross purposes by different recipients.

A 1964 G-10 ministerial working group document is credited with first using the term "multilateral surveillance" as it sought to develop an "early warning system" for financial crises.[16] It emphasized "key indicators (money supply, bank lending, bank liquidity, short-term interest rates, and use of central bank credit ... the function of the surveillance exercise was to focus attention on macroeconomic data that should initiate a policy change or policy response."[17] The G-10 document thus conceptualized a larger space in which national policies played out ("the international monetary system") and named the transnational technocratic vision *from which that space could be seen* "multilateral surveillance." During the 1970s the IMF was able to capture this work and make the case to the G-10 that it was the appropriate body to carry it on, but it was still private and indeed generally secret. What is most new about the "second IMF" is the public face of its multilateral surveillance.[18]

The key publication was the *World Economic Outlook (WEO)*. It began as an internal IMF analytical exercise in the early 1970s. But in 1979 the Fund's Managing Director leaked a copy to the press to gauge reception, and secured Executive Board approval to publish the *WEO*, or at least a redacted version of it, twice a year.[19] The *WEO* emphasized financial flows from the beginning, and emerged conjointly in 1980 with another new IMF publication, *International Capital Markets*. In 2002 *International Capital Markets* was folded into the quarterly *Global Financial Stability Report*. The IMF has taken a keen interest in the *WEO*'s public uptake.[20]

The distinguishing analytic and rhetorical feature of the *WEO* is its focus on a medium-term future, in the 3 to 5-year range. This is partly a consequence of the analytical achievements noted above – the question the *WEO* sought to answer was how current policies and other relevant phenomena could be expected to interact over this period. It also resolved a diplomatic problem: direct criticisms of the policies of member nations could be avoided. The Fund's staff could not write that, for example, Argentina's current fiscal policy was wrong. But it *could* write that Argentina's current fiscal policy was, according to staff analysis and projections, "unsustainable." By staking a claim to the medium-term future, and moreover the future *of the world* which Fund staff could claim to be uniquely able to envisage and warn about, it became possible to voice the same critique. Consider two passages from the April 2008 *WEO*, not so much for content as for rhetoric:

> The sustainable current account of the United States is estimated to be a deficit in the range of 2 to 3 percent of GDP, determined as a function of medium-term fundamentals including demographics and the structural fiscal position. The U.S. current account deficit is projected to come down to about 4 percent of GDP in 2013, but will still exceed the estimated sustainable deficit level.
>
> (WEO April 2008, pp. 19–20)

> To be sure, concerns remain, including that government spending has been allowed to rise too quickly on the basis of rapidly rising tax revenues that may be unsustainable when growth slows, that domestic credit booms could weaken financial institutions' balance sheets, and that some countries, particularly in emerging Europe, have built up large current account deficits financed at least in part by short-term and debt-related flows.
>
> (WEO April 2008, p. 25)

The passive voice, well-honed prolepsis, and even tone are necessary requisites of this bureaucratic policy discourse. These rhetorical characteristics mark the voice of the "world economy" the Fund has conjured into existence. This ventriloquized world economy is large and threatening. It chastens national governments. It is somewhat remote (you need specialized expertise to make full sense of the passages quoted above) and difficult to challenge.[21] It moves mysteriously, but inevitably humbles those who try to defy it. For example Guitián:

> The growing freedom of capital movements and their increasing importance in international transactions only add urgency to the need for economic policy consistency across countries; in effect, capital flows have made national boundaries increasingly porous so that pursuit of national objectives to the neglect of international considerations has become more and more futile.
>
> (Guitián 1992, p. 49)

None of this, I hasten to add, is to deny that rash, crisis-inviting policies exist in the world. It is simply to point out that we have both a particular scale – the IMF as the voice of a level of international reality that national governments and private actors cannot see – and a new temporality, in which the Fund staff become the voice of the medium-term future.

The original Bretton Woods treaty conceptualized a world divided into nations and a world economy broken into pieces under national governments. Its concept of the international economy emphasized trade. When the international financial system, which had repressed between the wars, re-emerged, the technocratic response was not to rethink its foundational assumption of a compartmentalized world, but to supplement it by naming an additional, global-scale "international financial market" with the IMF staff as its oracle. The characteristic mode in which this market spoke was to *warn*.

Discipline and punish

Pinning down precisely what "surveillance" means for the IMF is not easy or necessarily productive, because it has become a catch-all term for almost all Fund activity aside from actual lending. Nonetheless from the point of view of Foucauldian analysis there is the striking coincidence that only a few years after the 1975 publication of *Surveiller et Punir*, a powerful organization with an annual budget of hundreds of millions of dollars set itself the task of achieving global power through persuasion and routinized bureaucratic information-gathering and assessment. Moreover the neoliberalism Foucault examined in his late-1970s lectures was in part an argument that governments were constrained by a more powerful "market." I have found no evidence that the French sage influenced IMF intellectuals. But I will suggest that the IMF has influenced Foucault's legatees in the humanities and interpretive social sciences when they think of the global economy. The Fund has been since the 1980s strongly interested in its public face, building a large internal media relations unit and hiring international public relations firms. It conducts regular audits of its media impact. While there is no easy measure of its popular or cultural success (and we should not conflate popularity with success), I point in coming chapters to the adoption of IMF tropes by IMF critics.

The very fact of the Fund's keen interest in its public face, though, complicates questions about how to interpret success. One school of thought, of which Michel Callon is the most prominent, argues that postwar "Economics," broadly construed, has been successful not because it studies economy, but because it *makes* economy.[22] This view avoids simple positivism (economists understand economy the way astronomers understand stars) by leaping to a strong constructivism (economists understand economy like builders understand houses). Callon's view cannot be entirely wrong: economists' efforts to shape subjectivities and institutions are too numerous and vigorous to ignore. But such accounts overstate the smooth integration of knowledge and power, and understate contingency, difficulty, disagreement, and failure. Butler's (2010, p. 149) caution, that this account fails to "tell us when and why performativity fails to work," is precisely on target. Lacking a category for the unpredictability, opacity, and intractability of the social and material world, Callon's approach risks naively accepting the boasts of economists. However sophisticated their critical apparatuses, constructivists routinely end up with even greater complacency than positivism: say what you like about positivists, they at least entertain the possibility that scientists can be wrong. Callon and his followers seem to believe that the social world has sprung out of the minds of intellectuals, who are therefore uniquely well placed to run it.

The sophisticated constructivism of Callon and allied scholars is ultimately yet another variant of modernity: the world has become (or is becoming) rationalist/modern because industrious economists have built it like that. I emphatically agree that economy is performative in that it requires persuasion: not merely individual acts of persuasion, but larger cultural ensembles that people find compelling. But "performative" does not mean anything goes and everything works. The next part of the book asks what made this particular performance so recognizable.

Notes

1 Histories include Boughton (2001), James (1996), de Vries (1986a) and de Vries' multi-volume account. Interesting shorter assessments include Coats (1986, pp. 18–20) Best (2005), and Crockett (1992).
2 On the longer history and development of surveillance, please see Schäfer (2006), James (1995), Moschella (2012), Pauly (1997, 2008). It is perhaps the central theme of Boughton (2001), whose second chapter provides a careful and illuminating discussion of the role of surveillance in the 1976 revision of the IMF's Articles of Agreement. Guitián (1992) is an especially forceful and compact presentation of the IMF staff view on surveillance. Manuel Guitián (1939–2000) was a consistent advocate of capital account openness whose work deserves further study. Other studies include Bossone (2008) and Lombardi and Woods (2008).
3 On changes in international financial markets, see Rajan and Zingales (2003). On the IMF and this transition, Crockett (1992).
4 Rauchway (2015, pp. 203–226) describes the Truman administration's campaign to obtain passage, which was more difficult than the ultimate votes in the U.S. Congress (348–18 House, 61–16 Senate) might suggest.
5 See, in Coats (1986, p. 157) the remarks by Margaret de Vries:

> We've moved historically – grown right away from World War II when international cooperation was an ideal, to the present, when international cooperation is a dirty word. The kind of international organizations represented here today [UN, IMF, World Bank, GATT, OECD] probably wouldn't be set up today, because people don't believe in international cooperation.

6 Guitián (1992) explicitly casts surveillance as the counterpoise to "the sheer weight of the strongest." The Executive Board also established a tradition of taking decisions by consensus rather than by vote, skirting the embarrassment of a formal vote in which unequal voting power would come into play. There is much more on board dynamics in Blustein (2002).
7 In this early phase of the Fund's operations, the government whose recalcitrance was the greatest spur to the development of this doctrine was the United Kingdom. James

(1996, pp. 184–185) writes that British governments in the 1960s refused to accept that their domestic monetary policies had balance of payments implications and refused to discuss the matter in international forums. This failure

> gave an indication of the extent to which the practice of surveillance was handicapped by the absence of a common intellectual framework to guide responses to major economic problems or an agreement on policy choices.... Without a shared understanding of the functioning of the economy, surveillance can easily degenerate into a rehearsal of cases based solely on perceptions of national interest.

National interest is counterposed to surveillance. The monetary macroeconomic apparatus structuring surveillance is more comprehensive than national income accounting, including data on central bank operations, the national financial system as a whole, and balance of payments at a somewhat higher level of disaggregation. A history of the balance of payments, as concept and data, is yet to be written.

8 See also Coats (1986, p. 121), recounting remarks in discussion by Jacques Polak to the effect that "the decision on whether or not to accept exchange-rate changes, required quite a bit of economic theory." See in the same forum de Vries' remarks (p. 141) about the Fund's version of monetrarism – "It wasn't monetarism as a doctrine, but monetary statistics – the way in which a country's balance of payments could be seen and quantified."

9 Accounts include Lucatelli (1997), Helleiner (1994), and Abdelal (2009).

10 Eichengreen (1996). Crotty and Epstein (1996) examine the political economy of this shift. Abdelal (2009, pp. 131–136) argues that Fund staff had begun to support capital account openness as early as the mid-1950s. Guitián (1992) is an especially forceful staff argument for abolishing capital controls, in the interest of "conformity with economic logic" and "establishment of universality." 1992 was arguably the high-water mark of neoliberalism in the economic policy sense.

11 See in particular Cohen (1982) and James (1996, Chapter 11).

12 Blustein (2002, p. 28). For examples see Beaufort Wijnholds (2011, pp. 13–14) on "clientelism" in the IMF's Western Hemisphere Department before the 1994 Mexican crisis and Pisani-Ferry *et al.* (2011) and Blustein (2015) on the European Department.

13 Harper (1998). See also Oshima (1957, p. 169).

14 This does not mean the figures arrived at are necessarily "right," it just means there has been a ritual that has produced an agreement. Blustein (2002) is instructive on the limits of these consultations.

15 On this theme see P. Miller (2003, p. 573) and Holmes (2013, pp. 22–23).

16 Another instance in which OEEC staff may have been responsible for the crucial intellectual innovations – see James (1995, p. 767) and Pauly (1997).

17 Group of Ten Ministerial Statement, quoted in James (1995, p. 768).

18 Though as de Vries (1986b, p. 60) notes, the IMF's Annual Report, issued since 1946, included assessments of the world economy and "gradually became larger and more extensive, in some ways being the forerunner of the *World Economic Outlook*."

19 James (1995), de Vries (1986a); Pauly (2008), Boughton (2001, Chapter 5).

20 Hacche (2009, pp. 196–197) discusses "three external evaluations [of the WEO] commissioned by the IMF or its Independent Evaluation Office." These are Crow *et al.* (1999), Mishkin *et al.* (2000), and Takagi *et al.* (2006).

21 Tellmann (2003), examining a different series of IMF documents, makes essentially this point: that "the market" becomes the producer of truth about economy and indeed "the subject of knowledge, which is authorized to speak the truth about the economy" (p. 49). Foucault (2008, pp. 30–38) makes the further point that markets not only speak economic truth, but speak the truth about government's success or failure.

22 Callon and Muniesa (2005, 2007), Muniesa *et al.* (2007), MacKenzie *et al.* (2007), Mirowski (2015), Mirowski and Nik-Kah (2008).

Part II
Romantic responses

Introduction to Part II

To summarize, romantics and rationalists agree that:

1 What determines whether an act is "economic" is what is in the mind of the actor.
2 Fully modern economic reasoning is rational, and rationality is attained by putting aside love. Economy is made out of these bits of detached rationality.
3 The split in individual consciousness that produced economy-making rationality is an historical fact (at least, for some value of "historical").
4 Rational economy, having emerged historically, has claimed the global scale, relegating love to the smallest scales. The nation occupies a contested middle, partly rational and partly familial.

Romantics and rationalists collaborated in splitting political economy away from natural science during the nineteenth century, and did so by making "its proper domain of inquiry mental phenomena."[1] Romantics had a particularly strong interest in detaching Economics from natural science, which they saw as mechanistic, materialist, and universalist. They were also, like rationalist modernists, deeply invested in the idea of correspondence between individual psychology and a social whole. Both romantics and rationalists came to identify the social whole with the nation, ending up with a thin and socially evacuated conception of the global. This shared understanding of scale became the basis for a shared investment in portraying global capitalism as a mighty world-spirit.

The essential points of divergence between rationalists and romantics are these:

1 Individual psychology: rationalists view the break from traditional to modern consciousness with equanimity; romantics believe it produced enduring trauma.
2 In consequence romantics are more likely to favor efforts to recover the alleged loss of traditional community and closeness to nature, efforts which have taken many shapes including nationalism, communitarianism, and some forms of environmentalism.

3   Rationalists, from John Stuart Mill to the IMF's *WEO*, perform rationality by cultivating a calm, measured, impersonal tone. Romantic writing is more likely to perform trauma and distress.
4   Rationalist writing leans toward formalization and the style of the natural sciences. Much romantic writing is allegorical, mourning losses that cannot be named.

Points (3) and (4) are not just superficial matters of style, but go to the heart of what makes different kinds of writing persuasive to different audiences. Moreover, each style needs to be read in relation to the other: there is a larger formation of mutual rhetorical repulsion. Mill and Marshall wrote in a way that distinguished themselves from Carlyle and Ruskin, and vice versa. In the example described in this book's Introduction, Nicolas Sarkozy spoke the language of pride, mourning, anger, and resentment. None of these registers were accessed by the economists, who reproduced their practiced rhetoric of universal reason. What has perhaps changed over the last century-plus is that reading-across has almost ceased, something you can confirm for yourself by examining the bibliographies of scholars in the different streams. Each has shut out the other, both by their own choice of what to read, and by developing modes of writing difficult for the other.

This part of the book has two tasks. The first is to present romantic political economy as a positive doctrine. The *rationalist* tradition is well enough known that it requires much less exposition: I do not need to defend the idea that it exists, or that it has content, heft, coherence, achievements. But today figures like Ruskin, Carlyle, Roscher, and Schmoller are almost forgotten, or remembered only in derision. In the end, Mill won: the idea that a *romantic* political economy exists, or existed, requires a defense today. That is the burden of Chapter 7. Doing this also helps flesh out the dual genealogy of modernist economic thought that is the book's larger goal: that modernist economic thought consists of two parts, covertly interconnected even as they play off each other.

After that I narrow the genealogy to one influential strain of contemporary anti-globalization writing, in order to explain why it has resonated so strongly with the IMF's claims about the world economy. Chapter 8 discusses Georg Simmel and Werner Sombart, who originated the core theory of a powerfully alien capitalism. Chapter 9 is devoted to Fredric Jameson, and Chapter 10 to Saskia Sassen, Arjun Appadurai, and David Graeber. This is a tradition devoted to the cultural study of capitalism that retains strong romantic assumptions about what culture is, how it works, and how it can be studied. Writers in this school have moved past the simple view that capitalism is the solvent of culture. But they have kept the underlying ontological precepts that "culture" is integrally whole and bounded, and that there is a close mapping between a "culture" and the minds of the individuals nestled within it. In other words, an ideal "culture" is treated as a space of clarity and *knowledge* for its inhabitants, a space of shared meaning to which their minds have been shaped. This is the influence of Herder. If you start with these (rather strong) assumptions, then *failures* of understanding become significant. In other words, someone who is *not* steeped in Herder's doctrine might regard confusion, misreading, ignorance, and a degree of general bewilderment as a normal part of life. But for Herder's descendants culture *ought* to be doing a lot of work for you, organizing meanings and tuning you in to shared truths. If you find yourself confused, something has gone badly wrong.

Broadly speaking, the thinkers discussed in Chapters 8, 9, and 10 theorize capitalism as a new and strange culture, a new and strange order of meaning that is displacing the old. Because they make strong assumptions about the ties between individual psychology and larger cultures, they theorize the change as a crisis in individual consciousness, as people unwillingly find themselves in a new cultural system they do not understand. These writers attain a certain rhetorical and emotional power by evoking and performing shock, bewilderment, and distress, and arguing that their readers' sense of shock, bewilderment, and distress is not idiosyncratic, but a direct consequence of history and capitalism.

This is why this school of writers has resonated so deeply with the depiction of global finance that appears in the IMF's *WEO*, with the larger genre of "bankers' boasts" and neoliberal policy advocacy that arose in the 1980s (F. Cooper 2005, p. 93). Neo-romantics needed no persuading that "capitalism" has a single, terrible, animating spirit. The voice ventriloquized by the IMF was just what they thought capitalism would sound like.

I write as an advocate, not a detractor, of a thickly cultural understanding of economy. What lies behind this part of the book is an effort to work out why scholarly traditions equipped with sophisticated tools of cultural analysis, and asking important questions, have come back time and again with thin, schematic, and uncritical descriptions of economy.

Note

1 Gallagher (2006, p. 134). On this period and the relationship between Psychology and Economics see also Kornbluh (2013).

7 Romantic political economy

The idea of *romantic* political economy might seem odd today, but it is actually much easier to set out the romantic approach to economic questions than it is to characterize romanticism as a whole. The material I draw on in this chapter comes from the late 1700s and 1800s, and mainly from the German states and Great Britain. The intellectual heavy lifting was German: such figures as Goethe, Herder, Müller, Schelling, and Fichte. They directly influenced the British romantics, notably via Coleridge and Carlyle. But while the British romantics included major creative artists like Wordsworth and Coleridge, their social thought was less systematic and more polemical. German romanticism inspired a substantial school of academic economists, sometimes called the "German Historical School," that flourished in German universities during the 1800s.[1] While British romantics fought pitched battles with rationalist economists for popularity and policy influence, their German counterparts enjoyed uncontested institutional access and considerable policy success: in its nationalist form, German romanticism contributed to nineteenth-century German unification and the economic policy of the emerging German state.

I will not attempt a complete intellectual history but will proceed analytically, setting out core ideas and prioritizing exposition over critique.

Transactions, meanings, and society

The rationalist and romantic doctrines can be approached as divergent responses to the eighteenth-century critique of knowledge. David Hume (1711–1776) and Immanuel Kant (1724–1804) launched a powerful, fundamental critique of *all* knowledge: on what basis, they asked, can we claim that our perceptions and internal intuitions correspond to the outside world? This is not just a challenge to the knowledge claimed by scientists, natural or social. It is also a challenge that any theory *of* society must answer: what does *any* individual know about the society she moves in, and how is that knowledge made? If significant *shared* understandings exist, where do they come from, and how does the sharing work? If it is so hard to know the world outside our minds, why is the social world not sheer blundering chaos?

Broadly speaking, rationalists have argued that large social institutions do much of the work of coordinating, reducing the burden on individuals to observe much, or to understand what they observe very deeply. Orthodox market theory is a prime example: you can produce and sell rubber without caring how it will be used; you can buy rubber bands without knowing that rubber comes from a tree. All you need to do is respond to prices; markets manage the rest. Hume's friend Adam Smith carefully avoids arguing that individuals know much or reason well. They do not have to: a providential order coordinates their actions.

But there is an alternative response to the Hume/Kant challenge. Suppose society is *already* in our minds, because it has *formed* our minds. Or suppose society is something we more or less wittingly *make*, on a daily basis, so that we have insight into it that way.[2] If there is already a close and necessary link between our internal understandings and the external "society" in which we move, the Kantian locked-in-your-own-head problem starts to recede.[3] At the foundation of romantic social thought is the idea that a society is built out of and *depends* on common understandings and shared meanings. Just at we expect co-religionists to share common understandings via texts, images, songs, and rituals, so a romantic social analyst looks for the shared core of ideas and understandings in society in general, and then asks *how* they are shared.

This is why art is so vital to romantics: it is how communities develop and share meaning. Ruskin approached Gothic cathedrals as public, shared, assemblages of meaning. Moreover the romantic model of knowledge comes from the *practice* of art and the *scholarship* of art, which are bodies of common knowledge and tradition learned with difficulty and discipline. While romantics praise individual genius in the arts, it is always genius *at* accessing collective truth and communicating it back to the collective.

How do meanings circulate? Think about a family dinner, a religious ceremony, a civic festival – events with multiple participants that re-affirm commonly understood meanings. Their repetition makes and remakes society; we feel any alteration in these rituals as social change. Romantic thought puts economic transactions in the same category as ritual events. In this view economic transactions do not just, or even mainly, satisfy the momentary and idiosyncratic needs of a buyer and a seller. Rather, they carry powerful meanings that make, remake, or change the character of the society they knit together. When you buy a sandwich, the romantic thinker asks: what kind of society are you making? What relationships are you building, and what shared understandings are you supporting? Those considerations weigh more heavily than whether your sandwich is tasty or cheap. To repeat the passage from Coleridge quoted in the Chapter 1:

> You talk about making this article cheaper by reducing its price in the market from *8d.* to *6d.* But suppose, in so doing, you have rendered your country weaker against a foreign foe; suppose you have demoralized thousands of your fellow-countrymen, and have sown discontent between one class of society and another, your article is tolerably dear, I take it, after all. Is not its real price enhanced to every Christian and patriot a hundred-fold?
>
> (Coleridge 1884, pp. 186–187)

This is the core of the romantic approach to economy: *if* human society rests on knowing, on interpretation, on shared meaning, and *if* every interaction affects those shared meanings, *then* we can ask about the social and moral implications of buying a sandwich. How odd, a romantic would say, to think that the paid work that shapes our lives and fills many of our waking hours, or the commercial purchases that provide most of our needs, are nothing but technical solutions to technical problems.

To take an early example, in Johann Goethe's 1795 novel *Wilhem Meister's Apprenticeship* the artistically inclined hero chafes against his businessman father, who sold his grandfather's serious art collection to buy a big new house stuffed with fashionable opulence. Wilhelm laments the banal "striped walls, with their endless rows of flowers, their scrolls and baskets and figures" that his father bought. Early in the story he runs into an art connoisseur:

> "Aren't you a grandson of old Meister who had such a fine art collection?" the stranger asked.
> "Yes, I am," said Wilhelm. "But my grandfather died when I was ten, and I was very grieved to see these lovely things sold."
> "But your father got a great sum of money for them."
> "How do you know that?"
> "Oh, I saw those treasures when they were still in your house. Your grandfather was not just a collector, he knew a great deal about art ..."
> "Then you can imagine what a loss we children felt when all those things were taken down and packed"
>
> (Goethe 1959, pp. 36–37)

Wilhelm's father may be a philistine, but he is no puritan: he spends lavishly on decoration. The problem is that Wilhelm's father has dreadful taste, and he has dreadful taste because he chases fashion. Good taste, Goethe reminds us in the exchange above, is the product of internal cultivation and knowledge. The German keyword is *Bildung*, or personal development – the kind of cultivation for which Wilhelm's grandfather is praised ("not just a collector") and which Wilhelm seeks. The enemy of *Bildung* is superficial fashion, because when we follow fashion we adopt the views of others rather than cultivating our own traditions and our own deep knowledge.

We can pin down three points. First, romantics are concerned with shared knowledge and understanding, not just feelings. Second, they are attentive to scarcities of time and attention: in their view people do not have infinite time to learn; artists do not have infinite time to create. Bad art crowds out good art. Third, one characteristic of bad art is irresponsible circulation of signs: the stripes, flowers, and scrolls on Wilhelm's father's fashionable wallpaper have escaped their original context, and are now nothing but designs to catch the eye. Romantic critiques of fashionable clothing, popular novels, and *money* (Chapter 10) all sound the alarm that signifiers have gotten loose, and are reproducing irresponsibly.[4]

A similar argument was presented a century later by art and social critic John Ruskin (1819–1900).[5] He starts by proposing a general category of "life" for whatever is good or valuable.

> Intrinsic value is the absolute power of anything to support life. A sheaf of wheat of given quality and weight has in it a measurable power of sustaining the substance of the body; a cubic foot of pure air, a fixed power of sustaining its warmth; and a cluster of flowers of given beauty a fixed power of enlivening or animating the senses and heart.
>
> (Ruskin 1891, p. 12)

Here Ruskin rolls up aesthetic and physical nurture in the same large category of "life." His next move is to argue that *realizing* such value requires capacity, understanding, knowledge:

> But in order that this value of theirs may become effectual, a certain state is necessary in the recipient of it. The digesting, breathing, and perceiving functions must be perfect in the human creature before the food, air, or flowers can become of their full value to it. The production of effectual value, therefore, always involves two needs: first, the production of a thing essentially useful; then the production of the capacity to use it.... A horse is no wealth to us if we cannot ride, nor a picture if we cannot see.
>
> (Ruskin 1891, pp. 12–13)

In this way Ruskin moves the question of value out of the good itself – the book, the dress, the flower, the house – and into what you *do* with the good, which depends on what you *know*.[6] The rationalist political economists against whom Ruskin railed were uninterested in what people *did* with their purchases: they assumed that if a person chose to buy something it must do them some good, and that was the end of it.[7] But for Ruskin, the doing is all-important – we can do good *or* bad things (Craig 2006). Doing good things requires well-cultivated knowledge, a knowledge that tunes us in to larger truths. The same chain of knowing extends back to the producer of the good. For example, Ruskin laments that wealthy newlyweds get their inherited silverware melted down for new plate in the latest fashion. What is the harm in that? He explains

> so long, observe, as fashion has influence on the manufacture of plate – so long *you cannot have a goldsmith's art in this country*. Do you suppose any workman worthy the name will put his brains into a cup, or an urn, which he knows is to go to the melting-pot in half a score years? ... You ask of him nothing but a little quick handicraft – a clever twist of a handle here, and a foot there ... But you don't suppose that that's goldsmith's work? Goldsmith's work is made to last, and made with the men's whole heart and soul in it; true goldsmith's work, when it exists, is generally the means of education of the greatest painters and sculptors of the day.
>
> (Ruskin 1906, pp. 51–52, emphasis in original)

And so the circle is complete: production ought to be thoughtful and skilled, and consumption educated and discerning. Goods, like the well-made cup, convey knowledge and ideas. Common participation in shared ideas cements society. While Ruskin is drawn to elaborately wrought goods like silver plate or Gothic churches, his argument extends to any commodity and indeed any service, no matter how humble. Wheat or coal, he would admonish, should be produced with the purpose of sustaining good lives and consumed in the same spirit. Their use binds producers and consumers in a larger social compact. Hence Ruskin's bitter denunciations of fashionable dress that, he contends, diverts the labor of poor seamstresses away from wholesome craft, and toward gratifying the vanity of wealthy philistines. This is a recurring worry for romantics: as more people get more spending power, and as markets widen purchasing options, popular taste will gain more influence over the cultural landscape, at the expense of cultivated elites.

To take one more example, Thomas Carlyle, an important channel for German romantic ideas, translated Goethe's *Wilhelm Meister's Apprenticeship* into English in 1824. In his translator's introduction, Carlyle doubts the novel's success with

> the great mass of readers, who read to drive away the tedium of mental vacancy, employing the crude phantasmagoria of a modern novel, as their grandfathers employed tobacco and diluted brandy.
>
> (Goethe 1959, vii)

If you want entertainment, he says, look elsewhere:

> Of romance interest there is next to none in "Meister"; the characters are samples to judge of, rather than persons to love or hate; the incidents are contrived for other objects than moving or affrighting us; the hero is a milksop, whom, with all his gifts, it takes an effort to avoid despising.
>
> (Goethe 1959, p. vii)

Rather, continues Carlyle, the novel is written for the discerning few "who have penetrated to the limits of their own conceptions, and wrestled with thoughts and feelings too high for them."

Now, there is no question that *Wilhelm Meister* has philosophical dimensions. But notice the way Carlyle sets the surface and philosophical readings *against* each other, and assigns them to opposed classes of people. On the one hand there are people who read to be "moved or affrighted," and on the other hand people who read allegorically for higher truth. Consider the term "phantasmagoria" in Carlyle's dismissal of shallow modern novels. This is the name of a kind of theatrical performance invented in France in the mid-1700s. Phantasmagoria were a proto-cinema, in which ingenious optical machines projected images on screens and made them appear to move, complemented by sound and even olfactory effects (Castle 1988). Originally phantasmagoria were fake séances, with spirits appearing and vanishing on thin scrims. But even as they moved toward frank entertainment, their content remained weird and terrifying: ghosts and demons. You sat in a dark room to be scared by illusions. Hence Carlyle's metaphor: phantasmagoria were unedifying, disorienting, and *false*, appealing to a taste that wanted only cheap stimulation.[8] This is what made entertaining novels like tobacco and brandy; this passage presages the drug analogies that have been a recurrent feature of dystopian romanticism.

So tastes are a flashpoint: for rationalist Economics, uncultivated tastes are no problem.[9] People know what they want. But for romantics cultivation, *Bildung*, is everything. A material/cultural environment that distracts and dazzles us, offering cheap thrills and light entertainment, undermines cultivation. Additionally, foreign fashion and foreign books draw the minds of consumers away from shared national cultures toward alien ideas. The rapid growth of the book trade in the eighteenth and nineteenth centuries revealed a popular taste for escapist fiction and shallow novelty among the literate public. Literary reviews in the German states and in Britain sought to educate readers and shape their tastes, but it was not easy to persuade readers to grapple with difficult texts (Hohendahl 1988). Concerns over the superficiality of popular taste, from Goethe to Nietzsche to Adorno to Allan Bloom, are not just snobbery. They sound an alarm over the extinction of traditions of art and literature that bind us across time, across space, and to serious larger purposes.

What distinguishes nineteenth-century romanticism is a certain (though not universal) optimism that the decline in popular taste could be stopped and even reversed through expanded secular and religious education, diligent work by critics to shape popular tastes, and the *writing* of new national literature when the existing stock was inadequate.[10] Goethe and Wordsworth intended their literary output to have a moral, social, and political effect.

Units

Up to this point, we have pursued the argument that a "society" is cemented via the creation of shared meanings, but we have not specified how big or small that society is. At the large extreme, it is possible to conceive the relevant unit as a single global society, united by international commerce and international culture. At the small end many romantic thinkers have idealized little rural communities, mistrusting cities as large, alienating, and cosmopolitan.[11]

Nonetheless, nineteenth-century romanticism is strongly associated with the mid-level unit of the nation. The key theorist is Johann Gottfried Herder (1744–1803), a student of Kant who turned against Kant's universalism to develop a carefully thought local relativism (Barnard 1966; Berlin 2000). Herder's legacy is the doctrine (1) that the language, thought, culture, natural environment, and material life of a given place are closely intertwined with each other, and (2) that the world is made up of many distinct, discrete social wholes, sufficiently different from each other that it is not easy to think or translate across them. What *makes* a society whole, what binds it together and distinguishes it from other societies, is that its members understand each other, and language is the medium of understanding. A language, for Herder, is not just grammar plus vocabulary. It is song, poetry, and legend; it is idiom and allusion; it is the full repertoire of expression and reference a native speaker deploys.

A consequence of Herder's doctrine was that it is difficult for a person in one society to understand another society. We can recognize here an origin of immersive fieldwork as the method of cultural Anthropology: only by learning the language, living in the place, and participating in the rituals for some time can one begin to figure another society out. But this argument put in question the very possibility of a universal social science.

Herder's theory is essentially descriptive, though it had obvious political implications. Herder was for example a principled opponent of imperialism, because he did not believe one society could rule another well. For intellectuals working to bring a German nation into existence out of a ragged patchwork of smaller states, his ideas had implications for economic policy. Johann Gottlieb Fichte (1762–1814) drew them out in his (1800) *Geschlossene Handelsstaat* (closed commercial state) which proposed an autarkic planned economy strictly regulated to exclude foreign influence.[12] The bare minimum of foreign trade would be conducted by government in order to avoid creating private cross-border business ties. Most foreign travel and communication were forbidden. Fichte was insistent that there could be no world money, only national money, because national money symbolized and enabled nation-unifying commerce. Fichte's successors continued to approach markets not as arms-length exchanges but as ongoing *communication*: they took a keen interest in railroads and telegraphs as means of binding a nation.

Nineteenth-century romanticism was a powerful *scale-making project*, in the terminology (Tsing 2000) used elsewhere in this book. In 1800 not only was there no German nation, but the concept of nation as economic unit was far from obvious. As already noted, the root-stock of the romantic argument is an idealization of small, face-to-face, rural communities. In the eighteenth century Justus Möser had sought to preserve the peculiar local laws of Osnabrück against Frederick the Great's efforts to standardize them (Muller 2002). One of the streams flowing into British romanticism was Tory agrarianism. But after this, a transition happens. You can argue that Möser was genuinely rooted in a traditional local society. But Fichte's closed state was radically unlike anything then existing. Carlyle and Ruskin were hardly isolated rustics: they were cosmopolitan intellectuals addressing a national audience and trying to shape an urban-centered culture. The agrarianism and medievalism of nineteenth-century romanticism should be read as utopian fiction.[13] The politics of nineteenth-century romanticism make its radicalism harder to see today. Müller, Novalis, Southey, Coleridge, and Ruskin were deeply committed to inegalitarian societies. Carlyle defended slavery, fiercely. It is tempting to classify these figures as mere reactionaries. But they were not, in fact, voices of a vanishing past, nor were they defenders of any obvious status quo. They were radical thinkers working to build new social, cultural, and political models.

Romantic critique of economic policy

Most of the thinkers discussed above developed their economic thought in con-
scious, sometimes strident, opposition to British political economy. Indeed, one
wonders how much of this doctrine would have developed without rationalist
political economy as a convenient foil. Rationalists thought economy should get
people what they wanted. For a romantic, the essential question is not "what will
give me pleasure" but "what are my duties"; indeed they saw "what will give *me*
pleasure" as calculated to make people neglect their duties (Briefs 1941).

Rationalist political economy celebrated competition between producers as
they vied to give consumers pleasure. Romantics thought competition wasteful,
cruel, and corrosive of social solidarity. Even worse, Adam Smith and David
Ricardo (not to mention Ricardo's follower Karl Marx), theorized society in
terms of contending classes with opposed interests: landlords, capitalists, and
workers. Nothing could be more corrosive of the social comity and national
unity romantic thinkers desired. In other words romantics did not just think
rationalist political economy was misguided: they saw it as a deliberate effort to
encourage individual irresponsiblity and sow social discord. As Poovey shows,
nineteenth-century political economy was not just dry technical writing for specialists: it included popular writings with an explicitly pedagogical function, and
romantics reacted to its popularity (Poovey 2008).

Rationalist political economists thought they were developing a universal,
abstract science, derived from first principles true across space and time. Smith
set out to develop a theory applicable anywhere in the world. Ricardo, his most
prominent successor, used mathematics to extend Smith's insights and sort out
some of his confusions. For Ricardo and *his* successors mathematics is at the
very least a tool for achieving conceptual clarity. Romantics tended to regard
mathematical abstraction as a deliberate effort to escape the moral and cultural
significance of economic interactions (Welch 2000).

Finally, romantic political economists tended to oppose free trade.[14] Friedrich
List's 1841 *National System of Political Economy* became a globally famous critique of Ricardian Economics, which was drawn on by economic nationalists in
Japan, Argentina, India, and the United States, where List spent several years.
List and Wilhelm Roscher (1817–1894), the founder of the German Historical
School, argued against Ricardo's policy conclusions, against his abstract analytical method, and against his emphasis on the different interests of classes within
the nation.[15] Romantics rejected the idea of a "world economy" as a meaningful
unit, and favored national currencies over international money because they saw
national currencies as facilitating *national* commerce. The critique of foreign
imports follows readily: they disrupt national circuits of meaning because commerce with foreigners cannot be culturally meaningful.

Romantic critics from Fichte to Ruskin, therefore, took issue with the free-
trade conclusions of rationalist political economy and traced their logic back to
fundamental assumptions of individualism and abstract method. However shrill
some of those criticisms sound today, they had a logical structure.

Was Marx a romantic political economist?

Marx is sufficiently prominent in the theoretical landscape, and sufficiently important to some of the figures discussed in the next few chapters, that a few words on him many be useful.

During his lifetime, Karl Marx (1818–1883) dismissed "the German philistine" Friedrich List as a hack protectionist and a shill for German capitalists. He argued, on straight Ricardian grounds, that tariffs, which List favored, siphoned spending from the pockets of consumers to the pockets of national capitalists.[16] Marx abused Wilhelm Roscher in the footnotes to *Capital*.[17] He and Engels (1850) published a penetrating critique of Carlyle. Marx was internationalist while the romantics were nationalist, and assailed their belief in the unifying capacities of national capitalism (Szporluk 1991). Marx mocked idealizations of agrarian life and praised capitalism for demolishing feudal society – not just for demolishing feudalism as an exploitive relationship, but for demolishing feudal culture.

So Marx emphatically distinguished himself from contemporary romantic political economy. Moreover his respect for Ricardo, his internationalism, his cosmopolitalism, his own experience as an exile, his support for free trade, and the fact that he dedicated most of his life to developing a single economic theory applicable across the world – all these factors put him in close dialog with rationalist political economy. Marx's critique of bourgeois political economy was not a root-and-branch rejection of the project, but an effort to sort out science from ideology. He spent decades developing a single theory applicable across time and space, the kind of effort that was, as we have seen, anathema to romantic Economics.

But we cannot quite leave it there. Marx shared the romantic interest in social commonality, and the idea that people come to understand themselves by sharing their experience with others. He agreed with romantics that a person's internal experience might be at *odds* with prevailing social ideology. Such conflict is not a possibility in Adam Smith, whose writings are conspicuously silent on community-binders like nationalism and religion. Such conflict is something John Stuart Mill avoided by crudely compartmentalizing society into an economic part and a cultural/ideological part. Marx rejected the Millian split and avoided Smith's culturally thin theory, seeking instead a single theoretical plane in which ideas and things circulated. In other words Marx shared an important chunk of social ontology with romantics: he recognized that the material and the cultural are intertwined, understood that collectivities matter for how we understand ourselves, and was highly aware of the historical and political salience of nationalism despite his anti-nationalist politics.

It is the romantic-rationalist *split* that now makes is difficult to bring all these features of Marx's thought into a single view. The divide that produced a culturally attuned "Western Marxism" in the twentieth century is usually, and plausibly, presented as a rejection of the dogmatic "Eastern" Marxism of the Soviet Union (Anderson 1976; Jay 1984, 1996). But it was also, *effectively*, a sidestepping of political economy as a critical and creative project. "Economics" got conflated with "economism" and thus with crude base-superstructure analyses that flattened culture. Even though figures like Adorno had highly nuanced understandings of the relationship of cultural analysis to social science, their work has been read in recent decades through neo-romantic assumptions in which economy is the enemy of culture.[18] The same evasion can be seen in recent scholarship on globalization (e.g., Jameson and Appadurai, in coming chapters) which hastens to announce some qualitatively "new" (and more cultural) stage of capitalism in order to claim that the world has so fundamentally changed over the last century or so that Marx's economics can be left on the shelf. There are three problems with this move. First, it grants Marx too *much* authority as a theorist of nineteenth-century capitalism: his work, however insightful, needs to be read critically and in light of other scholarship. Simply giving Marx the nineteenth century is symptomatic of a left nostalgia for an allegedly simpler time when exploitation was obvious and class politics dominant. Second, it assumes without warrant that there have been sufficiently large changes in material life over the last century or so to require an entirely new economic theory. Third and relatedly, this move undersells Marx – a monetary macroeconomist with much to say about finance – as a theorist who might be useful today. It sidesteps Marxian political economy as an ongoing, contemporary project.

Concluding note

The romanticism of the late eighteenth and nineteenth centuries was a radical project. It assailed on cultural grounds the rapid social and economic changes accompanying the commercial and industrial revolutions. It resisted the globalizations of that era, whether intellectual (Enlightenment universalism) or material (trade, especially of meaning-bearing things like fashionable clothing). Not merely critical, romantics advocated the formation of a new unit, the nation, and worked out the cultural and material basis necessary to integrate this new unit. They achieved a degree of success in Germany that belies the aura of impracticality still lingering around the term "romantic," and the ideas and structures of feeling they developed remain powerful today. Start with an individual's yearnings and hurts. Add a nation, which amplifies those yearnings and hurts at the same time that it succors and completes the individual. Then consider the nation's negations: the nation is not sectionalism, regionalism, or class, all things that might divide it. The nation's other negation is the *international*, which becomes a thin space without culture or attachment.

Notes

1 See Přibram (1983, Chapters 14, 15, and 25); this was part of the larger historicist tradition, on which please see Beiser (2012), Nau (2000), and Nau and Steiner (2002). For contrasting treatments of romantic political economy in relation to rationalist Economics see Bronk (2009) and Levy (2002). On romanticism itself a starting point is Sayre and Löwy (1984), whose opening section treats different understandings of the term.

2 I explore these alternatives more fully in Danby (2015).
3 Přibram (1983, pp. 209–212). There is an alternative genealogy of this concept through Rousseau and Kant (Jay 1984, pp. 39–49) that gets us to the same place, but with greater emphasis on the crisis for individual consciousness when the social whole fails to do its work, and different timing for that crisis: eighteenth century for Rousseau, nineteenth for the British romantics.
4 See Desaulniers (1995, pp. 12–17).
5 For treatments of Ruskin please see Hobson (1898), Fain (1956), Henderson (2000), Craig (2006), and Winch (2009).
6 The knowledge Ruskin describes is at least partly tacit, felt, embodied: how to ride a horse is not something you can write down. This bears comparison to Burke and Oakeshott, providing another glimpse of resonances between the rationalist and romantic schools.
7 Compare Chapter 3, where we saw that once a good was exchanged for money it was regarded as "consumed," and thus disappeared from the sight of Economics.
8 For the rationalist inheritors of the Enlightenment, vision and light were central metaphors for knowing. Carlyle turned the metaphor around. Light is an instrument of trickery; we are fooled through our sense of sight. See Jay (1993).
9 For economists there may be "externalities" e.g., environmental harm caused by heedless gratification of individual tastes, but those are understood precisely as external, large-scale problems, not problems of individual cultivation.
10 See Jay (1984, p. 43) on the idea of building a "second nature" to resolve alienation.
11 Radhakamal Mukherjee is a good example among romantic economists. See also Justus Möser (Muller 2002). See Williams (1987) for more on the urban/rural question.
12 Gray (2008, 2011). Among the more interesting extensions of early nineteenth-century German romantic political economy was an embrace of national (credit) money as opposed to an international commodity money like gold. See (Gray 2003). The national money (this anticipates Simmel) symbolizes and enacts national commercial unity. Adam Müller is the other great theorist of national money in this tradition.
13 The same ambiguous reference to an imagined past will appear in Jameson. Sayre and Löwy (1984, p. 56) write: "the Romantic orientation towards the past can be – and is in general in a certain sense – a look into the future; for the image of a dreamed-of future beyond capitalism is inscribed in the nostalgic vision of a pre-capitalist era."
14 For more extended accounts please see Přibram (1983) and Helleiner (2002).
15 Tribe (1995, 2002). See also Nau (2000) and Nau and Steiner (2002) on Schmoller, and Szporluk (1991) on List.

16   Since the bourgeois now hopes to become rich mainly through "protective tariffs," and since protective tariffs can enrich him only insofar as no longer Englishmen, but the German bourgeois himself, will *exploit* his *fellow-countrymen*, indeed exploit them even more than they were exploited from abroad, and since protective tariffs demand a sacrifice of exchange values from the consumers (chiefly from the workers who are to be superseded by machines, from. all those who draw a fixed income, such as officials, recipients of land rent, etc.), the industrial bourgeois has therefore to prove that, far from hankering after material goods, he wants nothing else but the sacrifice of exchange values, material goods, for a spiritual essence.

(Marx 1845, p. 275)

17 The German Historicists, in return, regarded Marx as a wayward Ricardian. Writes Tribe (2002, p. 5): "Hence the political economy of Karl Marx was firmly linked to the classical economics of early nineteenth century Britain, and he should consequently be understood as the last of the English classical economists." Also (2002, p. 11): "as far as the Older School was concerned, these two polar extremes – economic liberals and

Marxist socialists – in fact had a common source for their economic ideas: the classical economics of early nineteenth century Britain. German historical economics was therefore a path between these two extremes..."

18 For a recent example of the enduring effect of this split, see Butler and Athanasiou (2013, pp. 38–43). The authors recognize the problems of economic representation, but see the horizon of economic analysis as containing only neoliberalism and an economistic, culture-denying Marxism.

8   Shock of the modern

The simplest romantic critique of markets and capitalism pits rich, organic cultures against an *absence* of culture. Markets set people in competition with each other, undermining social solidarity. Markets popularize cultural products, like fashion or novels, whose exciting novelty and cheap sensations distract us from serious cultivation. Rationalist political economists encourage this cultural rot, praising irresponsible hedonism and denying any distinction between cultivated and shallow tastes. In this theory, then, markets and consumer culture erode cultural solidarity, undermining the psychic integration that individuals gain by being part of a serious shared tradition. The result is emptiness, shallowness, atomization, anomie.

In the late nineteenth and early twentieth centuries there arose a variant of this critique, which argued that markets and capitalism possess a serious *culture of their own*. If that was case, the struggle was between *different* cultures, rather than between culture and no culture. This move opened the door to a rich stream of cultural analyses of capitalism.[1] Just as Herderian cultural analysis privileged the shared language of a culture, theorists trying to build cultural analyses of capitalism fixated on the language-like qualities of money. Alert to shared ritual and magic, they saw sorcery in finance. So this new version of the romantic critique retained the basic opposition between the rootedly local and the elusively global, but added a twist: local culture was not merely being eroded; it was being attacked by a malign and elusive counter-culture.

Once you make this move, you open the question of individual consciousness under these different cultures. As we have seen, romantics made tight links between an individual's subjectivity and whatever larger "culture" shaped and contained the individual. So if capitalism was a "culture" in this sense, who were its people?

The two theorists discussed in this chapter, Georg Simmel and Werner Sombart, had somewhat different answers to that question. But they agreed that people enmeshed in capitalist culture had sharply different subjectivities from those who were not, even if they lived next door. These theorists thus introduced a geographical theory: the world is inhabited by one kind of people who are place-bound, possessing the traditional culture and language and customs of particular places, and another kind of people who are mobile and participate in a global culture of markets and capitalism. In Simmel the difference was extended to a doctrine of the body and the somatic correlates of consciousness.

These theorists also agreed that between these two kinds of people, the decisive advantage lay with those who were embedded in the worldwide, placeless capitalist culture. That advantage, moreover, lay in their superior understanding. Here is a key asymmetry. If we start from simple Herderian premises, then if you meet someone from a profoundly different culture, you are *both* at a loss. One of you might prevail in a struggle because of greater capacity for force, but not because of superior understanding. But in Simmel and Sombart the capitalist is able to read the place-bound person, but not vice versa. The upshot is a theory of *confusion*, and I mean that quite seriously: place-bound people's *experience* of confusion, their deeply-felt bafflement and loss, is approached by these theorists as an important phenomenon to be understood on its own terms, and as a sign that something else is happening.

Bourgeois nerves

In 1881 U.S. physician George Miller Beard (1839–1883) published *American Nervousness: Its Causes and Consequences* in which he announced the new malady "neurasthenia," and explained it as a consequence of recent changes in the environment (Taylor 2001; Killen 2006):

> Particularly during the past quarter of a century, under the press and stimulus of the telegraph and railway, the methods and incitements of brain-work have multiplied far in excess of average cerebral development. It is during this period that various functional nervous disorders have multiplied with a rapidity for which history gives us no analogy. Modern nervousness is the cry of the system struggling with its environment.
>
> (Beard 1881, p. 138)

Beard and his followers fixated on electricity, which was only then coming into widespread use in cities to power lights, telephones, trams, and telegraph networks. Beard contended that the human nervous system functioned like a telegraph network, and was vulnerable to overloading and electrical faults. The neurasthenic suffered from a deluge of artificial stimuli. The railways, telegraphs, newspapers, telephones, and electric light that changed their physical surroundings overcharged their nerves. Modern bodies condensed charges from global circuits; nearby non-modern bodies were left vulnerable and confused, tied to obsolete localities and materialities. Rapid railway travel, abruptly shifting people between localities and exposing them to rushed, flickering views, also figured as a strain on modern nerves.

Intellectual workers in the professions, finance, and business were most vulnerable to neurasthenia because of the demands work placed on their minds. Businessmen suffered because "increased facilities for agriculture, manufactures, and trades have developed sources of anxiety and of loss as well as profit, and have enhanced the risks of business" (Beard 1881, p. 116). Beard considered himself a sufferer, as did many of the medical professionals in Germany who applied his electrical treatments to themselves and their patients (Killen 2006). In other words neurasthenia was not just a malady but an *identity*. Beard's book can be read as a manifesto, a declaration by a group of people that they were different, somatically and mentally: early cyborgs, perhaps. The self-theorization lifts Beard's work above mere quackery. His was a reflexive theoretical project of impressive ambition, linking individual psychology, social theory, and history. The pattern is more general: to declare oneself "modern" is to declare oneself both special and damaged, wounded by the blow of modernity *and* granted special powers by virtue of that blow.

Beard's work had wide influence in Germany, not only in the medical profession but also among social scientists (Killen 2006). Sociologist George Simmel depicted neurasthenia as the "blasé condition," an altered consciousness characteristic of capitalist modernity.

> The metropolis exacts from man as a discriminating creature a different amount of consciousness than does rural life. Here the rhythm of life and sensory mental imagery flows more slowly, more habitually, and more evenly.
> [...]
> Thus metropolitan man reckons with his merchants and customers, his domestic servants and often even with persons with whom he is obliged to have social intercourse. These features of intellectuality contrast with the nature of the small circle in which the inevitable knowledge of individuality as inevitably produces a warmer tone of behavior ... The modern metropolis, however, is supplied almost entirely by production for the market, that is, for entirely unknown purchasers who never personally enter the producer's actual field of vision.... The money economy dominates the metropolis; it has displaced the last survivals of domestic production and the direct barter of goods.
>
> (Simmel 1950, pp. 410–411)

This is the standard romantic lament about mass markets, discussed in the previous chapter. The critique to this point is the markets-as-solvent argument, that older community solidarities are washed away by mass markets. Then he adds the Charles Beard part:

> There is perhaps no psychic phenomenon which has been so unconditionally reserved to the metropolis as has the blasé attitude. The blasé attitude results first from the rapidly changing and closely compressed contrasting stimulations of the nerves. From this, the enhancement of metropolitan intellectuality, also, seems originally to stem. Therefore, stupid people who are not intellectually alive in the first place usually are not exactly blasé.
>
> (Simmel 1950, pp. 410–411)

Neurasthenia is a disease of intellectuals. Overlaid is an argument about pleasure:

> A life in boundless pursuit of pleasure makes one blasé because it agitates the nerves to their strongest reactivity for such a long time that they finally cease to react at all. In the same way, through the rapidity and contradictoriness of their changes, more harmless impressions force such violent responses, tearing the nerves so brutally hither and thither that their last reserves of strength are spent; and if one remains in the same milieu they have no time to gather new strength.
>
> (Simmel 1950, pp. 410–411)

The blasé are smarter, richer, and get more pleasure. Neurasthenia is the price they pay, as modernity alters their bodies. Simmel's "matter-of-fact" and "intellectualistic" mentality bears comparison with Alfred Marshall's "deliberateness" (Chapter 1), though Marshall said nothing about nerve damage. Simmel closely aligned the blasé attitude with money; unlike Beard he entertained the possibility that it might be cause as much as consequence of that money economy:

> The matter-of-fact attitude is obviously so intimately interrelated with the money economy, which is dominant in the metropolis, that nobody can say whether the intellectualistic mentality first promoted the money economy or whether the latter determined the former.
>
> (Simmel 1950, pp. 410–411)

In this sense he aligns with Ferdinand Tönnies, who had distinguished between natural and rational will, between the different mentalities underlying Gemeinschaft and Gesellshaft, and also Max Weber, who argued that a distinct Protestant ethic had made capitalism possible (Frisby 1985; Frisby 1992; Hamlin 2005).

The Philosophy of Money (Simmel 2004) is also one of the great arguments in romantic political economy about scale: money functions as it does because it is a large-scale, disembedding institution. Both Beard and Simmel can be read as theorists of scale, linking large-scale networks (railway, telegraph) to the intimate wiring of the human body and also using each as a metaphor for the other. The blasé are the plugged-in, the jangling nodes in a humming global network. They live differently and think differently from people who may be physically proximate, but who are not plugged in.

Alien spirit

Werner Sombart's 1911 *The Jews and Modern Capitalism* shifted the encounter between tradition and capitalism back to early modern Europe. Sombart claimed that rooted-in-the-land Northern Europeans were incapable of conceiving of capitalism, and in particular finance, because those things were alien to their cultures and minds. It was left to Jews, who in Sombart's view had always possessed a radically different culture and mentality, to develop those things. Sombart asserted that abstraction is the essence of capitalism, and that Jewish capacities for calculation, numbers, and abstract thought in general were radically better than Christian Europeans: "the conflict between Jewish and Christian merchants was a struggle between two outlooks, between two radically differing – nay, opposite – views on economic life" (Sombart 1951, p. 86). In a passage filled with romantic tropes about land and climate, he describes Jews as quintessentially non-Northern-European:

> The Jews are rational, are fond of abstraction.... The sharp outlines of the landscape in hot, dry countries, their brilliant sunshine and their deep shadows, their clear, starlit nights and their stunted vegetation – cannot all these be summed up in the one word abstraction? The opposite to this is surely what is concrete, as all things of the North are, where the water flows abundantly, where the landscape is as varied as it is rich, where Nature is prolific in wood and field, and the earth sends up its fragrance. Is it accidental that astronomy and the art of reckoning first arose in the hot lands where the nights are ever brilliant, and was developed among peoples whose pastoral pursuits taught them to count? ... can we imagine the peasant of the misty North as he follows his plough, or the huntsman chasing deer in the forest, as either of them able to conceive the abstract idea of numbers?
>
> (Sombart 1951, p. 340)

Sombart stressed rationality and abstract thought, interpreted in Herderian fashion as integral to one culture and alien to another. His discussion of cities echoes Simmel.

> And as the desert, so the town, in depriving man of his piece of fruitful mother earth destroys in him the feeling of communion with all living things, breaks the bond of fellowship between him and animals and plants, and so deadens all true understanding of organic Nature. On the other hand, the city sharpens his intellectual capacities, enabling him to search, to spy-out, to organize, to arrange. To be constantly on the alert is the nature of the nomad; to have to be constantly on the alert was what their fate forced on the Jews – to be constantly alive to new possibilities, new goals, new combinations of events; in a word, to order life with some end in view.
>
> (Sombart 1951, p. 340)

Sombart avoided cruder anti-Semitic tropes about cheating in favor of the idea that a peculiar genius for abstraction allowed Jews to tap into capitalism's explosive potential.[2] In Sombart's view this capacity for abstraction allowed polyglot, well-traveled Jews to transcend space, whisking their wealth away when local authorities turned hostile, transmitting information across borders, and developing global financial markets. This is not much different from how Simmel and

Beard imagined neurasthenics: the Jew may live in the same city as the non-Jew, but inhabits space in an entirely different way.

Most importantly, wrote Sombart, Jews understood "the secret power of money ... the mechanism of lending" in a way Christian Europeans, even the most powerful and wealthy, could not: "With the fine threads of money-lending a people who were socially of little moment were able to bind the feudal giant, much as the Lilliputians did to Gulliver" (Sombart 1951, p. 347).

He spends chapters tracing the history of financial development in Europe and finding (or, when necessary, asserting) Jews present at every innovation, and brilliantly successful in every kind of financial market. Christians, less intellectual and innovative, were on Sombart's account time and again caught flat-footed. This intellectual culture reshaped Europe:

> Before capitalism came, exchange was a many-sided, multicoloured and technical process; now it is just one specialized act – that of the dealer: before there were many relationships between buyer and seller; there is only one now – the commercial. The tendency of capitalism has been to do away with different manners, customs, pretty local and national contrasts, and to set up in their stead the dead level of the cosmopolitan town.
>
> (Sombart 1951, p. 275)

The Jews and Modern Capitalism is a tendentious anti-Semitic tract, and terrible history.[3] Nonetheless it bequeathed a complex romantic theory of capitalism, emphasizing finance.[4] If you remove all the specific references to Jews, you are left with a theory that capitalism and finance:

1 span international distances, humble national governments, and thus reshape space;
2 are ontologically different from the production of tangible goods;
3 not only obey an alien logic confusing to ordinary, rooted people who make tangible goods (which could be mere cultural difference), but obey a logic that has a decisive *advantage* over rooted people;
4 contain a strange and unnatural secret of wealth and transformation.

Capital is alien and insatiable. Brentano wrote that for Sombart capital works "not merely like an automaton, but like a Moloch, driven by its nature to devour everything" (Brentano 1916, p. 81). This is a theory about scale, a theory about the split between a materially "real" economy and abstract signs, and a theory about the upheaval and confusion this split creates among those who cannot understand it. It emphasizes mentalities and logics. It dramatizes a clash between two opposed logics: one rooted and concrete, the other rootless and abstract. The abstract logic is not merely a little better at generating wealth. It is shockingly *incomprehensible* to people whose way of thinking is rooted and concrete, and runs rings around them. Sombart's book is full of stories of bewildered Christian merchants unable to figure out why they were losing business to outsiders.

This theme, of a rooted *Volk* versus an alien capitalist spirit, of stolid local tradition versus quicksilver opportunism, survives in many contemporary theories of globalization. The spirit may be portrayed as benign or malign, but its opposition to the settled and traditional is a constant. It bears at least a family resemblance to the way the IMF portrays financial markets (Chapter 6) as everywhere and nowhere, powerful, and obeying a rationality that requires a specialized intellectual discipline to understand. This is why neo-romantic anti-globalizers have responded so strongly to that portrayal.

There are some important distinctions. Beard and Simmel understood themselves as members of the new mobile urban elite, while Sombart positioned himself alongside fellow place-rooted Germans who were puzzled and threatened by this elite. Sombart's rhetorical mode has been more influential in recent anti-globalization writings, even among people who would be horrified by his politics, because it lets writers invoke a shared bond of confusion, distress, and alarm with their readers. Fredric Jameson, as we will see, argues that the place from which capitalism might be understood has disappeared.

Notes

1 I am using "capitalism" and "capitalist" here as terms of convenience. Exactly what this thing is – markets, finance, bourgeois culture – is not always easy to pin down in this literature.
2 See discussion of Sombart and his reception in Ferguson (1988).
3 Brentano (1916, p. 159) termed it "one of the most distressing phenomena in German scholarship." See also Ferguson (1988), Rivkin (1952), Mendes-Flohr (1976), Trevor-Roper (1951).
4 Harris (1942) is particularly good on this, and on pointing out where and how Sombart parted company with Marx.

9   Jameson's postmodern

In his 2003 *After the New Economy*, Doug Henwood examines the tropes employed by financial journalists and by government figures like U.S. Federal Reserve Chair Alan Greenspan during the mid-1990s "new economy." He shows that the essentially the same arguments were made by academics, in only slightly transformed language. After quoting Castells and Baudrillard, he writes:

> But the weightlessness discourse infects even highly admirable writers like Fredric Jameson, who argues in his essay "Culture and Finance Capital" (1988) that capital has become deterritorialized and dematerialized in this "global" era. All the weightless postindustrial nostrums [in press accounts] are represented: "profit without production" ... and "globalization," defined as "rather a kind of cyberspace in which money capital has reached its ultimate dematerialization," as messages which pass instantaneously from one nodal point to another across the former globe, the former material world. Globalization becomes here the triumph of nothingness, and finance capital becomes "deterritorialized," and "like cyberspace can live on its own internal metabolism and circulate without reference to an older type of content."
>
> (Henwood 2003, p. 27)

This chapter and the next flesh out and explain what Henwood observed.

Jameson merits a full chapter for several reasons. He has been enormously influential, one of the developers, in the 1980s, of contemporary doctrines of globalization, postmodernity, and the rise of finance. He is one of the most prominent legatees of the Frankfurt School. And his work is, very simply, of great depth and scope. His contribution to romantic political economy has been to bring out its latent doctrine that modernity is ignorant of itself – that capitalism dazzles, obscures, and achieves monstrous proportions beyond human capacities of comprehension.

The first part of this book explored the representational power of national income accounting and the IMF's *WEO*. The Jamesonian perspective denies economy's representability. But both share the modernist story of the irresistible destruction of the local and socially close by the global and socially individuated.

For both, commerce and finance are an inexorable globe-bestriding force, chastening national governments and imposing a uniformly impersonal market logic. On the IMF's account markets triumph through sheer rationality, on Jameson's account capitalism prevails because it dazzles and confuses us. In this shared frame anything that operates via thicker sociality, like gender, is pushed back in time and down the spatial scale. The "economic" *makes* the global scale.

How we fell

The idea that primitive humans lived at one with each other and with nature, with a shared consciousness, arose in late nineteenth-century Anthropology and is perhaps best known in Durkheim.[1] Jameson sets the imagined point of total social closeness far back in the past as a point of social origin: history itself becomes the product of a great force that began splitting people up (Dowling 1984, p. 21). How that original "moment of plenitude" felt is in Jameson's view irrecoverable, but we sense its loss in our present condition, which he describes as impoverished, alienated, fragmented, maimed, and mutilated.[2]

> How many modern philosophers have described the "damaged existence" we lead in modern society, the psychological impairment caused by the division of labor and by specialization, the general dehumanization of modern life in all its aspects?
>
> (Jameson 1971a, p. 61)

Literature and art ever since have sought to cope with the traumatic loss of social wholeness; utopian fiction in particular offers "a distorted dream of a more humane collectivity."[3] So when Jameson (1971a, p. 36) writes about contemporary economy that "the entire business system ... depends for its very existence on the automatic sale of products which no longer correspond to any kind of biological or indeed social need" this is not idle rhetoric. The two neglected needs correspond to the two dimensions of this primal loss: our alienation from nature, and from each other.

Jameson (1977, 1981) argues that our lost wholeness, and the trauma of its dissolution, are *unrepresentable*. Commerce and money, on this account, constitute a powerful symbolic system that overrides older codings, impoverishing our being in the world.[4]

> where before there was a qualitative difference between the objects of production between, say, shoes and beef, or oil-paintings and leather belts or sacks of grain – all of them, in the older systems, coded in unique and qualitative ways, as objects of quite different and incommensurable desires, invested each with a unique libidinal content of its own – now suddenly they all find themselves absolutely interchangeable, and through equivalence and the common measure of a money system reduced to the grey tastelessness of abstraction.
>
> (Jameson 1975, p. 14)

Commerce divides us from each other as we become independent producers (Jameson 1990, p. 23), but worse, it obliterates use-values and beclouds our experience of the world.[5] The "quantification by the market system of the older hierarchical or feudal or magical environment" appears as a social and aesthetic crime (Jameson 1975, p. 9). When Jameson speaks (1979b, p. 70) of "the commodified daily life, reified spectacles, and the simulated experience of our plastic-and-cellophane society" he is not just complaining about the banality of consumerism, but lamenting the success of commodification in destroying our lost social wholeness, ritual unity, and integration with nature.

The first two counts in the indictment of commerce, therefore, are (1) that by dividing labor and selling things to each other we lose an older social wholeness, (2) that commerce commodifies, and this commodification suppresses the "use values" of things. A third count is that in this process art changes: it is disembedded from the ritual, magic, and lore that bound the community and becomes instead yet another fragmented and commercialized activity.[6] (All three points come from the nineteenth-century romantic critique of markets, discussed in Chapter 7.) So the story goes something like this: once we lived in little bands, and we made simple things and gave them to others and enjoyed them as use values: a roasted yam or a pair of sandals were different things, made, used, and experienced as part of a vibrant and varied physical world.[7] Our art ritualistically expressed and enacted our social solidarity. But then, at some point, the yamroaster and sandal-maker became separate people who traded their products for money. Exchange value trumped use value, direct physical experience yielded to the abstract logic of markets, and we lost the solidaristic wholeness of our original society. But our loss stays with us – we *feel* that something wonderful has been taken from us, without quite knowing what.

This fragmented, maimed, impoverished condition, then, is not a matter of hunger or cold or subordination or denial of social dignity. It afflicts the prosperous and the poor alike.[8] Indeed, when Jameson imagines the past reproaching the present, the reproach is *not* about power or domination, but an unfavorable comparison between the past's gritty authenticity, its immediate violences and pleasures, and our present artificiality:

> the primacy of collective ritual, or the splendor of uncommodified value, or even the transparency of immediate personal relations of domination, at once stigmatize the monadization ... of our own way of life.
>
> (Jameson 1979b, p. 70)

Simply to exist within a money economy is to be trapped by a grotesque symbolic system whose elaboration and extension intensifies our distance from direct, wholesome, experience.[9]

In Jameson's writings, the original social big bang that splits solidaristic human society does not immediately do away with all human social closeness, cultural authenticity, or connection with nature: that happens only over many thousands of years, gradually taking over all production, seizing control of all nature, and ultimately colonizing all cultural production.[10] During this long period the modern and premodern coexist and intermingle. What brought Jameson wide attention in the 1980s was his announcement that this process had reached, or was on the point of reaching, its end, the point at which all traces of nature, social solidarity, and non-commercial culture were obliterated, and memory itself disappeared. This moment, the extreme opposite of the imagined primordial moment of complete social wholeness, he named the postmodern.

From the postindustrial to late capitalism

The route to the postmodern runs through Jameson's seminal 1970's writings on Lukács and Adorno, and the difficulties he encountered using a prior term, "postindustrial."

For people in the last half century who think of themselves as working in the Marxian tradition, the resilience of capitalism and scarcity of proletarian revolution require explanation. One genre of explanation posits later "stages" in which the free-wheeling, brutal, unstable capitalism of the nineteenth century lost its self-destructive impulses and lubricated its contradictions. Another genre of explanation holds that capitalism has clouded our minds and bought us off with superficial pleasures. In the 1971 *Marxism and Form*, Jameson combined the two in the notion of a "postindustrial" stage.[11] The idea is straightforward. Start with Georg Lukács' argument that capitalism creates a proletariat with a privileged epistemological standpoint because workers have a direct, lived understanding of their work and exploitation (unlike, says Lukács, the intellectual elite). Jameson takes this to mean that a Lukácsean proletariat derives its knowledge from the experience of making physical, tangible goods, so that *service*-providers are denied this kind of understanding.[12]

> for the most part, and particularly in the United States, the development of postindustrial monopoly capitalism has brought with it an increasing occultation of the class structure through techniques of mystification practiced by the media and particularly by advertising in its enormous expansion since the Cold War. In existential terms, this means that our experience is no longer whole ... In psychological terms, we may say that as a service economy we are henceforth so far removed from the realities of production and work on the world that we inhabit a dream world of artificial stimuli and televised experience.
>
> (Jameson 1971a, pp. xvii–xviii)[13]

This concern over distance from the kind of goods that you can heft and smell makes sense in terms of Jameson's overarching historical vision, discussed in the last section, in which history moves us from immediate, physical sense-experience to treacherous artificiality. Though alienated, the millworker still has a relation to real cloth, to the production of a physical good. In Jameson's account, the service economy snaps that link with physical reality. But once the millworkers are gone and the proletariat is only providing intangible services, you have a Lukácsean world without a Lukácsean proletariat, which means *nobody understands capitalism.* There exists no subject-position from which it can be seen and grasped.

But two years later, Daniel Bell's *The Coming of Postindustrial Society* grabbed the word "postindustrial" to make the opposite argument, that a service economy is socially *enriching*, because service work is by its nature more inter-personal than industrial or agricultural work.[14] Bell inverted Jameson's history by denying any epistemological or ethical virtue to closeness to nature or to physical labor. In Bell's view capitalism's reshaping *of production* is socially progressive.[15]

Jameson's response to this challenge was to propose a third, "postmodern," stage of capitalism.[16] First, he posited that the aesthetic forms of realism and modernism corresponded to two successive phases of capitalism, market capit-alism and monopoly capitalism:

aesthetic form:	realism	modernism
phase of capitalism:	market	monopoly

You can think of the transition as happening late in the nineteenth century. Jameson then suggested that, dialectically, these two successive moments required a third stage to resolve them.[17] In the early 1980s Jameson named this third stage "late capitalism," and christened its corresponding aesthetic form "postmodernism."[18]

aesthetic form:	realism	modernism	postmodernism
phase of capitalism:	market	monopoly	late

In Jameson's account the transition from monopoly to late capitalism was roughly pegged to the 1970s.

A third move and culminating move follows. In the two diagrams above I dis-tinguish an upper row called "aesthetic form" from a lower row called "phase of capitalism": this is the old, troublesome, Marxian split between ideological superstructure and economic base. In its third, postmodern phase, Jameson pro-poses, capitalism has leapt *out* of its old base of factories and machinery, sweat and dust, and *into* the superstructure. It has transformed itself into a creature of meanings and symbols. The postmodern world is one in which there is no longer nature or even things. Instead there is a world of pure symbols and cultural manipulation.

Capitalism's cultural turn has the largest implications, because culture encom-passes not just elite art but the entire sphere of representation. But having become a creature *of* representations, capitalism is farther than ever from being *representable.* This vision shares the paranoid flavor of the late twentieth-century science fiction of William Gibson or Philip K. Dick, in which powerful corporate forces so saturate our surroundings and fill our senses that we can never know what is true. Jameson in 1996 refers to "this peculiar existential and epistemological dilemma, comparable to the science-fictional one of beings inhabiting a cosmos they do not have organs to perceive and identify" (Jameson 1996, p. 17). Late capitalism creates "confusion and feelings of helplessness" in us because it "confronts us with new measures and quantities to which no one has ever adjusted, and with new geographical processes (and temporal ones too ...) for which we have not yet grown organs."[19] While the core of Jameson's system was developed in the 1970s, what emerges in the 1980s and 1990s is an audacious interpretive doctrine to the effect that we can know things about the world *from the way we are confused by it*. Hence the argument in his pivotal 1984 article that:

> our faulty representations of some immense communicational and computer network are themselves but a distorted figuration of something even deeper, namely the whole world system of present-day multinational capitalism. The technology of contemporary society is therefore mesmerizing and fascinating, not so much in its own right, but because it seems to offer some privileged representational shorthand for grasping a network of power and control even more difficult for our minds and imaginations to grasp – namely the whole new decentred global network of the third stage of capital itself.
>
> (Jameson 1984b, pp. 79–80)[20]

He identifies manifestations of this fact in "contemporary entertainment literature" in which "circuits and networks of some putative global computer hook-up are narratively mobilized by labyrinthine conspiracies ... in a complexity often beyond the capacity of the normal reading mind" (80).

> This literature of conspiracy must be seen as a degraded attempt – through the figuration of advanced technology – to think the impossible totality of the contemporary world system. It is therefore in terms of that enormous and threatening, yet only dimly perceivable, other reality of economic and social institutions that in my opinion the postmodern sublime can alone be adequately theorized.
>
> (Jameson 1984b, p. 80)

(David Graeber, discussed in the next chapter, makes a similar argument that luridly implausible conspiracy theories gesture toward unthinkable totalities.) Two broad themes come together here: the non-representability of the Truth about society, and the commodification of the means of representation under postmodern late capitalism.[21]

Finance and knowledge

It is troublesome enough, for Jameson and indeed for the whole romantic tradition, that goods and services are easily exchanged for money. But what happens when money buys money? The link between money and things snaps.

Speculation – the withdrawal of profits from the home industries, the increasingly feverish search, not so much for new markets ... as for the new kind of profits available in financial transactions themselves and as such – is the way in which capitalism now reacts to and compensates for the closing of its productive moment. Capital itself becomes free-floating. It separates from the concrete context of its productive geography. Money becomes in a second sense and to a second degree abstract ... Now, like the butterfly stirring within the chrysalis, it separates itself from that concrete breeding ground and prepares to take flight.

(Jameson 1997, pp. 250–251)

This paragraph proceeds from the assumption that the most real is the most tangibly physical.[22] On this story commerce began to push the old world of physical things and direct experience out of sight, pressing down on it a powerful, vast, commodifying logic. Finance, then, is doubly alienated: it is money paying for money, it is the signifying system snapping any link to real objects but acquiring a weird energy of its own. And because it is so far removed from the ground of tangible things (which is for Jameson the ground of understanding and knowledge) it cannot make sense.

Jameson's own prose sometimes performs this failure of sense.[23]

The rich were certainly doing something with all this new income that no longer needed to be wasted on social services; rather than go into new factories, it seemed to get invested in the stock market. Whence a second perplexity: The Soviets used to joke about the miracle of their system, whose edifice seemed comparable only to those houses kept standing by the swarm of termites eating away inside them. But some of us had the same feeling about the United States. After the disappearance (or brutal downsizing) of heavy industry, the only thing that seemed to keep it going (besides the two prodigious American industries of food and entertainment) was the stock market. How was this possible, and where did the money keep coming from? And if money itself rested on so fragile a basis, why did "fiscal responsibility" matter so much in the first place, and on what was the very logic of monetarism itself grounded?

(Jameson 1997, pp. 267–268)[24]

Please note the terms "seem," "sense," and "feeling," which are *the only ways* the nature of capitalism can appear to our senses, in Jameson's epistemology. Start with the second sentence, and take the terms "perplexity" and "miracle" seriously – despite the rueful tone, Jameson does not mean this as a joke. Move now to the third sentence, and "same feeling." The characteristic understanding *must* be perplexity, because the thing being understood cannot make sense. The reason for this is explained in the next sentence. A characteristic claim on Jameson's part, noted in the discussion of Daniel Bell, is that capitalist production *used* to be a matter of tangible, physical, thing-making and was therefore to some degree intelligible to the people who worked in it, but that it has subsequently changed in such a way that it is no longer transparent. The assertion about the decline of heavy industry is a marker of the shift that Jameson believes has taken place away from legibly material production and toward incomprehensibly immaterial profit-making.

So if you read the sequence of questions that end the above-quoted paragraph like a social scientist, they make little sense. The questions are not clearly stated and the logical links between them are missing. It sounds like half of a telephone conversation. But if you read these instead as sentences mocking the very *idea* of logical connections, lampooning the representability of economy, they make excellent sense and fit the rest of Jameson's text. *If* the truth of capitalism is hidden from us and *if* its visible signs do not cohere, *then* discourse generated by it *must* have a disjointed quality. The paragraph is performative.

Assessment

It should now be clear that the Jamesonian system has a logical shape and a certain explanatory power. It offers an explanation for why capitalism is experienced as frightening and disorienting. It can handle simultaneously the ideas that capitalism is powerful and succesful and that it arouses grave cultural disquiet, even among those who apparently do well by it. It retains some of the oppositional energies of Marxism, and shrewdly avoids dissipating them in apologetics for the passivity of the proletariat or the failures of twentieth-century socialist revolutions. Jameson jettisons crude formulations like base versus superstructure, reconciles Adorno and Lukács, and appears to offer an historicist Marxism bulletproofed against the attacks on teleology, totalization, and grand narratives launched by waves of structuralists, post-structuralists, and early postmodernists (e.g., Lyotard). And even if you doubt his overall system you cannot deny that he has produced compelling critical performances, bravura pieces of analysis like those of Warhol and the Bonaventura Hotel (1984b).

Under the name of postmodernity Jameson offers an account of a recent present in which economy and culture, including high culture, have become disturbingly intermingled. Now, it is my contention that these levels have *always* been intermingled. But to readers intellectually formed in a modernist framework, to readers convinced that a separation of economy and culture *actually occurred and was the foundational event of their culture and society*, such re-mingling comes as news – shocking news.[25] So Jameson can stage a re-discovery of what (in my view) was always there as a sign of an epochal historical shift. If we think of modernity as a secular cosmogonic myth, the energies unleashed by the Jamesonian postmodern become more explicable.

If Jameson's history is psychoanalytic it is an Oedipal conflict without the father; if it is Marxist it is a Marxism without class protagonists. Its drama comes down to scale: the large swallows the small; that is history. The drama depends on imputing, by hints and gestures, agency to the large scale without ever quite naming that agency: history/capitalism is a dark force operating outside our sight, but its work is evident in what we can and cannot do.[26] For Jameson "history is what hurts," the equivalent IMF rhetoric speaks of that which is not "sustainable." Like the IMF, Jameson relies on projecting a scale larger than all of us, and *giving that scale historical agency and power*.

When capitalism owns the scale of the world[27] everything else is demoted to the local – the quaint, powerless local:

> The only authentic cultural production today has seemed to be that which can draw on the collective experience of marginal pockets of the social life of the world system: black literature and blues, British working-class rock, women's literature, gay literature, the *roman québecois*, the literature of the Third World; and this production is possible only to the degree to which these forms of collective life or collective solidarity have not yet been fully penetrated by the market and by the commodity system.[28]
>
> (Jameson 1979c, p. 140)

There are no other historical actors. Neither gender, race, nor sexuality operates on large scales.[29]

Traces

The ideas that generate the Jamesonian postmodern – the emptiness of consumer culture, the grievance over lost wholeness, the privileging of tangible goods, the unnaturalness of finance, the way capitalism is experienced as confusion, the alarming intrusion of markets and profit-seeking into cultural production – were deeply theorized, as an ensemble, by earlier romantic thinkers. Jameson's elegaic tone is romantic, as is his use of terms like violent, spasmodic, maimed, and damaged. The effort to theorize allegorically is romantic.

This is not to say there are no resonances with the Marxian corpus. But Jameson's magpie-like forays into contemporary Marxian Economics, plucking out attractive phrases and theorists, belie a rejection of Marxian political economy as open-ended inquiry. It is instead the Chicago School of Gary Becker that gets authority to speak about economy: "as description, then, Becker's model seems to me impeccable and very faithful indeed to the facts of life as we know it."[30]

With this Becker-Jameson accord over the nature of economy comes the consequences of the rescaling already described: gender is demoted to the smallest scale, cultural units are naturalized, state power vanishes, and all difference recedes except for difference in relation to a single, great, scandalous, globe-bestriding neoliberalism or capitalism. The next chapter turns to a different group of theorists who also reenact this accord, starting with romantic critical energies and ending up with the IMF's view of the world.

Notes

1 Stocking (1995); Durkheim (1915). This is echoed, for example, in Jameson (1975, p. 2), on the "unspecialized ritualistic world of primitive social life." See also Jameson (1981, p. 290).

2 Jameson (1971a, p. 38; 1971b, p. 17; 1975, p. 19; 1979a, p. 14; 1981, p. 20; 1995, p. 131).

3 Jameson (1981, p. 70; 1971b, p. 17). See also Jameson (1971a, p. 113) and (1977, p. 392).

4 See, for example Jameson (1971a, p. 20): "the commercial universe of late capitalism" and (1975) and (1979c), all of which emphasize the global, systemic nature of commodification and consumerism as what is most characteristic of capitalism; the competitive, individualist, robber-baron period of the nineteenth century having been eclipsed by a monopolizing process so vast that nobody understands it. See also (1995, p. 212): "doctrines of reification and commodification which played a secondary role in the traditional or classical Marxian heritage, are now likely to come into their own and become the dominant instruments of analysis and struggle."

5 Jameson 1979c, p. 131):

> by its transformation into a commodity a thing, of whatever kind, has been reduced to a means for its own consumption. It no longer has any qualitative value in itself, but only insofar as it can be 'used': the various forms of activity lose their immanent intrinsic satisfactions as activity and become means to an end.

6 See Jameson (1971a, p. xvi) ("the healthier, socially-functional art of the past") and pages 11–13 and *passim* on savage art; also (1982, pp. 75–76) and (1979c, p. 136).

7 Jameson's writings place less emphasis on the loss of religious experience than others in this genre (though see O'Neill (1989)), but I suggest nature plays the role for him that religion does for other writers, as a category of unmediated contact with the vibrant non-human that has been overwritten by commodification. Note too that if Jameson is right and the primal social split is unrepresentable, then one cannot represent it in *any* words, including these. Jameson frequently contends that the most profound matters can only be addressed via allegory and hints, so we must be wary of over-literalism in the exegesis of his writings (for which Dowling has been criticized). Very possibly Jameson does not believe that the Edenic wholeness described here ever *really* existed in human history, but is instead making an historical myth to point toward social potentials and harms that cannot be named directly.

8 Sayre and Löwy (1984, p. 55) underline the connections to nineteenth-century romanticism:

> Although there is sometimes an awareness of the exploitation of one class by another ... this awareness is by no means always present in Romanticism. All of the diverse currents of Romantic anti-capitalism, on the other hand, in one way or another point to and protest against those characteristics of capitalism of which the negative effects are felt throughout the social classes, and which are experienced as misery everywhere in capitalist society.

9 Dowling (1984, p. 35) shows that it is easy to extend this to the argument that Economics is a direct expression of this alienating symbolic system, an argument that would apply to any sort of Economics, heterodox or orthodox.

10 Hence Jameson's understanding of the third world as the place where commodification lags and doomed pockets of solidarity and cultural authenticity remain.

11 Jameson (1991, p. xix). See also Jones (1971) and Sayre and Löwy (1984) on Lukács.

12 See Jameson (1971a, pp. 184–188), for an exposition that emphasizes the tangible nature of this production, and p. 204 ("transparent"). The contrast, "but in our own time ... concealed," is drawn on p. 296. See also (1998b, p. 32).

13 Kellner (1989, p. 20) calls this passage Jameson's "urtext"; see also Anderson (1998, p. 51).
14 The first edition appeared in 1973. I quote from the second, 1976 edition.
15 Though see O'Neill (1989, p. 155).
16 The larger story of the emergence of the term "postmodern," amid a vivid narrative of Jameson's writings in the early 1980s, can be found in Anderson (1998), especially pp. 54–68. For Jameson, this stage also worked as a ground for reconciling Lukács and Adorno. Adorno had argued that modern music, painting, literature, and other forms contained at least the potential to criticize capitalism, and that elite art preserved a realm of autonomy from the bourgeoisie and the philistinizing forces of the market. Lukács retorted that high modernism *was* bourgeois art, and that its nonrepresentational, chaotic qualities, far from being critical, encouraged passive acceptance of capitalist alienation. He argued instead for a return to realism as a model for socialist literature. Haslett (2000) has a useful account.
17 In Hegelian fashion history is logic; logic is history; logic follows a narrative progression. The logical sequence works itself out in historical time, so that history is the record of a certain logic, or if you like the space in which narrative logic unfolds. Time is the dimension along which meaning is produced.
18 Jameson ostentatiously drew the phrase "late capitalism" from Marxist economist Ernest Mandel (e.g., Jameson (1984b, p. 55)) and repeatedly set Mandel in opposition to Bell e.g., "with Ernest Mandel's theorization of a third stage of capitalism ... there exists a properly Marxian alternative to non- or anti-Marxist theories of 'consumer' or 'postindustrial' society today, theories of which Daniel Bell's is no doubt most influential" (1984a, p. xiv). Other conjoint mentions are (1982, p. 76) and (1996, p. 22); and implicitly (1991, p. 400). But there is no textual evidence that Jameson relied on Mandel for anything more than the two words "late capitalism," despite uncritical acceptance, by exegetes such as Anderson and Dowling, of the claim that Jameson drew theoretical substance from Mandel. Jameson ignored Mandel's rather different periodization of stages. None of Mandel's key theoretical and analytical innovations – his version of Marxian value theory, his ideas around regulation, investment, or crisis – appear in the Jameson texts that invoke him. See Davis (1985), Shumway (1989), and especially Norton (1995).
19 Jameson (1996, pp. 38–39). Note similarities to neurasthenia in the previous chapter.
20 See also Connor (1997, pp. 47–48) on this passage.
21 Key passages on this theme are Jameson (1971a, p. 57), on our ideas about society, and the parallel and more famous "history is what hurts" passage (1981, p. 102).
22 Contrast the butterfly image to the same article's discussions of how capitalism "powerfully undermines and destroys the logic of more traditional or precapitalist societies and economies," which display a marked violence of metaphor and language: *penetration, spasmodic, leap, virus, epidemic* (Jameson 1997, pp. 248–249). See further discussion of his language in Gibson-Graham (1990, pp. 120–147). This hardboiled style became popular in the globalization literature.
23 Some of Jameson's most perceptive interpreters agree that much of his thinking happens in the difficulties, oppositions, and deliberate obscurities on the surface of his writing e.g., Eagleton (1982), Dowling (1984), Homer (1998).
24 See also Homer (2002) on the financial sublime. La Berge (2015) situates Jameson in a larger literature on financial complexity.
25 On the question of the separation of economy as an event, please see Butler (2010).
26 Hence the extended argument (Jameson 1979b) that all modes of production are, ultimately, one, and the insistence (e.g., 1971a) that the current mode of capitalism is centralized and monopolistic. This should be read in light of his remarks on Marxism and history, for example (1989, pp. 19–20). See Larsen (1988, 1971, p. xxiii) and Homer (1998, p. 63) for more exegesis; among critics see Bennington (1982), White (1982), Young (1990), and Norton (1995).

27 Jameson (1971b, 10): "as we become a single world system, as the other cultures die off..."; (1975, p. 3): "We all know that capitalism is the first genuinely global culture"; (1995, p. 3): "disappearance of specifically national cultures and their replacement, either by a centralized commercial production for world export of their own mass-produced neotraditional images"; (1995, p. 10) "... the world system of late capitalism (or post-modernity) is however inconceivable without the computerized media technology which eclipses its former spaces and faxes an unheard-of simultaneity across its branches..." (1998a, p. 57): "standardization on an unparalleled new scale." On scale please see also Kayatekin and Ruccio (1998), Bergeron (2001, 2004), and Li (2000).
28 See (Jameson 1981, p. 54, footnote).
29 Anderson (1998, p. 62) also makes this point. See also Ahmad (1987), Radhakrishnan (1989), Hestetun (1993), and Homer (1998).
30 Jameson (1991, p. 269). See Norton 1995.

10 Spirit of finance

Like an event foretold in legend, the voice of global financial liberalization that broke out in the 1980s was recognized by legatees of romanticism because their theory told them to expect it. The IMF positioned global finance within its own special dimension, a world space outside national spaces. They gave it a God-like ability to step outside time and see the inevitable consequences of wrong policies. They invested it with remorseless rationality. The ideas that finance slid through a secret dimension, followed a cryptic rationality, and ran rings around the local and the material had already been theorized by Sombart in 1911 (Chapter 8). You could say this theory was just awaiting the revival of international finance after several decades of eclipse. But it would be more accurate to say that it was awaiting the revival of a certain *performance* of international finance. International financial flows are quite real, but real finance is messy, flighty, and lacks any necessary unifying rationality. Thus we need to work out the conditions for the contemporary uncritical reception of the *performance* of finance as a powerful world-spirit.

This chapter is more structural and illustrative than genealogical, which is to say that its purpose is to demonstrate that the neo-romantic system of ideas visible in Jameson, and their resonance with orthodox Economics, is not peculiar to his work. The chapter discusses writings by Saskia Sassen and Arjun Appadurai, prominent figures in scholarship on "globalization" in the 1990s and early 2000s who have deepened their focus on financial markets in recent years.[1] I also discuss David Graeber, an influential theorist of money and debt. What these theorists have in common is:

1   A *geographical* theory in which finance claims the space of the global as a special, hidden, lubricated space of international flows.
2   A theory that such flows, and the logic that drives them, are innately more powerful than anything that is nailed down geographically, whether a household, or a traditional business, or a national government.
3   A theory that the overpowering logic of this immaterial, slippery force is alien, confusing, and deeply frightening to ordinary people.

These theorists start from a fundamental split between a tangible, real economy and a financial economy. The material economy is natural and material; it is rooted in space, ordered, and therefore comprehensible. By contrast the financial economy is magically immaterial, ubiquitous, arcane, and dangerous.

The split

Some of this recent work also draws on ideas that long pre-date the romantics. Appadurai, for example, writes that:

> Financialization may be broadly defined as the process that permits money to be used to make more money through the use of instruments that exploit the role of money in credit, speculation, and investment.
>
> (Appadurai 2016, p. 2)

> In a world of derivative assets, money breeds more money, if risks can be bought and sold through securitization, the process by which debts can be bundled, repackaged, and sold time and again. This dynamic, which liberates money almost entirely from Marx's famous formula M-C-M, allows money to grow, as if magically, on its own, through risk-based credit trading.
>
> (Appadurai 2016, p. 10)

Where have we heard this before?

> For it is a work of nature to provide sustenance to the newly born, everything deriving sustenance from what remains of that from which it is born. Expertise in business relative to crops and animals is thus natural for all. But since it is twofold, as we said, part of it being commerce and part expertise in household management, the latter necessary and praised, while expertise in exchange is justly blamed since it is not according to nature but involves taking from others, usury is most reasonably hated because one's possessions derive from money itself and not from that for which it was supplied. For it came into being for the sake of exchange, but interest actually creates more of it. And it is from this that it gets its name: offspring are similar to those who give birth to them, and interest is money born of money. So of the sorts of business this is the most contrary to nature.
>
> (Aristotle 2013, p. 18)

Households, said Aristotle, channel the products of farmers and artisans to people who need them, and uphold a larger social and political order. Commerce can *serve* these purposes; though "expertise in exchange" by itself is not admirable. But finance is crazy. When he writes "get its name," Aristotle plays on the way the Greek term for "interest," *tokos*, also means birth or offspring. Interest is the child of money and that is monstrous, because money ought to be sterile. Such unnatural breeding is dangerous because it knows no bounds: "all those who engage in money-making increase their wealth without limit" (Aristotle

2013, p. 19). Finance has a disturbingly *unnatural* fecundity, from which decent people recoil.

This is the moral ordering Appadurai invokes: the unnaturalness of finance explains both its power and its menace. Ignoring Marx's extensive writings on money and finance, he asserts that Marx dealt only with the production of "commodities by means of commodities" and thus cannot help us "understand a form of capitalism that was barely born when he lived, that is, that sort of financialized capitalism in which the production of money by means of money ... is the regnant form" (Appadurai 2016, p. 5).

Here is Sassen:

> Profit is realized from automobile manufacture in about nine months; the duration of a financial service transaction could be a day or less.... The sharper the differentiation between these two temporalities grows (with dematerialization/digitalization), the more abundant the business opportunities become. This is one way in which economic globalization today is constituted: temporal features of finance capital empower it to subject other forms of capital to its rhythms.
>
> (Sassen 2001, p. 220)

Old-fashioned bolted-to-the-floor physical capital yields to "hypermobile dematerialized financial instruments" (Sassen 2001, p. 218); the result is the "ascendancy of finance and the dematerialization of many economic activities" (Sassen 2001, p. 222). Sassen does not follow Aristotle in assailing *all* finance, but instead seeks to draw a bright line between safe and conservative "traditional banking" and "innovative and invasive" contemporary finance (Sassen 2014, p. 118), between "healthy" and "unhealthy" debt. Contemporary finance preys on healthy real activity, says Sassen; Appadurai contends it has figured out how to transmute precarity into profit.

The temporal argument is tied to a spatial argument. Appadurai writes that

> Globalization ... extends the earlier logics of empire, trade, and political dominion in many parts of the world. Its most striking feature is the runaway quality of global finance, which appears remarkably independent of traditional constraints of information transfer, national regulation, industrial productivity, or "real" wealth in any particular society, country, or region.
>
> (Appadurai 2001, p. 4)

Thus "traditional constraints" and "real" things are tied in space; "runaway" finance eludes locality. Sassen theorizes a geography of globalization that is superimposed across an older world of more stable places and borders.

Their basic analytical template remains romantic (Chapter 8), but these writers have reached back to Aristotelian reasoning for a booster shot of moral repulsion, a re-affirmed conviction that a virtuous, life-sustaining natural economy is threatened by an antagonistically unnatural economy. The very existence of financial profits, in their view, is evidence that something has gone very wrong. (Jameson, though he sometimes taps into the rhetorical energies of the Aristotelian view, is working from a more Hegelian ontology in which the transformation of economy from material to immaterial is the result of the working-out of long-standing internal dynamics, not a sudden ambush.)

Signs on the loose

The romantic addition to Aristotle's doctrine is a Herderian theory of culture and knowledge. Herder understood cultures as internally coherent units, bound by complex shared understandings and bounded off from other cultures with very different shared understandings. As noted in Chapter 8, this produced two distinct romantic theories of economy, what we might call the money-as-solvent and money-as-competing-culture theories. In the money-as-solvent theory, markets and commodification dissolve older, local, face-to-face community economies. But in money-as-competing-culture theories, the sphere of money, finance, and commerce (or "business" or "capitalism") constitutes a separate culture of its own, however strange and parasitical. This licenses a cultural analysis of commerce and finance *along romantic lines*: in other words if we start with the Herderian assumption that it is the shared language, circulation of songs and legends, and repeated exchanges of meanings that define a culture and make it work, we will look for those features in commerce and finance. A result of this strategy, however, has been fixation on those properties of money and finance that look most language-like. The common functional definition of money names three distinct roles: "unit of account," "means of exchange," and "store of value." The neo-romantic literature emphasizes "unit of account," and recognizes "means of exchange," because those are the aspects of money that can most easily be analogized to language. But it tends to skip over the "store of value" role that is the key *financial* function of money: its role as one asset among others (financial or real) that a person may choose to hold. An unfortunate result has been theorizations of finance that neglect the substance of finance.

There is another troubling consequence of starting from romantic premises. Herderian theory assumes that a "culture" is animated by a singular spirit. If you make that assumption, you have drastically reduced and simplified the kinds of evidence you need to "read" a culture. In the neo-romantic view financial capitalism may be a dark, shape-shifting spirit, but it is still *a* single spirit whose nature and will can be read from the disturbances it causes, like clues to the murderer in a detective story. You can see this in a passage in which Sassen *warns* against dropping the assumption that we are studying a single unified logic:

> disaggregation also renders invisible the deeper vortex and in many ways veils what is happening: a large-scale destruction of healthy economies, healthy government debt, and healthy households. In case after case, this destruction takes the form of a flow of capital and resources to financial firms and the impoverishment of other economic sectors.
>
> (Sassen 2014, pp. 119–120)

Sassen *assumes* a moral and ontological division between "healthy" economies, debt, and households, and destructive finance. She *assumes* the essential unity of all finance in one principle, one force, one malign world-spirit, even *if* finance appears to take multiple forms in multiple places. For Sassen it is the work of the analyst to perceive the global unity of the unhealthy parts. She personalizes finance and imputes a single will: "Finance was aggressive, invasive, and self-interested, and rather than being regulated firmly, it was too often left to risk our money for its own gain" (Sassen 2014, p. 146).

Appadurai's *Banking on Words* draws further linguistic parallels in its discussion of derivative financial instruments (derivatives are financial assets whose value derives from other assets, like a bond backed by a pool of mortgages). Appadurai understands money as a symbolic system overlaying real goods, the signs by which people "have reckoned both value and price." In this view finance is troubling because money begins symbolizing *itself* rather than real goods, and derivatives represent runaway signification.

> The derivative is an asset whose value is based on that of another asset, which could itself be a derivative. In a chain of links that contemporary finance has made indefinitely long, the derivative is above all a linguistic phenomenon, since it is primarily a referent to something more tangible than itself: it is a proposition or a belief about another object that might itself be similarly derived from yet another similar object.
>
> (Appadurai 2016, p. 4)

Financial assets refer to other financial assets; "securitization" permits the monstrous, limitless, proliferation of chains. Appadurai writes of the way derivatives "allow money to generate more money without the intervening step of industrial commodity production" and argues that the possibility of "shorting" an asset (that is, taking a position that pays off if its price falls), demonstrates that finance has become "independent of the real course of commodity values in the real world of goods and services."[2] He assumes, in short, a "real world" with real values, and a competing false world with false values.[3]

Appadurai has been especially attentive to the Sombartian theme that finance is an alien logic, too hard for ordinary people to understand.

> Global capital in its contemporary form is characterised by strategies of predatory mobility (across both time and space) that have vastly compromised the capacities of actors in single locations even to understand, much less to anticipate or resist, these strategies.
>
> (Appadurai 2000, p. 16)

Likewise Sassen writes that "Goldman Sachs's backroom is well stocked with physicists. The mathematics of the backroom is mostly well beyond the understanding of the highly paid executives of the boardroom" (Sassen 2014, p. 119).

David Graeber's (2011) *Debt: The First 5000 Years* contends that the 1971 de-linking of the U.S. dollar from gold precipitated the world economy into a new era of confusion: "once the global system of credit money was entirely unpegged from gold, the world entered a new phase of financial history – one that nobody completely understands." He segues into "When I was growing up in New York, I would hear occasional rumors of secret gold vaults..." and relays lurid rumors about those vaults and the September 11 2001 attacks. He sums up:

> Reality, then, has become so odd that it's hard to guess which elements of grand mythic fantasies are really fantasy, and which are true. The image of collapsed vaults, the melted bullion, of secret workers scurrying deep below Manhattan with underground forklifts evacuating the world economy – all this turns out not to be. But is it entirely surprising that people were willing to consider it?
>
> In America, the banking system since the days of Thomas Jefferson has shown a remarkable capacity to inspire paranoid fantasies.
>
> (Graeber 2011, p. 363)

This is the same rhetorical mode we saw in Jameson: rueful reflection on the strangeness of it all, and then a move to posit one's own (and others') confusion as *evidence* that something deeply strange is going on.[4] He describes (p. 370) a Federal Reserve operation as "yet another piece of arcane magic that none of us could possibly understand," and adopts a Jamesonian register when he writes (p. 367) that "the advent of the free-floating dollar marks not a break with the alliance of warriors and financiers on which capitalism was originally founded, but its ultimate apotheosis." Like Appadurai, Graeber appears to believe that a natural monetary system would tie values down; finance becomes a story of the disembedding of economy from the natural order.

Credulity

A recent article by Sassen traces the IMF's development, and almost precisely reproduces its claims about global finance:

> The global capital market represents a concentration of power capable of systemically, not just through influence, shaping elements of national government economic policy and, by extension, other government policies. The powerful have long been able to influence government policy ... But today it is also the operational logic itself of the global financial system that becomes a norm for "proper" economic policy ... These markets can now exercise the accountability functions formally associated with citizenship in liberal democracies: they can vote governments' economic policies out or in; they can force governments to take certain measures and not others. Given the properties of the systems through which these markets operate – speed, simultaneity, and interconnectivity – the resulting orders

of magnitude give them real weight in the economies of countries and their policymaking.

(Sassen 2012, p. 7)

These last few chapters have tried to work out where this comes from: why "globalization," "financialization," and so forth are theorized as something that has spun off from the real, from the locatable and understandable. These writers depend on a division between a weighty and material economy, and a weightless non-place into which capitalism has escaped. Again, Jameson:

> Capital itself becomes free-floating. It separates from the concrete context of its productive geography. Money becomes in a second sense and to a second degree abstract ... Now, like the butterfly stirring within the chrysalis, it separates itself from that concrete breeding ground and prepares to take flight.
>
> (Jameson 1997, pp. 250–251)

I do not contend that finance is always and everywhere benign. What I want to put under pressure is the rapid generalization in this literature toward finance, debt, securitization, or derivatives as creatures of a single malign and monstrous logic, a logic that, to invoke Brentano's criticism of Sombart, works "not merely like an automaton, but like a Moloch, driven by its nature to devour everything" (Brentano 1916, p. 81). The Moloch theory is sweeping and indiscriminate. It fixates on superficial features of money and finance. It crowds out any discursive space for heterodox economics, or even for the more critical and interesting parts of mainstream economics.

This style of explanation has left its practitioners defenseless in the face of the IMF's claims, all too ready to be impressed by what Fredrick Cooper (2005, p. 93) aptly terms the "banker's boast." An all-powerful global finance with a single inexorable logic is precisely what this school of thought wants to hear; its fondest fear. Like the IMF, they see global credit markets as a single powerful world-scale rationality that has floated free of the merely material. Unlike the IMF, they have drawn on the tradition discussed in Chapter 7 to emphasize the opacity of globalization and finance. In the view of the romantic anti-globalizers finance is opaque, malign, and violent; and we know about it not directly, via our senses and reason, but indirectly via our confusion, dread, and alarm.[5] For all their rhetorical truculence, these anti-globalization theorists re-affirm the IMF's view of the world. If we are to escape this trap we need to rethink the modernist priors that reproduce this agreement on the shape and nature of the world.

Notes

1 I examine just a few prominent academics for reasons of compactness. In a more expanded discussion the obvious figure to add would be journalist and activist Naomi Klein.

2 Appadurai (2016, p. 12). Appadurai appears to use shorting as evidence about the nature of derivatives. But shorting has no necessary connection with derivatives. To spell this out: in a typical "short sale," you borrow, say, a thousand shares of General Electric stock for a month. You immediately sell them for cash, hold the cash, and then buy the shares back in a month and return them to the owner you borrowed them from. If the price of the shares dropped over the month, it costs you less to buy them back than you sold them for, so you make a profit. If the price has risen, it costs you more and you take a loss. This is of course *speculative*, but no derivatives are involved (and it is no more *speculative* than taking a "long" position in an asset in hopes of profiting from a rise in its price). Appadurai appears to believe that the fact that a short position pays off when the price of the shorted asset falls demonstrates that meanings have become unmoored from the real.

3 Appadurai reproaches mainstream economics for what he claims is its inability to account for money, yet relies on that the traditional view that money is a "veil" spread over a real economy of genuine goods and services and labor, a view that has been a recurrent (though not universal) feature of the mainstream economics that he deplores. He ignores not only Marxian monetary economics (e.g., Volume 3 of *Capital*) but also the Keynesian and Post Keynesian traditions. Appadurai also invokes "Knightian uncertainty," which doubts the calculability of certain risks, but ignores Keynesian fundamental uncertainty, which is an *ontological* uncertainty – the problem for Keynes is not simply knowledge and calculation, but the underlying nature of the thing we are trying to predict. There is a reason for this: for Appadurai, the real, natural, virtuous world *must* be a stable and predictable world, while risk is a property of capitalism and finance. For anthropological critique of this view see Ho (2009, pp. 31–38) and Maurer (2005, pp. 85–89, 2006).

4 See La Berge (2015, p. 15) on the resonance between Jameson and LiPuma and Lee (2004), on which Appadurai draws.

5 Bergeron (2001), Gibson-Graham (1990), Kayatekin and Ruccio (1998).

Part III
Opening up

11 Time and finance

Ellen Oxfeld's *Blood, Sweat, and Mahjong: Family and Enterprise in an Overseas Chinese Community*, describes a community of Hakka Chinese families whose lives and businesses span India, China, and Canada (Oxfeld 1993). People, money, ownership, and management expertise move across borders; Oxfeld examines the familial logics, sentiments, rivalries, and ambitions that inform these movements. Such family businesses illuminate the artificiality of splitting family from business for the sake of creating a measurable national economy. Oxfeld has much to say about the cross-national movement of capital and people, about the capacity of families to coordinate economic activities across multiple countries. Yet a book like Oxfeld's is reviewed in Anthropology and Ethnic Studies journals, not Economics journals. It remains hard to see Oxfeld's familial entrepreneurs as more than just "a few people somewhere," in Anna Tsing's phrase.[1]

Tsing demonstrates that scales like national or global are not obvious features of the world but made, "conjured" into existence. The family/business split described in Chapter 1 was not only a division of a complex society into two simple realms with opposed ethical characteristics. It was also a scale-making project that scaled *up* economy to the national level at the same time that it scaled families *down* to nuclear households. "Family" in Economics excludes cousins and aunts and grandparents, much less Godparents, fictive kin, neighbors, colleagues, co-religionists, or any of the myriad ways people build, maintain, or just find themselves enmeshed in relations of moral responsibility to particular other people. It means a small consuming unit under one roof, and was initially theorized around the self-sacrificing care of an isolated mother. At the same time economy, manifest as employment, production, income, investment, wealth, and so forth, claims the larger scales.

The family relationships described by Oxfeld were already gone from the scale of the national, and were thus excluded from the conception of global economy. At the same time the conception of the world as intercommunicating national units ignored structural inequality at the global level. All that was left at the global level, in this conceptualization, were mechanical, impersonal, "flows" of goods and finance.

My working assumptions, by contrast, are that we live in a world in which the cultural and material have *always* been deeply intermingled. We also live in *one* world, and have done for centuries. That world is untidy, loosely structured, and cruelly unequal. I have found this disclaimer necessary: when I say that our world does not fit the modernist template, that it is shaggier and more intermingled than modernist social science believes, I am making a purely ontological claim. I am not claiming that it is a nicer or better world than we think it is. Nor am I proposing any political alternative. To the extent that I offer any political argument in this book, it is simply that the modernist template limits our ability to understand the world and restricts political choices.

What I hope to show in this chapter is that it is quite possible to do social science about material life and economic relations – include monetary and capitalist relations and multiple scales – without the crutch of modernist assumptions, and that those assumptions hide much of the world from view, like Oxfeld's transnational kinship. I will also offer one possible alternative via the heterodox literature called Post Keynesian Economics.

To summarize the critique and alternative: the modernist carving-up of society we have been exploring is an ontological position that economic society really *is* fundamentally in tension between the two opposed principles of loving households and competitive markets. This commitment pre-theorizes the household as solidaristic and the market as arms-length and asocial. My critique of this is that (a) loving households versus competitive markets is a poor way of sorting out the complex social world (b) to the extent that a distinct realm of kinship and face-to-face sociality really exists, it is poorly captured by pre-theorizing it as solidaristic (c) to the extent that a distinct realm of business and finance and impersonal transactions really exists, it is poorly captured by pre-theorizing it via competitive markets.

In Post Keynesian theory business and finance may be institutionally heterogeneous. Some markets are competitive, some oligopolistic, some monopolistic, and some government regulated. Large and small firms may be very different creatures. Firms are often linked in enduring ways. Key prices like interest rates, exchange rates, and wages may be as much a product of political as market forces. This framework is capable of incorporating productive activity that goes on under the name of household and kinship, and working out its complex interactions with activity under other names. By starting from concepts of time and fundamental uncertainty that stretch across institutionally heterogeneous kinds of production, we can avoid presuming modernist ontology. Moreover, a theory of this kind is better able to understand patterns of dispossession, exclusion, and abjection that are ignored by a social ontology that boils down to loving families, plus impersonal markets on which anyone can buy or sell.

Diachrony and the inevitability of finance

Production takes time. Weeks, months, and sometimes years elapse between planting and harvesting, between fattening animals and eating them, between buying raw materials and selling finished manufactures. Any arrangement of production, under any social dispensation, needs to bridge this temporal gap. In a purely agricultural setting with no money, I would still need to put aside food to eat between planting and harvesting. If I am a manufacturer in a money-using environment, I must spend money for inputs, wages, and so forth well before I "get the money back" by selling output. In a money-using milieu we commonly say that production has to be "financed" – whether I use my own money or borrow it, I need money up front before I can begin a time-consuming productive process.

The temporal gap becomes larger when we acquire capital goods. To go back to a moneyless milieu, I might spend years digging an irrigation system before I began to get any benefit in higher crop yields. In a similar way a manufacturer might borrow money to buy a machine tool that will provide additional returns only gradually, over 20 years. So the time-gaps that have to be bridged can be quite long, and require considerable resources up front; such time-gaps also imply higher levels of risk if our plans do not work out.

A second implication of the time-gap between committing resources and getting back usable or saleable output is that there must be planning and coordination if more than one person is involved. *Some* institution or institutions must handle this – and I use "institution" in the general sense of some regularized system of interaction with rules, whether it is embodied in an organization, enforced by contract law, despotically coerced, or supported by an informal social code.[2] One of the more interesting questions that we can ask, in any particular place or time, is how this coordination works.

The things that we commonly call households, for example, typically produce a variety of services for their members. Many household services are time-sensitive: meals need to be served at dinnertime, children need to be gotten ready in the morning, laundry needs to be done. Households need to be flexible enough to handle unexpected occurrences like sick children, and may participate in ritual calendars that demand extra household production at certain times in the year. Producing these services entails the timely acquisition of inputs, investment in and maintenance of household capital, and timely availability of labor. In money-using contexts, food and beverages, new clothes, and other inputs need to be bought regularly and in advance of their use. We do not think of households as having the *purpose* of making money, but in money-using settings they face cash-flow challenges in covering gaps between the availability and expenditure of money.[3] As Marjorie DeVault (1991) emphasizes, household production does not just require devoting a certain number of hours of labor per week, but entails a high level of ongoing planning that takes into account budget and cash-flow constraints, the needs, likes, and dislikes of different household members, and the exigencies of dealing with merchants, service-providers, and repair specialists.

Formally established businesses sort these processes out as specified management tasks, and use specialized accounting tools to manage cash flow. The cash-flow perspective developed by Post Keynesian economists Paul Davidson (1994) and Hyman Minsky (1982) highlights the time-dated promises that firms have made to other entities, and that others have made to them. Anyone who has worked for a small, tenuous business understands this dimension: a firm may be profitable over some long period in the sense that total income exceeds total expenditure, but nonetheless face crippling cash-flow squeezes in the short run. When business owners talk about "meeting payroll," they mean the very specific challenge of managing cash flows so that there is enough money in the bank on payday to cover paychecks.

Households, individuals, firms, and any other relevant units can therefore be characterized, at any moment in time, by (a) their commitments to do or provide things for others in the future, and (b) others' commitments to do things for them or provide things to them. These commitments may be precise and precisely time-dated (e.g., bill payments) or imprecise and heavily contingent on circumstance (e.g., a parent's open-ended obligations to a child). They may or may not be monetized, and they will reflect differing types of obligations and norms and power in terms of who meets obligations to whom and how. (All obligations, even those written in contracts, can be renegotiated and contested and exist in cultural, political, social fields that condition how those contestations work.) There may be long-term patterns of commitment between units substantial enough that we may wonder whether the two units are really separate at all. In any case, for any specified unit you can imagine a temporal map showing commitments to and from others, stretching into the future (Charusheela and Danby 2006).

Once we think of a person, household, or firm as enmeshed in future commitments, our attention is drawn to the large range of institutions that in various ways enable, condition, encourage, discourage, thwart, constrain, or enforce commitments, which may include government, law, community, family, friendship, and religious institutions.[4] It is bears repeating that "ties" and institutions can be systematically and cruelly oppressive, and that some institutions, like race or class differences, work in part by *limiting* the kinds of social ties people are able to draw on, make, and sustain. This is one obvious point at which culture enters. Contracts, formal or informal, are things of symbols and codes that partake of larger symbolic systems. A material world filled with forward commitments is irreducibly, necessarily, filled with meanings, systems of meaning, and specialized practices of meaning-making and meaning-interpretation. It is not news that economy is cultural, always deeply culturally embedded. How could it be anything else?

We can then move from the examination of small units to the larger network of ties they entail. Once you imagine each individual's time-map of commitments to others and from others, you can then imagine the ensemble of *all* of these maps, with all their interconnections. This gives us one possible vision of a larger "economy," and it will quickly be apparent that such an economy is global – such ties have never been stopped by national borders – and that it is not cleanly bounded off from other spheres of social existence. The resultant networks have properties of their own. One, explored canonically by Walter Bagehot (1873), is the relation between speculative finance and liquidity. Financial instability may be built into the capitalism rather than something that just happens because of external shocks or bad regulation.

Finance

So in a robustly diachronic material world, finance is everywhere. Finance is a specific institutional manifestation of the more generalized phenomenon of the *forward transaction*, to introduce another piece of jargon. Essentially the distinction is between a "spot" transaction, in which both sides are completed at the same time, and a forward transaction, in which the two sides are separated by some period of time. Buying a newspaper from a vending machine is a spot transaction, subscribing to a newspaper is a forward transaction. Thus many of the linked future commitments that this chapter described earlier could be seen as parts of forward transactions. Every time you pay money now to get something in the future, or accept something now in exchange for a promise to pay later, or provide a good or service before or after you get paid for it, you are making a forward transaction. All of these in some way could be described as either "financing" activity (if money is provided in advance) or requiring finance (if the seller gets your money later). If specialized financial institutions develop within this pervasive environment of forward-transacting, we should not be surprised. Nor should we be surprised that dense complexes of persuasion arise around efforts to get people to part with large amounts of money in anticipation of a future benefit. If the future is unknowable because it is yet to be made, then there are no bright lines between sound and worthy projects and crazy boondoggles. Your persuasive success in getting finance for your project may have a lot to do with whether it succeeds or fails.

If we start from this point of view, it makes no sense to portray production as inherently good and necessary and finance as inherently dodgy or parasitic. Production implies finance; diachronic material life must be financed. You can't evade finance: you're soaking in it. That does not mean that everything that happens under the name of finance is good or useful – nor is everything that happens under the name of production.

Related arguments apply to money. In the contemporary world, virtually everything that goes under the name of "money" is a financial asset. To call an asset "financial" means that it is simultaneously the liability of some other person or institution. The cash in your pocket is a liability of a central bank, the money in your bank account is a liability of the commercial bank where you have the account. Money, then, is simply one aspect of a larger financial system that includes other assets that are not money, and is for that reason *integral* to material life, not something that stands outside it. We thus end up with a very different ontology from the previous three chapters. In those chapters theorists began by imagining a simple, wholesome, economy producing tangible goods to meet genuine needs, and portrayed money and finance as monstrous parasites on that "real" economy. A Post Keynesian social ontology starts *in* time, and thus always already *in* finance. Finance generates the conditions for making goods and services, and generates money as part of a spectrum of financial assets.

In sum: the thin modernist theory that sorts production into (a) solidaristic households which know and meet members' needs, and (b) competitive take-it-or-leave-it spot markets in goods and services, has to abstract away from time and uncertainty and from the myriad social and cultural acts and institutional forms by which forward commitments are made and ideas about the future conveyed and contested. These are blinders we can remove.

Implications

The robustly diachronic, non-modernist approach outlined above can be pushed in two directions: toward history and large-scale power on the one hand, and toward subjectivity and knowledge on the other.

History and power: Synchrony allows analysts to limit the scope of economic actors. That is, it erects an analytic barrier between the unchangeable institutions through which people act (whose origin, modification, and demise are outside the slice of time that we analyze), and the scope allowed to actors in the slice of time considered (e.g., questions like what to produce and by what technique or what to buy). In a robustly diachronic approach institutions are contingent and reproduced through repeated performances.[5] There is not just the short and long term of the neoclassical economist (in which the long term allows changes in the physical capital stock), there is also a genuine political history in which law, government, states, and other relevant institutions may be changed.

This kind of analysis is especially prominent in a group of economists active in the mid-twentieth century who took a particular interest in institutional change, including Celso Furtado, Michał Kalecki, Juan Noyola, and K. N. Raj. all of these authors took a strong interest in sectoral conflict within nations, with the relevant sectors or classes drawn from observation. For example Furtado examines the struggle between two groups of Brazilian business owners, those producing for export and those producing for the domestic market. Depending on historical circumstances other analyses emphasize landlords, peasants, different groups of capital owners, and urban workers. This approach *looks for* distinct groups, classes, or sectors with competing interests, and is attentive to the way competition plays out in politics. But it is not the cardboard Marxism in which every nation is understood to pass through a standard series of modes of production.

This approach has been attentive to the possibility that conflict may be as much over power and position as resources. One of the characteristics of political struggle is that it is played for keeps: losers may not survive to fight another day. The Mexican Revolution, for example, effectively eliminated the old landed aristocracy as a political player. So while there may be instances in which different groups just fight over shares of the pie, of far greater importance are conflicts over enduring position and power. It is not difficult to see that this extends to conflict over the fundamental nature and composition of the state.

Accordingly, existing states are never neutral arbiters. There is no "outside" to politics or to economy; there are no neutral referees or apolitical technocrats. The Furtado-Kalecki-Noyola-Raj tradition was particularly alive to large discontinuities in institutional structure, for example in the financial system. If people within a given nation were divided, this division was likely to be not one of mere "interest," but of institutional position and linkages.

Finally, while the theorists under discussion phrased most of their interventions in terms of national policy questions, the nation was not the sole frame of reference or limit of analysis. If particular groups within a nation had particular kinds of foreign connections, then national policymakers could find themselves constrained in interesting ways. Business elites might deliberately transnationalize themselves, in order to reduce the leverage of any one state over their activities. Groups of workers may also deliberately cultivate foreign work or business opportunities so as to widen their options, and many national borders straddle long-term transmigration and commercial routes.

Two points about this tradition may strike readers familiar with the globalization literature. One is that it does not reduce politics or history to economy, and for that reason does not theorize power as necessarily emerging from economy. Economy and material life matter, but they are not a free-standing realm, nor an adequate basis for explaining history.

Subjectivity and knowledge: Work on Post Keynesian subjectivity is less well-developed, and potentially-relevant insights are spread across literatures that do not reference each other. The interdisciplinary feminist literature on care[6] and the Austrian Economics literature on fundamental uncertainty[7] possess ideas relevant to Post Keynesian work, but the three literatures are sufficiently separated by other theoretical and political commitments that cross-fertilization has been difficult.[8] Work in Anthropology, like the book by Oxfeld mentioned at the start of this chapter, may be a more useful starting point.

Two large questions confront us on subjectivity.

The first is the relation of subjectivity to conversations, interactions, and relations with others, fleeting or enduring. At every stage, from our perception of the world, our interpretation of it, our formation and revision of projects, to our capacity to act, social relations are relevant. We learn from others, test our perceptions and ideas with others, and include each other in our plans – for example if part of your life-project includes falling in love or raising a child, that project is relational from the outset. Think of the way drama, tragic or comic, typically revolves around complex relations of three or more people, following stories of efforts to extend or break ties, and conflicting efforts by different people to include each other in their projects. Easily recognizable from experience, this thick, fraught relationality has never been described by any sort of Economics; even a very simple idea of responsibility to others remains difficult to capture, and it is usually avoided either by sticking to asocial self-gratifying individuals, or by appealing to overarching concepts of structure.

The second problem has to do with how knowledge works. Controversies or distinctions in Economics tend to stop at very simple ignorance/knowledge splits: you know something or you don't. For example the Post Keynesian literature on fundamental uncertainty, discussed earlier in this chapter, asserts that the future is unknowable but tends to assume that the present is fairly readily knowable. Neoclassical discussions of "information asymmetries" tend to assume that certain facts are hidden from certain people, but still assume that when facts become visible, we "know" things without difficulty. But it is one thing to, say, model a consumer's purchase as response to a quoted price. It is quite another matter to ask how an entrepreneur understands a potential new market or how a banker understands an entrepreneur who applies for a loan. It has largely been left to Austrian Economics, which places great store in the role of the entrepreneur, to raise the question of interpretation and to remind Post Keynesians that while the future may indeed be invisible, the present is a challenge too.[9]

This has been perforce a brief sketch of a few of the possibilities in heterodox Economics. I hope at least to persuade non-economist readers that the field is open, and that it cannot be reduced to ideological positions.

Notes

1 Tsing (2000, 2005). On scale see also Ferguson and Gupta (2002). On more recent anthropology of finance see Maurer (2012).
2 For example, in a matrilineal agrarian society it might be understood that I will help my mother's brothers with their harvests. This is an institutional pattern that allows my uncles to plan production with less worry over being short-handed at critical moments.
3 Heyman (1994) provides a penetrating historical analysis of householding patterns in Northern Mexico, distinguishing "flow-conserving" and "flow-through" patterns, the former yielding to the latter as households become more dependent on earning money.
4 For one discussion around this see Danby (2000), Davidson (2000), Danby (2004b). A larger point is that even institutions that *present* themselves as bureaucratically-formal and rule-bound are in practice often reliant on particularist social ties. This is one of the points made by Critical Legal Studies about law.
5 Coddington (1982, p. 486) is thus mistaken to say that "uncertainty and subjectivism in themselves have no bearing on the institution of private property in the means of production, nor on any other institution."
6 See references in Danby (2004a).
7 Boettke *et al.* (2001); Froman (2001).
8 The Post Keynesian-feminist disjuncture is examined in Danby (2004b).
9 If the Austrian interpretive literature has a weakness, it is that its hermeneutics is heavily textual. The feminist care literature has by contrast devoted attention to kinds of knowledge that require observing bodies and formulating understandings of the condition of others that those others do not or cannot (in the case of infants) articulate. This literature has only begun (e.g., Dalmiya 2001, 2002) to come under epistemological critique. For more see Danby (2000, 2010).

12 Numbered things

In the Second Book of Samuel, King David commanded a census. The census counted 1.3 million military-aged men in Israel and Judah. Angered, God sent a plague to kill 77,000 of them. Why? The text presents David's census as accurate and, at least in secular terms, favorable: carefully gathered by scrupulous officials, it demonstrated the kingdom's growth and strength. Today we would call these "good numbers," signifying prosperity and sound government. The offense to God lay in the *goodness* of the numbers: the census was a troubling and boastful way of representing His people. The medieval Talmudist Rashi explained: "for the evil eye has power over numbered things, and pestilence comes upon them, as we find in David's time."[1]

Behind much of the literature on economic representation flickers the hope that if only we had truer numbers, we could have better government, better policy, better lives. Bad numbers bring wrong policies and confusion; good numbers might clear all this up. With better numbers we would all see ourselves as we are; and then voters, politicians, and technocrats would choose properly. Yet it is seldom clear how revised data would have the desired political effect. For example, an improved economic understanding of how women's labor absorbs the shocks of austerity policies *might* lead to more "family friendly" policies than before, but it might just as easily lead to the policy conclusion that a given national economy is more resilient than it appears, and can therefore absorb harsher levels of austerity. The Introduction noted the complaints of Nicolas Sarkozy that French GDP figures were both too high (and thus did not show enough French suffering) *and* too low (because they omitted the ineffable qualities of French life). That is why this book has bracketed off the question of whether the numbers are true, and asked about the role numbers have played in the fabrication of the nation, the fabrication of a scale built around that kind of nation, the fabrication of a global symbolic order. I have offered two main claims.

The first is that the relevant history is the emergence of modernist political economy over the last two centuries, which is to say a kind of political economy built within modernist social ontology. This ontology highlights individual psychologies and the large national units to which those individual psychologies correspond. It contains a stylized history in which national units and the psychologies of those within them move from "traditional" to "modern." Fully modern economic reasoning is rational, and rationality puts aside love. One consequence of the emphasis on individual psychology, nation, and the communion between them is corresponding neglect of kinship, community, and religious institutions, and other sources of division and solidarity. Another consequence is that the international is evacuated of social content, at the expense, among others, of people who may find themselves living and working between nations or without recognition by a national government. A more subtle consequence is that we look to the nation to supplement what the individual lacks, and vice versa. All the characteristics of modernist political economy noted so far in this paragraph are shared by two contending moieties within modernist political economy, rationalists and romantics. I have sought to reframe the showy hostilities between them as a ritual combat atop a substantial, consequential, and troubling platform of agreement.

The second main claim is that this kind of modernity came fully into its own after WWII. Before the war, there was a world of frank imperialism and inequality. After the war, there arose a symbolic order of formal equality – everyone got rights-bearing citizenship in a formally equivalent nation. But former colonies became independent into an order of nations that made their governments and governed populations perennial objects of discipline and punishment, confined in national compartments.[2]

It is here that Tsing's concept of "scale-making projects" proves so fruitful. What Tsing shows is not just that such scales as the national and global are made things, but that they are complex assemblages that do much work, incorporating not only the voices of governments and large businesses, but also, simultaneously, rhetorics of suspicion and conspiracy. Her "Inside the Economy of Appearances" (Tsing 2000) followed the failure of a Canadian transnational mining concern, tracking the voices of the business in question, the Indonesian state, Indonesian and Canadian media, and ruined Canadian investors. Investors resonated to stories of miraculous discovery and profits to be made on wild frontiers and later consoled themselves with rumors of hidden plots against the bankrupt vehicle of their hopes. Where Appadurai and Graeber see a disturbing "magic" in finance, Tsing perceives "conjuring," a deliberate, skilled performance. Where Jameson and Graeber see conspiracy theories as demotic strivings to grasp the unknowable, Tsing shows that they are allied fictions, lurid retracings of the same notions of power and scale.[3]

My suggestion is that the world is not in fact very tightly organized, and that financial markets are flighty and unreliable. Apologists and critics alike risk pareidolia, that is to say a tendency to read signals that are not there, and attribute more coherence than really exists. What is the warrant for assuming that international financial markets, or global capitalism or what have you, function according to any *single* inexorable logic, whether that is the logic of Moloch or Adam Smith?

At the global level, we risk being frightened by a creature of our own minds, an inflated image of international capitalism. At the level of the nation, the close alignment of society, population, and nation promoted by this kind of data has authorized the disciplining of households, and hindered migration and transnational kin and community ties. Scales and units of aggregation of data take on troublesome lives of their own. Concepts developed to make consistent data-collection possible become reified as the data itself becomes an argument for their obviousness.

Notes

1 Alter (2004, p. 486), Miller and Schneerson (2005, p. 228). Additional discussion in Alter (2000, p. 354). Rashi is writing about a related passage in Exodus.
2 I am indebted to postcolonial studies like Chatterjee (1993) and Mbembe (2001) that put the national form under pressure.
3 Ho (2009, pp. 295–324) provides a compelling account of the performance of the global by U.S. investment banks.

Bibliography

Abdelal, Rawi. 2009. *Capital Rules: The Construction of Global Finance*. Cambridge, MA: Harvard University Press.

Abraham, William I. 1952. *The National Income of the Philippines and Its Distribution*. United Nations. ST/TAA/K/Philippines/2. New York: United Nations. Technical Assistance Administration.

Ady, Peter. 1952. *Economic Statistics in Burma*. New York: United Nations. Technical Assistance Administration.

Ahmad, Aijaz. 1987. "Jameson's Rhetoric of Otherness and the 'National Allegory.'" *Social Text* 17 (October): 3–25.

Alter, Robert. 2000. *The David Story: A Translation with Commentary of 1 and 2 Samuel*. New York: W. W. Norton.

Alter, Robert. 2004. *The Five Books of Moses: A Translation with Commentary*. New York: W.W. Norton.

Alway, Todd. 2009. "Accounting for Globalization: National Statistics, International Comparisons and the Emergence of the Global Economy." Doctoral thesis, Carleton University.

Anderson, Perry. 1976. *Considerations on Western Marxism*. London: Verso.

Anderson, Perry. 1998. *The Origins of Postmodernity*. London: Verso.

Apffel Marglin, Frédérique, and Stephen A. Marglin. 1990. *Dominating Knowledge: Development, Culture, and Resistance*. Oxford: Clarendon Press.

Appadurai, Arjun. 2000. "Grassroots Globalization and the Research Imagination." *Public Culture* 12 (1): 1–19.

Appadurai, Arjun. 2001. *Globalization*. Duke University Press.

Appadurai, Arjun. 2016. *Banking on Words*. Chicago: University of Chicago Press.

Aristotle. 2013. *Aristotle's "Politics": Second Edition*. Edited by Carnes Lord. Chicago: University Of Chicago Press.

Asad, Talal. 1993. "Afterword: From the History of Colonial Anthropology to the Anthropology of Western Hegemony." In *Colonial Situations: Essays on the Contextualization of Ethnographic Knowledge*, edited by George Stocking. Madison: University of Wisconsin Press.

Aukrust, Odd. 1994. "The Scandinavian Contribution to National Accounting." In *The Accounts of Nations*, edited by Zoltan Kenessey, 16–65. Amsterdam: Washington DC: IOS Press.

Averch, Harvey A., John E. Koehler, and Frank H. Denton. 2015. *The Matrix of Policy in the Philippines*. Princeton: Princeton University Press.

Bagehot, Walter. 1873. *Lombard Street: A Description of the Money Market*. New York: Scribner, Armstrong and Co.

Barnard, F. M. 1966. "Metaphors, Laments, and the Organic Community." *The Canadian Journal of Economics and Political Science* 32 (3): 281–301.

Barr, Nicholas. 1988. "The Phillips Machine." *LSE Quarterly* 2 (4): 305–337.

Barr, Nicholas. 2000. "The History of the Phillips Machine." In *A. W. H. Phillips: Collected Works in Contemporary Perspective*. Cambridge University Press.

Beard, George Miller. 1881. *American Nervousness, Its Causes and Consequences*. New York: Putnam.

Beaufort Wijnholds, Onno de. 2011. *Fighting Financial Fires: An IMF Insider Account*. Basingstoke; New York: Palgrave Macmillan.

Becker, Gary. 1981. *A Treatise on the Family*. Cambridge, MA: Harvard University Press.

Beckerman, Wilfred. 1968. *An Introduction to National Income Analysis*. London: Weidenfeld and Nicolson.

Beiser, Frederick C. 2012. *The German Historicist Tradition*. Oxford; New York: Oxford University Press.

Bennington, Geoff. 1982. "Not Yet." *Diacritics* 12 (3): 2–13.

Bergeron, Suzanne. 2001. "Political Economy Discourses of Globalization and Feminist Politics." *Signs* 26 (4): 983–1006.

Bergeron, Suzanne. 2004. *Fragments of Development: Nation, Gender, and the Space of Modernity*. Ann Arbor: University of Michigan Press.

Berlin, Isaiah. 2000. *Three Critics of the Enlightenment: Vico, Hamann, Herder*. Princeton: Princeton University Press.

Best, Jacqueline. 2005. *The Limits of Transparency: Ambiguity and the History of International Finance*. Cornell Studies in Money. Ithaca: Cornell University Press.

Bissell, Chris. 2007. "The Moniac: A Hydromechanical Analog Computer of the 1950s." *Control Systems, IEEE* 27 (1): 69–74.

Blustein, Paul. 2002. *The Chastening*. Oxford: Public Affairs.

Blustein, Paul. 2015. *Over Their Heads: The IMF and the Prelude to the Euro-Zone Crisis*. CIGI Papers No. 60, Centre for International Governance Innovation, Waterloo, Ontario. http://site.ebrary.com/lib/celtitles/docDetail.action?docID=11048625.

Boettke, Peter J., Don Lavoie, and Virgil Henry Storr. 2001. "The Subjectivist Methodology of Austrian Economics and Dewey's Theory of Inquiry." Paper Prepared for the First Annual Symposium on the Foundation of the Behavioral Sciences. http://econfaculty.gmu.edu/pboettke/pubs/the_subjectivist_methodology.pdf.

Bollard, Alan. 2011. "Man, Money and Machines: The Contributions of A. W. Phillips." *Economica* 78 (309): 1–9.

Bollard, Alan. 2016. *A Few Hares to Chase: The Life and Times of Bill Phillips*. Oxford: Oxford University Press.

Bos, Frits. 2009. "The National Accounts as a Tool for Analysis and Policy; History, Economic Theory and Data Compilation Issues," MPRA Papers. http://mpra.ub.uni-muenchen.de/23582/.

Bossone, Biagio. 2008. *IMF Surveillance: A Case Study on IMF Governance*. BP/08/10. Washington, DC: International Monetary Fund, Independent Evaluation Office.

Boughton, James M. 2001. *Silent Revolution: The International Monetary Fund, 1979–1989*. Washington, DC: International Monetary Fund.

Bowley, Arthur Lyon. 1942. *Studies in the National Income, 1924–1938*. Cambridge: Cambridge University Press.

Bratich, Jack Z., Jeremy Packer, and Cameron McCarthy. 2003. *Foucault, Cultural Studies, and Governmentality*. Albany: State University of New York Press.

Breit, William. 2013. "Stone, Sir John Richard N." In *An Encyclopedia of Keynesian Economics, Second Edition*, edited by Thomas Cate. Cheltenham: Edward Elgar Publishing.

Brentano, Lujo. 1916. *Die Anfänge Des Modernen Kapitalismus*. München: Verlag der K. B. Akademie der Wissenschaften.

Breslau, Daniel. 2003. "Economics Invents the Economy: Mathematics, Statistics, and Models in the Work of Irving Fisher and Wesley Mitchell." *Theory and Society* 32 (3): 379–411.

Briefs, Goetz A. 1941. "The Economic Philosophy of Romanticism." *Journal of the History of Ideas* 2 (3): 279–300.

Bronk, Richard. 2009. *The Romantic Economist: Imagination in Economics*. Cambridge: Cambridge University Press.

Buck-Morss, Susan. 1995. "Envisioning Capital: Political Economy on Display." *Critical Inquiry* 21 (2): 434–467.

Burchell, Graham, Colin Gordon, and Peter Miller, eds. 1991. *The Foucault Effect: Studies in Governmentality*. Chicago: University of Chicago Press.

Butler, Judith. 2010. "Performative Agency." *Journal of Cultural Economy* 3 (2): 147–161.

Butler, Judith, and Athena Athanasiou. 2013. *Dispossession: The Performative in the Political*. Malden, MA: Polity.

Callon, Michel, and Fabian Muniesa. 2005. "Peripheral Vision: Economic Markets as Calculative Collective Devices." *Organization Studies* 26 (8): 1229–1250.

Cameron, Angus. 2003. *The Imagined Economies of Globalization*. London: SAGE Publications.

Cammack, Paul. 2002. "The Mother of All Governments: The World Bank's Matrix for Global Governance." In *Global Governance: Critical Perspectives*, edited by Rorden Wilkinson and Steve Hughes, 36–53. London: Routledge.

Carson, Carol S. 1975. "The History of the United States National Income and Product Accounts: The Development of an Analytical Tool." *Review of Income & Wealth* 21 (2): 153–181.

Castells, Manuel. 1989. *The Informational City: Information Technology, Economic Restructuring, and the Urban-Regional Process*. Oxford: Basil Blackwell.

Castle, Terry. 1988. "Phantasmagoria: Spectral Technology and the Metaphorics of Modern Reverie." *Critical Inquiry* 15 (1): 26–61.

Chandavarkar, Anand. 1990. *Keynes and India: A Study in Economics and Biography*. Basingstoke: Palgrave Macmillan.

Charpin, Jean-Michel. 2010. "Statistiques: Les Voies de La Confiance." *Revue Économique* 61 (3): 371–393.

Charusheela, S. 2001. "Women's Choices and the Ethnocentrism/Relativism Dilemma." In *Postmodernism, Economics and Knowledge*, edited by Stephen Cullenberg, Jack Amariglio, and David Ruccio, 197–220. New York: Routledge.

Charusheela, S. 2010. "Gender and the Stability of Consumption: A Feminist Contribution to Post-Keynesian Economics." *Cambridge Journal of Economics* 34 (6): 1145–1156.

Charusheela, S., and Colin Danby. 2006. "A Through-Time Framework for Producer Households." *Review of Political Economy* 18 (1): 29–48.

Chatterjee, P. 1993. *The Nation and Its Fragments: Colonial and Postcolonial Histories*. Princeton: Princeton University Press.

Clark, Colin. 1985. "Development Economics: The Early Years." In *Pioneers in Development*, edited by Gerald M. Meier and Dudley Seers, 59–77. New York: Oxford University Press.

Coats, A. W. 1986. *Economists in International Agencies: An Exploratory Study*. New York: Praeger.

Coats, A. W. 1992. *On the History of Economic Thought*. London ; New York: Routledge.

Cochran, John P. 2014. "How Measuring GDP Encourages Government Meddling." *Mises Institute*. March 17. https://mises.org/library/how-measuring-gdp-encourages-government-meddling.

Coddington, Alan. 1982. "Deficient Foresight: A Troublesome Theme in Keynesian Economics." *American Economic Review* 72 (3): 480–487.

Cohen, Benjamin J. 1982. "Balance-of-Payments Financing: Evolution of a Regime." *International Organization* 36 (2): 457–478.

Coleridge, Samuel Taylor. 1884. *Table Talk of Samuel Taylor Coleridge: And the Rime of the Ancient Mariner, Christabel, &c*. London: George Routledge and Sons.

Collier, Jane Fishburne, and Sylvia Junko Yanagisako. 1987. *Gender and Kinship: Essays Toward a Unified Analysis*. Stanford: Stanford University Press.

Comim, Flavio. 2001. "Richard Stone and Measurement Criteria for National Accounts." *History of Political Economy* 33: 213–234.

Connell, Philip. 2001. *Romanticism, Economics, and the Question of "Culture."* Oxford: Oxford University Press.

Connelly, Matthew. 2010. *Fatal Misconception: The Struggle to Control World Population*. Cambridge, MA: Belknap Press.

Connor, Stephen. 1997. *Postmodernist Culture: An Introduction to Theories of the Contemporary*. Cambridge: Blackwell.

Cook, Simon J. 2009. *The Intellectual Foundations of Alfred Marshall's Economic Science: A Rounded Globe of Knowledge*. Cambridge: Cambridge University Press.

Cooper, Fredrick. 2005. *Colonialism in Question: Theory, Knowledge, History*. Berkeley: University of California Press.

Cooper, William W., and J. M. Crawford. 1953. "The Status of Social Accounting and National Income Statistics in Countries Other Than the United States." *The Accounting Review* 28 (2): 221–238.

Craig, David Melville. 2006. *John Ruskin and the Ethics of Consumption*. Charlottesville: University of Virginia Press.

Creamer, Daniel Barnett, and Henrietta L. Creamer. 1948. *Gross Product of Puerto Rico, 1940–1944*. Río Piedras, Editorial Universitaria.

Crockett, Andrew D. 1992. "The International Monetary Fund in the 1990s." *Government and Opposition* 27 (3): 267–282.

Crossman, Richard. 1946. *Palestine Mission: A Personal Record*. London: Hamish Hamilton.

Crotty, James, and Gerald Epstein. 1996. "In Defence of Capital Controls." *Socialist Register* 32: 118–149.

Crow, John W., Ricardo H. Arriazu, and Niels Thygesen. 1999. *External Evaluation of IMF Surveillance Report*. Washington, DC: International Monetary Fund.

Crum, Bartley Cavanaugh. 1996. *Behind the Silken Curtain: A Personal Account of Anglo-American Diplomacy in Palestine and the Middle East*. Jerusalem; New London, NH: Milah Press.

Dalmiya, Vrinda. 2001. "Knowing People." In *Knowledge, Truth, and Duty*, edited by Matthias Steup. Oxford: Oxford University Press.

Dalmiya, Vrinda. 2002. "Why Should a Knower Care?" *Hypatia* 17 (1): 34–52.

Dalton, George. 1962. "Traditional Production in Primitive African Economies." *The Quarterly Journal of Economics* 76 (3): 360–378.

Danby, Colin. 2000. "LDCs, Institutions, and Money." *Journal of Post Keynesian Economics* 22 (3): 407–422.

Danby, Colin. 2004a. "Lupita's Dress: Care in Time." *Hypatia* 19 (4): 23–48.

Danby, Colin. 2004b. "Toward a Gendered Post Keynesianism: Subjectivity and Time in a Nonmodernist Framework." *Feminist Economics* 10 (3): 55–75.

Danby, Colin. 2005. "Noyola's Institutional Approach to Inflation." *Journal of the History of Economic Thought* 27 (2): 161–178.

Danby, Colin. 2007. "Political Economy and the Closet: Heteronormativity in Feminist Economics." *Feminist Economics* 13 (2): 29–53.

Danby, Colin. 2010. "Interdependence through Time: Relationships in Post-Keynesian Thought and the Care Literature." *Cambridge Journal of Economics* 34 (6): 1157–1171.

Danby, Colin. 2012. "Postwar Norm." *Rethinking Marxism* 24 (4): 499–515.

Danby, Colin. 2015. "How Is Community Made?" In *Commerce and Community: Ecologies of Social Cooperation*, edited by Robert F. Garnett, Paul Lewis, and Leonore T. Ealy, 221–235. Abingdon; New York, NY: Routledge.

Davidson, Paul. 1994. *Post Keynesian Macroeconomic Theory: A Foundation for Successful Economic Policies for the Twenty-First Century*. Aldershot: Edward Elgar.

Davidson, Paul. 2000. "LDCs, Institutions, and Money: A Response to Danby." *Journal of Post Keynesian Economics* 22 (3): 423–426.

Davis, Mike. 1985. "Urban Renaissance and the Spirit of Postmodernism." *New Left Review* 151: 106–113.

Dawson, Thomas, and Charles Enoch. 2009. "Opening the Economic Books of Governments and of the IMF." In *Successes of the International Monetary Fund*, edited by Eduard Brau and Ian McDonald, 149–164. Palgrave Macmillan. http://link.springer.com/chapter/10.1057/9780230239494_8.

de Jasay, Anthony. 2008. "The Demise of GDP Is Premature." *Library of Economics and Liberty*. February 4. www.econlib.org/library/Columns/y2008/Jasaygdp.html.

de Vries, Margaret Garritsen. 1986a. *The IMF in a Changing World, 1945–85*. Washington, DC: International Monetary Fund.

de Vries, Margaret Garritsen. 1986b. "The International Monetary Fund: Economists in Key Roles." In *Economists in International Agencies: An Exploratory Study*, edited by A. W. Coats, 53–66. New York: Praeger.

Dean, Mitchell. 1999. *Governmentality: Power and Rule in Modern Society*. London: Sage.

Deane, Phyllis. 1948. *The Measurement of Colonial National Incomes, an Experiment*. National Institute of Economic and Social Research. Occasional Papers 12. Cambridge: Cambridge University Press.

Deane, Phyllis. 1953. *Colonial Social Accounting*. National Institute of Economic and Social Research. Economic and Social Studies 11. Cambridge: Cambridge University Press.

Deane, Phyllis. 1954. "The National Income of Nigeria, 1950–51. By A. R. Prest and I. G. Stewart. Colonial Research Studies No. 11, 1953. H.M.S.O. for the Colonial Office. Pp. Viii + 124. 8s. 6d." *Africa* 24 (3): 275–276.

Deane, Phyllis, and Nick Crafts. 1993. *Interviews with Historians: Phyllis Deane with Nick Crafts*. London: Institute of Historical Research.

Dequech, David. 2003. "Keynes's General Theory: Valid Only for Modern Capitalism?" *Journal of Post Keynesian Economics* 25: 471–491.

Desaulniers, Mary. 1995. *Carlyle and the Economics of Terror: A Study of Revisionary*

Gothicism in the French Revolution. Montreal; Buffalo: Mcgill-Queens University Press.

Desrosières, Alain. 1998. *The Politics of Large Numbers: A History of Statistical Reasoning*. Cambridge, MA: Harvard University Press.

Desrosières, Alain. 2003. "Managing the Economy." In *The Cambridge History of Science: Volume 7, The Modern Social Sciences*, edited by Theodore M. Porter and Dorothy Ross. Cambridge: Cambridge University Press.

DeVault, Marjorie L. 1991. *Feeding the Family: The Social Organization of Caring As Gendered Work*. Women in Culture and Society. Chicago: University of Chicago Press.

Doblin, Ernest. 1945. "Review: The National Income of Jamaica, 1942; the National Income of St. Vincent, 1942; the National Income of Barbados, 1942. by Frederic Benham." *The American Economic Review* 35 (1): 222–224.

Dorrance, Graeme. 2011. "Early Reactions to Mark I and II." In *A. W. H. Phillips: Collected Works in Contemporary Perspective*, edited by Robert Leeson, Reissue edition, 115–117. Cambridge: Cambridge University Press.

Dosser, Douglas. 1963. "Nigerian National Accounts, 1950–57 (Review)." *Journal of the Royal Statistical Society. Series A (General)* 126 (2): 330–331.

Dostaler, Gilles. 2007. *Keynes and His Battles*. Cheltenham; Northampton, MA: Edward Elgar.

Dowling, William C. 1984. *Jameson, Althusser, Marx: An Introduction to The Political Unconscious*. Ithaca: Cornell University Press.

Duncan, Joseph W., and William Chastain Shelton. 1978. *Revolution in United States Government Statistics, 1926–1976*. Washington: U.S. Dept. of Commerce, Office of Federal Statistical Policy and Standards: For sale by the Supt. of Docs., U.S. Govt. Print. Off.

Durkheim, Émile. 1915. *The Elementary Forms of the Religious Life, A Study in Religious Sociology*. Translated Joseph Ward Swain. London: Allen.

Durr, Kenneth D. 2013. *The Best Made Plans: Robert R. Nathan and 20th Century Liberalism*. Rockville: Montrose Press.

Eagleton, Terry. 1982. "Fredric Jameson: The Politics of Style." *Diacritics* 12 (3): 2–13.

Economist. 2010. "Have Your Roma Back," August 19. www.economist.com/blogs/east ernapproaches/2010/08/frances_expulsion_roma.

Edgeworth, Francis Ysidro. 1956. "Reminiscences." In *Memorials of Alfred Marshall*, edited by A. C. Pigou. London: Macmillan.

Eichengreen, Barry. 1996. *Globalizing Capital: A History of the International Monetary System*. Princeton: Princeton University Press.

Eke, I. I. U. 1966. "The Nigerian National Accounts – A Critical Appraisal." *The Nigerian Journal of Economic and Social Studies* 8 (3): 333–360.

Elson, Diane. 1993. "Gender-Aware Analysis and Development Economics." *Journal of International Development* 5 (2): 237–247.

Elson, Diane. 1995. "Gender Awareness in Modeling Structural Adjustment." *World Development* 23 (11): 1851–1868.

Englund, Harri, and James Leach. 2000. "Ethnography and the Meta-Narratives of Modernity." *Current Anthropology* 41 (2): 225–248.

Epstein, Roy J. 2014. *A History of Econometrics*. Amsterdam: North Holland.

Escobar, Arturo. 1995. *Encountering Development: The Making and Unmaking of the Third World*. Princeton: Princeton University Press.

Esquivel, Valeria. 2013. "Measuring Unpaid Care Work with Public Policies in Mind." *United Nations* EGM/MDG/EP.3. www.empowerwomen.org/en/resources/documents/2013/11/measuring-unpaid-care-work-with-public-policies-in-mind?lang=en.

Esty, Jed. 2009. *A Shrinking Island Modernism and National Culture in England*. Princeton: Princeton University Press.

Fabian, Johannes. 1983. *Time and the Other*. New York: Columbia University Press.

Fain, John Tyree. 1956. *Ruskin and the Economists*. Nashville: Vanderbilt University Press.

Ferguson, James. 1988. "Cultural Exchange: New Developments in the Anthropology of Commodities." *Cultural Anthropology* 3 (4): 488–513.

Ferguson, James. 1990. *The Anti-Politics Machine: "Development," Depoliticization, and Bureaucratic Power in Lesotho*. Cambridge: Cambridge University Press.

Ferguson, James. 1999. *Expectations of Modernity: Myths and Meanings of Urban Life in the Zambian Copperbelt*. Berkeley: University of California Press.

Ferguson, James, and Akhil Gupta. 2002. "Spatializing States: Toward an Ethnography of Neoliberal Governmentality." *American Ethnologist* 29 (4): 981–1002.

Fichtner, Ullrich. 2010. "Driving out the Unwanted: Sarkozy's War Against the Roma." *Spiegel Online*, September 15, sec. International. www.spiegel.de/international/europe/driving-out-the-unwanted-sarkozy-s-war-against-the-roma-a-717324.html.

Fisher, Irving. 1906. *The Nature of Capital and Income*. New York, Macmillan.

Fogel, Robert W. 2000. "Simon S. Kuznets: April 30, 1901–July 9, 1985." National Bureau of Economic Research. www.nber.org/papers/w7787.

Fogel, Robert W., Enid M. Fogel, Mark Guglielmo, and Nathaniel Grotte. 2013. *Political Arithmetic: Simon Kuznets and the Empirical Tradition in Economics*. Chicago: University Of Chicago Press.

Forman-Barzilai, Fonna. 2010. *Adam Smith and the Circles of Sympathy: Cosmopolitanism and Moral Theory*. Cambridge: Cambridge University Press.

Foucault, Michel. 1977. *Discipline and Punish*. New York: Pantheon.

Foucault, Michel. 1999. "Nietzsche, Genealogy, History." In *Aesthetics, Method, and Epistemology*, 1st edition, 369–417. New York: The New Press.

Foucault, Michel. 2008. *The Birth of Biopolitics: Lectures at the Collège De France, 1978–79*. Basingstoke: Palgrave Macmillan.

Foucault, Michel. 2009. *Security, Territory, Population: Lectures at the College De France*. Translated by Graham Burchell. Reprint edition. Basingstoke: Palgrave Macmillan.

Foucault, Michel. 2011. *The Government of Self and Others: Lectures at the College de France, 1982–1983*. Edited by Arnold I. Davidson. Translated by Graham Burchell. New York: Picador.

Frank, Andre Gunder, Dell Hymes, and George Dalton. 1971. "More on Issues in Economic Anthropology." *Current Anthropology* 12 (2): 237–241.

Frankel, S. Herbert. 1940. "Netherlands India: A Study of Plural Economy,' by J. S. Furnivall' (Book Review)." *South African Journal of Economics* 8 (4): 482–484.

Frankel, S. Herbert. 1949. "The Measurement of Colonial National Incomes: An Experiment. (Book Review)."

Frankel, S. Herbert. 1952. "'Psychic' and 'Accounting' Concepts of Income and Welfare." *Oxford Economic Papers*, New Series, 4 (1): 1–17.

Frankel, S. Herbert. 1953. "Concepts of Income and Welfare – In Advanced and Under-Developed Societies – With Special." *Review of Income and Wealth* 3 (1): 156–168.

Frankel, S. Herbert. 1978. *Two Philosophies of Money: The Conflict of Trust and Authority*. New York: St. Martin's Press.

Frankel, S. Herbert. 1980. *Money and Liberty*. AEI Studies; 293. Washington, DC: American Enterprise Institute for Public Policy Research.

Frankel, S. Herbert. 1992. *An Economist's Testimony: The Autobiography of S. Herbert Frankel.* Oxford: Oxford Centre for Postgraduate Hebrew Studies.

Frankel, S. Herbert, and Hans Herzfeld. 1943a. "European Income Distribution in the Union of South Africa and the Effect Thereon of Income Taxation." *South African Journal of Economics* 11 (2): 121–136.

Frankel, S. Herbert, and Hans Herzfeld. 1943b. "National Income and Outlay in Palestine 1936." *South African Journal of Economics* 11 (2): 64–65.

Frankenberg, Ronald. 2005. "A Bridge over Troubled Waters, or What a Difference a Day Makes: From the Drama of Production to the Production of Drama." *Social Analysis: The International Journal of Social and Cultural Practice* 49 (3): 166–184.

Frimpong-Ansah, J. H. 1991. *The Vampire State in Africa: The Political Economy of Decline in Ghana.* Trenton: Africa World Press.

Frisby, David. 1985. *Fragments of Modernity: Theories of Modernity in the Work of Simmel, Kracauer and Benjamin.* Cambridge: Polity Press.

Frisby, David. 1992. *Simmel and Since: Essays on Georg Simmel's Social Theory.* London: Routledge.

Froman, Wayne J. 2001. "The Question of 'Equilibrium' in Human Action and the Everyday Paradox of Rationality." *The Review of Austrian Economics* 14 (2): 173–180.

Fuerst, E. 1950. "The Presentation of National Income Statistics." *The Economic Journal* 60 (237): 170.

Gaathon, Arie L. 1978. *National Income and Outlay in Palestine, 1936.* Enlarged 2nd edition. Bank of Israel.

Galbraith, John Kenneth. 1980. "The National Accounts: Arrival and Impact." In *Reflections of America: Commemorating the Statistical Abstract Centennial*, edited by Norman Cousins, 75–80. Washington, DC: U.S. Bureau of the Census, U.S. Department of Commerce.

Gallagher, Catherine. 2006. *The Body Economic: Life, Death, and Sensation in Political Economy and the Victorian Novel.* Princeton: Princeton University Press.

Gibson-Graham, J. K. 1990. *The End of Capitalism As We Knew It.* Minneapolis: University of Minnesota Press.

Giddens, Anthony. 1977. *Studies in Social and Political Theory.* London: Hutchinson.

Gielis, Bart. 2014. "Analyse Critique Du Discours de Dakar de Nicolas Sarkozy et Commentaire de Sa Traduction Anglaise." Universiteit Gent. http://lib.ugent.be/fulltxt/RUG01/002/162/285/RUG01-002162285_2014_0001_AC.pdf.

Gilbert, Milton. 1942. "Measuring National Income as Affected by the War." *Journal of the American Statistical Association* 37 (218): 186–198.

Gilbert, Milton. 1943. "U.S. National Income Statistics." *The Economic Journal* 53 (209): 76–82.

Gilbert, Milton. 1955. "The National Income of Nigeria 1950–51. (Book Review)." *Economic Journal* 65 (258): 320–322.

Gilbert, Milton. 1958. *Comparative National Products and Price Levels; a Study of Western Europe and the United States.* Paris: Organisation for European Economic Cooperation.

Gilbert, Milton, and Irving B. Kravis. 1954. *An International Comparison of National Products and the Purchasing Power of Currencies.* Paris: OECD.

Gilbert, Milton, and Richard Stone. 1954. "Recent Developments in National Income and Social Accounting." *Accounting Research* 5 (1): 1–31.

Gilbert, Milton, George Jaszi, Edward F. Denison, and Charles F. Schwartz. 1948. "Objectives of National Income Measurement: A Reply to Professor Kuznets." *The Review of Economics and Statistics* 30 (3): 179–195.

Gilbert, Milton, Hans Staehle, W. S. Woytinsky, and Simon Kuznets. 1944. "National Product, War and Prewar: Some Comments on Professor Kuznets' Study and a Reply by Professor Kuznets." *The Review of Economics and Statistics* 26 (3): 109–135.

Gluckman, Max. 1955. "Anthropology in Central Africa." *Journal of the Royal Society of Arts* 103 (4957): 645–665.

Goethe, Johann Wolfgang von. 1959. *Wilhelm Meister's Apprenticeship.* Translated by Thomas Carlyle. New York: Heritage Press.

Gold, Joseph. 1967. "Interpretation by the International Monetary Fund of Its Articles of Agreement-II." *International & Comparative Law Quarterly* 16 (2): 289–329.

Gold, Joseph. 1975. *Uniformity as a Legal Principle of the International Monetary Fund.* Washington, DC: International Monetary Fund.

Goldhammer, Art. 2007. "Encore de L'audace." *French Politics.* November 30. http://art goldhammer.blogspot.com/2007/11/encore-de-laudace.html.

Graeber, David. 2011. *Debt: The First 5,000 Years.* Brooklyn: Melville House.

Gray, Richard T. 2003. "Economic Romanticism: Monetary Nationalism in Johann Gottlieb Fichte and Adam Müller." *Eighteenth-Century Studies* 36 (4): 535–557.

Gray, Richard T. 2008. *Money Matters: Economics and the German Cultural Imagination, 1770–1850.* Literary Conjugations. Seattle: University of Washington Press.

Gray, Richard T. 2011. *Inventions of the Imagination: Romanticism and Beyond.* Seattle: University of Washington Press.

Great Britain, Treasury. 1941. *An Analysis of the Sources of War Finance and an Estimate of the National Income and Expenditure in 1938 and 1940.* London: H.M. Stationery Office.

Groenewegen, Peter. 1994. "Alfred Marshall – Women and Economic Development: Labour, Family, and Race." In *Feminism and Political Economy in Victorian England,* edited by Peter Groenewegen. Aldershot Brookfield: Edward Elgar.

Grown, Caren, Diane Elson, and Nilufer Cagatay. 2000. "Introduction." *World Development* 28 (7): 1145–1156.

Guitián, Manuel. 1992. *The Unique Nature of the Responsibilities of the International Monetary Fund.* Pamphlet Series (International Monetary Fund); No. 46. Washington, DC: International Monetary Fund.

Guyer, Jane I. 1981. "Household and Community in African Studies." *African Studies Review* 24 (2/3): 87–137.

Hacche, Graham. 2009. "The IMF Staff's View of the World: The World Economic Outlook." In *Successes of the International Monetary Fund,* edited by Eduard Brau and Ian McDonald, 191–214. Basingstoke: Palgrave Macmillan.

Hacking, Ian. 1990. *The Taming of Chance.* Cambridge: Cambridge University Press.

Hall, Peter A. 1989. *The Political Power of Economic Ideas: Keynesianism across Nations.* Princeton: Princeton University Press.

Hamlin, David. 2005. "Romanticism, Spectacle, and a Critique of Wilhelmine Consumer Capitalism." *Central European History* 38 (2): 250–268.

Harper, Richard H. R. 1998. *Inside the IMF: An Ethnography of Documents, Technology and Organisational Action.* San Diego: Academic Press.

Harris, Abram L. 1942. "Sombart and German (National) Socialism." *The Journal of Political Economy* 50(6): 805–835.

Harrod, Roy. 1951. *The Life of John Maynard Keynes.* London: Macmillan.

Haski, Pierre. 2008. "Sarkozy et Edgar Morin: La Fable Du Président et Du Philosophe." *Rue 89, Nouvelle Observateur.* October 1. http://rue89.nouvelobs.com/2008/01/10/ sarkozy-et-edgar-morin-la-fable-du-president-et-du-philosophe-5204.

Haslett, Moyra. 2000. *Marxist Literary and Cultural Theories*. New York: St. Martin's Press.

Hawrylyshyn, Oli. 1976. "The Value of Household Services: A Survey of Empirical Estimates." *Review of Income and Wealth* 22 (2): 101–103.

Hayes, Brian. 2011. "Economics, Control Theory and the Phillips Machine." *Economia Politica* 28 (4): 83–96.

Helleiner, Eric. 1994. *States and the Reemergence of Global Finance*. Ithaca: Cornell University Press.

Helleiner, Eric. 2002. "Economic Nationalism as a Challenge to Economic Liberalism? Lessons from the 19th Century." *International Studies Quarterly* 46 (3): 307–329.

Henderson, Willie. 2000. *John Ruskin's Political Economy*. London: Routledge.

Henwood, Doug. 2003. *After the New Economy*. New York: The New Press.

Herskovits, Melville J. 1964. "Africa and the Problems of Economic Growth." In *Economic Transition in Africa*, edited by Melville Hersokits and Mitchell Harwitz. Northwestern University African Studies; No. 12, 3–19. Evanston: Northwestern University Press.

Hestetun, Øyunn. 1993. "A Prison-House Of Myth?: Symptomal Readings in Virgin Land, the Madwoman in the Attic, and the Political Unconscious." Thesis, Uppsala University.

Hewett, R., Yuval P. Yonay, and Arie Krampf, eds. 2015. "Israel." In *Routledge Handbook of the History of Global Economic Thought*, 189–201. London: Routledge.

Heyman, Josiah McC. 1994. "The Organizational Logic of Capitalist Consumption on the Mexico-United States Border." *Research in Economic Anthropology* 15: 176–238.

Hirschman, Dan. 2015. "Inventing the Economy." Thesis, University of Michigan.

Hirst, Paul, Grahame Thompson, and Simon Bromley. 2009. *Globalization in Question*. Malden, MA: Polity.

Ho, Karen. 2009. *Liquidated: An Ethnography of Wall Street*. Durham: Duke University Press Books.

Hobson, John A. 1898. *John Ruskin, Social Reformer*. London: J. Nisbet and Company.

Hohendahl, Peter Uwe, ed. 1988. *A History of German Literary Criticism, 1730–1980*. Lincoln: University of Nebraska Press.

Holmes, Douglas R. 2013. *Economy of Words: Communicative Imperatives in Central Banks*. Chicago: University Of Chicago Press.

Homer, Sean. 1998. *Fredric Jameson: Marxism, Hermeneutics, Postmodernism*. New York: Routledge.

Homer, Sean. 2002. "Fredric Jameson." In *Postmodernism: The Key Figures*, edited by Hans Bertens and Joseph Natoli, 180–188. Malden, MA: Blackwell Publishers.

Horowitz, David. 1953. *State in the Making*. New York: Knopf.

Horowitz, David, and Rita Hinden. 1938. *Economic Survey of Palestine, with Special Reference to the Years 1936 and 1937*. Tel Aviv: Economic Research Institute Of The Jewish Agency For Palestine.

Huxley, Julian, and Phyllis Deane. 1944. *The Future of the Colonies*. London: The Pilot Press.

International Monetary Fund. 1999. *External Evaluation of IMF Surveillance: Report by a Group of Independent Experts*. Washington, DC: International Monetary Fund.

Ironmonger, Duncan. 1988. "Statistical Perspectives and Economic Stability." In *National Income and Economic Progress: Essays in Honour of Colin Clark*, edited by Perkins, J. O. N., Tran Van Hoa, and Duncan Ironmonger, 32–48. London: Macmillan.

Irvine, Alexander G. 1955. "A Note on the National Income and Social Accounts of Northern Rhodesia 1945–1953." *South African Journal of Economics* 23 (4): 364–369.

James, Harold. 1995. "The Historical Development of the Principle of Surveillance." *International Monetary Fund Staff Papers* 42 (4): 762–791.

James, Harold. 1996. *International Monetary Cooperation Since Bretton Woods.* Washington, DC: International Monetary Fund.

Jameson, Fredric. 1971a. *Marxism and Form: Twentieth-Century Dialectical Theories of Literature.* Princeton: Princeton University Press.

Jameson, Fredric. 1971b. "Metacommentary." *Publications of the Modern Language Association of America* 86 (1): 9–18.

Jameson, Fredric. 1975. "Beyond the Cave: Demystifying the Ideology of Marxism." *Bulletin of the Midwest Modern Language Association* 8 (1): 1–20.

Jameson, Fredric. 1977. "Imaginary and Symbolic in Lacan: Marxism, Psychoanalytic Criticism, and the Problem of the Subject." *Yale French Studies* (55/56): 338–395.

Jameson, Fredric. 1979a. *Fables of Aggression: Wyndham Lewis, the Modernist as Fascist.* Berkeley: University of California Press.

Jameson, Fredric. 1979b. "Marxism and Historicism." *New Literary History* 11 (1): 41–73.

Jameson, Fredric. 1979c. "Reification and Utopia in Mass Culture." *Social Text* 1: 130–148.

Jameson, Fredric. 1981. *The Political Unconscious: Narrative as a Socially Symbolic Act.* Cornell University Press.

Jameson, Fredric. 1982. "Interview." *Diacritics* 12 (3): 72–91.

Jameson, Fredric. 1984a. "'Foreword.'" In *The Postmodern Condition A Report on Knowledge.* Minneapolis: University of Minnesota Press.

Jameson, Fredric. 1984b. "Postmodernism, or, The Cultural Logic of Late Capitalism." *New Left Review* 146: 53–92.

Jameson, Fredric. 1989. "Marxism and Postmodernism." *New Left Review* 176: 31–46.

Jameson, Fredric. 1991. *Postmodernism, Or, The Cultural Logic of Late Capitalism.* Durham, NC: Duke University Press.

Jameson, Fredric. 1995. *The Geopolitical Aesthetic: Cinema and Space in the World System.* Bloomington: Indiana University Press.

Jameson, Fredric. 1996. "Actually Existing Marxism." In *Marxism Beyond Marxism*, edited by Cesare Casarino Saree Makdisi and Rebecca E. Karl, 14–53. New York: Routledge.

Jameson, Fredric. 1997. "Culture and Finance Capital." *Critical Inquiry* 24 (1): 246–265.

Jameson, Fredric. 1998a. "Preface." In *The Cultures of Globalization*, edited by Jameson and Masao Miyoshi, xi–xvii. Durham, NC: Duke University Press.

Jameson, Fredric. 1998b. "The Brick and the Balloon: Architecture, Idealism and Land Speculation." *New Left Review* 228: 25–46.

Jaszi, George. 1986. "An Economic Accountant's Audit." *The American Economic Review* 76 (2): 411–417.

Jay, Martin. 1984. *Marxism and Totality: The Adventures of a Concept from Lukács to Habermas.* Berkeley: University of California Press.

Jay, Martin. 1993. *Downcast Eyes: The Denigration of Vision in Twentieth-Century French Thought.* A Centennial Book. Berkeley: University of California Press.

Jay, Martin. 1996. *The Dialectical Imagination a History of the Frankfurt School and the Institute of Social Research, 1923–1950.* Berkeley: University of California Press.

Jerven, Morten. 2013. *Poor Numbers: How We Are Misled by African Development Statistics and What to Do about It.* Ithaca: Cornell University Press.

Jewish Telegraphic Agency. 1946. "Gurion Testifies on Zionist Aims Before Anglo-American Inquiry Committee," March 12. www.jta.org/1946/03/12/archive/gurion-testifies-on-zionist-aims-before-anglo-american-inquiry-committee.

Jones, Gareth Stedman. 1971. "The Marxism of the Early Lukács: An Evaluation." *New Left Review* I/70 (November–December): 27–64.

Judah, Ben. 2010. "Europe's Most Persecuted People?" *Prospect Magazine*, September 9. www.prospectmagazine.co.uk/magazine/gypsy-roma-sarkozy.

Kalpagam, U. 2000. "Colonial Governmentality and the 'Economy.'" *Economy and Society* 29 (3): 418–438.

Kamen, Charles S. 1991. *Little Common Ground: Arab Agriculture and Jewish Settlement in Palestine, 1920–1948*. Pittsburgh: University of Pittsburgh Press.

Kane, Richard. 2012. "Measures and Motivations: U.S. National Income and Product Estimates During the Great Depression and World War II." MPRA Paper No. 4436. http://mpra.ub.uni-muenchen.de/44336/.

Karl, Alissa G. 2010. "Rhys, Keynes, and the Modern(ist) Economic Nation." *Novel: A Forum on Fiction* 43 (3): 424–442.

Kayatekin, Serap, and David Ruccio. 1998. "Global Fragments: Subjectivity and Class Politics in Discourses of Globalization." *Economy and Society* 27 (1): 74–96.

Kellner, Douglas, ed. 1989. *Postmodernism/Jameson/Critique*. Washington, DC: Maisonneuve Press.

Kendrick, John W. 1970. "The Historical Development of National-Income Accounts." *History of Political Economy* 2 (2): 284–315.

Kendrick, John W. 1972. *Economic Accounts and Their Uses*. New York, McGraw-Hill.

Kennedy, William Francis. 1958. *Humanist versus Economist; the Economic Thought of Samuel Taylor Coleridge*. Berkeley, University of California Press.

Keynes, John Maynard. 1919. *The Economic Consequences of the Peace*. London: Macmillan.

Keynes, John Maynard. 1936. *The General Theory of Employment, Interest, and Money*. London: Macmillan.

Keynes, John Maynard. 1940a. *How to Pay for the War: A Radical Plan for the Chancellor of the Exchequer*. London: MacMillan.

Keynes, John Maynard. 1940b. "The Concept of National Income: A Supplementary Note." *The Economic Journal* 50 (197): 60–65.

Keynes, John Maynard. 1956. "Alfred Marshall, 1842–1924." In *Memorials of Alfred Marshall*, edited by A. C. Pigou, 1–65. Kelly and Millman.

Keynes, John Maynard. 1971a. *A Tract on Monetary Reform (The Collected Writings of John Maynard, Vol. IV)*. London: Macmillan.

Keynes, John Maynard. 1971b. *The Collected Writings of John Maynard Keynes, Vol. X*. London: Macmillan.

Keynes, John Maynard. 1971c. *The Collected Writings of John Maynard Keynes, Vol. XXI*. London: Macmillan.

Keynes, John Maynard. 1971d. *Essays in Biography (The Collected Writings of John Maynard Keynes, Vol. XV)*. London: Macmillan.

Killen, Andreas. 2006. *Berlin Electropolis: Shock, Nerves, and German Modernity*. Berkeley: University of California Press.

Klein, Judy L. 2001. "Reflections from the Age of Economic Measurement." *History of Political Economy* 33 (5): 111–136.

Koopmans, Tjalling. 1947. "Measurement without Theory." *Review of Economics and Statistics* 29 (3): 161–172.

Kornbluh, Anna. 2013. *Realizing Capital: Financial and Psychic Economies in Victorian Form*. New York: Fordham University Press.

Korzeniewicz, Roberto Patricio, Angela Stach, Vrushali Patil, and Timothy Patrick Moran. 2004. "Measuring National Income: A Critical Assessment." *Comparative Studies in Society and History* 46 (3): 535–586.

Krampf, Arie. 2010. "Reception of the Developmental Approach in the Jewish Economic Discourse of Mandatory Palestine, 1934–1938." *Israel Studies* 15 (2): 80–103.

Kravis, Irving. 1957. "The Scope of Economic Activity in International Income Comparisons." In *Problems in the International Comparison of Economic Accounts*, edited by John Kendrick, 349–400. *Studies in Income and Wealth* 20. Princeton: Princeton University Press.

Kuiper, Edith. 2001. *The Most Valuable Of All Capital: A Gender Reading Of Economic Texts*. Amsterdam: Tinbergen Institute.

Kuznets, Simon. 1933. "National Income." *Encyclopaedia of the Social Sciences* Vol. XI.

Kuznets, Simon. 1937. "National Income and Its Composition; Discussion between Simon Kuznets, Clark Warburton and M. A. Copeland." *Studies in Income and Wealth*. New York: National Bureau of Economic Research.

Kuznets, Simon. 1941. *National Income and Its Composition, 1919–1938*. New York: National Bureau of Economic Research.

Kuznets, Simon. 1946. *National Income: A Summary of Findings*. New York: NBER.

Kuznets, Simon. 1948. "National Income: A New Version." *Review of Economics and Statistics* 30 (3): 151–179.

Kuznets, Simon. 1951. "Government Product and National Income." In *Review of Income and Wealth Series 1*, 178–244.

La Berge, Leigh Claire. 2015. *Scandals and Abstraction: Financial Fiction of the Long 1980s*. New York: Oxford University Press.

Lacey, James. 2011. *Keep From All Thoughtful Men How U.S. Economists Won World War II*. New York: Naval Institute Press.

Larsen, Neil. 1988. *"Foreword" to Fredric Jameson, The Ideologies of Theory*. Minneapolis: University of Minnesota Press.

Latham, Michael E. 2003. "Modernization." In *The Cambridge History of Science: The Modern Social Sciences*, 721–734. Cambridge: Cambridge University Press.

Latour, Bruno. 1993. *We Have Never Been Modern*. Cambridge, MA: Harvard University Press.

Lawson, Tony. 2015. *Essays on the Nature and State of Modern Economics*. Abingdon; New York: Routledge.

Leibler, Anat. 2004. "Statisticians' Ambition: Governmentality, Modernity and National Legibility." *Israel Studies* 9 (2): 121–149.

Leibler, Anat. 2008. "Nationalizing Statistics: A Comparative Study of the Development of Official Statistics during the 20th Century in Israel-Palestine and Canada." University of California, San Diego.

Leibler, Anat, and Daniel Breslau. 2005. "The Uncounted: Citizenship and Exclusion in the Israeli Census of 1948." *Ethnic and Racial Studies* 28 (5): 880–902.

Leontief, Wassily. 1953. *Studies in the Structure of the American Economy: Theoretical and Empirical Explorations in Input-Output Analysis*. New York: Oxford University Press.

Levy, David M. 2002. *How the Dismal Science Got Its Name: Classical Economics and the Ur-Text of Racial Politics*. Ann Arbor: University of Michigan Press.

Li, Victor. 2000. "What's in a Name?: Questioning 'Globalization.'" *Cultural Critique* (45): 1–39.

Link, Arthur S. 1948. "Samuel Taylor Coleridge and the Economic and Political Crisis in Great Britain, 1816–1820." *Journal of the History of Ideas* 9 (3): 323–338.

LiPuma, Edward, and Benjamin Lee. 2004. *Financial Derivatives and the Globalization of Risk*. Durham, NC: Duke University Press.

Lombardi, Domenico, and Ngaire Woods. 2008. "The Politics of Influence: An Analysis of IMF Surveillance." *Review of International Political Economy* 15 (5): 711–739.

Lucatelli, Adriano. 1997. *Finance and World Order: Financial Fragility, Systemic Risk, and Transnational Regimes*. Contributions in Economics and Economic History; No. 186. Westport: Greenwood Press.

Lury, Dennis A. 1964. "National Accounts in Africa." *The Journal of Modern African Studies* 2 (1): 99–110.

MacKenzie, Donald A., Fabian Muniesa, and Lucia Siu, eds. 2007. *Do Economists Make Markets?: On the Performativity of Economics*. Princeton: Princeton University Press.

Maddison, Angus. 2003. *The World Economy Historical Statistics: Historical Statistics*. Paris: OECD Publishing.

Maddison, Angus. 2004. "Quantifying and Interpreting World Development: Macromeasurement before and after Colin Clark." *Australian Economic History Review* 44 (1): 1–34.

Malaguerra, Carlos, ed., 2003. *50 Years of the Conference of European Statisticians*. Geneva: United Nations.

Mamdani, Mahmood. 1996. *Citizen and Subject: Contemporary Africa and the Legacy of Late Colonialism*. Princeton: Princeton University Press.

Margalit, Elkana. 1969. "Social and Intellectual Origins of the Hashomer Hatzair Youth Movement, 1913–20." *Journal of Contemporary History* 4 (2): 25–46.

Marshall, Alfred. 1949. *Principles of Economics*. 8th edition. Philadelphia: Porcupine Press.

Marx, Karl. 1845. "Draft of an Article on Friedrich List's book: *Das Nationale System der Politischen Oekonomie*." Translation pp. 263–291 in *Marx and Engels 1975, Marx–Engels Collected Works*, Vol. 4. London: Lawrence and Wishart.

Marx, Karl, and Friedrich Engels. 1850. "Latter-Day Pamphlets, Edited by Thomas Carlyle-No. I, The Present Time, No. II, Model Prisons" Original published in *Neue Rheinische Zeitung Politisch-ökonomische Revue* No. 4; translation pp. 301–310 in *Marx and Engels 1975, Marx–Engels Collected Works*, Vol. 10. London: Lawrence and Wishart.

Maurer, Bill. 2005. *Mutual Life, Limited: Islamic Banking, Alternative Currencies, Lateral Reason*. Princeton: Princeton University Press.

Maurer, Bill. 2006. "The Anthropology of Money." *Annual Review of Anthropology* 35: 15–36.

Maurer, Bill. 2012. "Finance 2.0: A Handbook of Economic Anthropology, Second Edition." In *A Handbook of Economic Anthropology*, edited by James Carrier. Cheltenham: Edward Elgar.

Mbembe, Achille. 2001. *On the Postcolony*. Berkeley: University of California Press.

Mbembe, Achille. 2011. "Provincializing France?" *Public Culture* 23 (1): 85–119.

McCann, Carole. 2016. *Figuring the Population Bomb: Gender and Demography in the Mid-Twentieth Century*. Washington DC: University of Washington Press.

McDowall, Duncan. 2008. *The Sum of the Satisfactions: Canada in the Age of National Accounting*. Montreal: Carleton University Press.

McNeely, Connie. 1995. *Constructing the Nation-State: International Organization and Prescriptive Action*. Westport: Greenwood Press.

McRobie, Alan. 2016. "Video & Audio: The Phillips Machine Demonstrated by Allan McRobie – Metadata." Accessed June 17. www.sms.cam.ac.uk/media/1094078.

Mehmet, Ozay. 1999. *Westernizing the Third World: The Eurocentricity of Economic Development Theories*. London: Routledge.

Mendes-Flohr, Paul R. 1976. "Werner Sombart's The Jews and Modern Capitalism: An Analysis of Its Ideological Premises." *The Leo Baeck Institute Yearbook* 21 (1): 87–107.

Metzer, Jacob. 1998. *The Divided Economy of Mandatory Palestine*. Cambridge; New York: Cambridge University Press.

Mill, John Stuart. 1848. *The Principles of Political Economy*. London: Parker.

Mill, John Stuart. 1948. *Essays on Some Unsettled Questions of Political Economy*. Series of Reprints of Scarce Works on Political Economy, No. 7. London: Reprinted by the London School of Economics and Political Science.

Mill, John Stuart. 2006. *Essays on Ethics, Religion and Society*. Indianapolis: Liberty Fund.

Miller, Chaim, and Menachem Mendel Schneerson. 2005. *The Gutnick Edition Chumash – Book of Exodus*. Brooklyn: Kol Menachem.

Miller, Peter. 2003. "Management and Accounting." In *The Cambridge History of Science: The Modern Social Sciences*, 565–576. Cambridge: Cambridge University Press.

Minsky, Hyman. 1982. *Can "It" Happen Again?* Armonk: M.E. Sharpe.

Mirowski, Philip. 1994. "Tit for Tat: Concepts of Exchange, Higgling and Barter in Two Episodes in the History of Economic Analysis." In *Higgling: Transactors and Their Markets in the History of Economics*, edited by Neil DeMarchi and Mary S. Morgan. Durham, NC: Duke University Press.

Mirowski, Philip. 2001. *Machine Dreams: Economics Becomes a Cyborg Science*. Cambridge: Cambridge University Press.

Mirowski, Philip. 2015. *Science-Mart: Privatizing American Science*. Cambridge: Harvard University Press.

Mirowski, Philip and Edward Nik-Kah. 2008. "Markets Made Flesh: Performativity, and a Problem in Science Studies, Augmented with Consideration of the FCC Auctions." In *Do Economists Make Markets? On the Performativity of Economics*, edited by Donald A MacKenzie, Fabian Muniesa, and Lucia Siu. Princeton: Princeton University Press.

Mishkin, Frederic S., Francesco Giavazzi, and T. N. Srinivasan. 2000. *External Evaluation of IMF Economic Research Activities*. Washington, DC: International Monetary Fund.

Mitchell, Timothy. 1998. "Fixing the Economy." *Cultural Studies* 12 (1): 82–101.

Mitchell, Timothy. 2002. *Rule of Experts: Egypt, Techno-Politics, Modernity*. Berkeley: University of California Press.

Mitchell, Timothy. 2005. "Economics: Economists and the Economy in the Twentieth Century." In *The Politics of Method in the Human Sciences: Positivism and Its Epistemological Others*, edited by George Steinmetz, 126–141. Durham, NC: Duke University Press.

Mitchell, Wesley Clair. 1937. *The Backward Art of Spending Money, and Other Essays*. New York: Augustus M. Kelley.

Mitra-Kahn, Benjamin. 2011. "Redefining the Economy." City University London Department of Economics. https://mitrakahn.wordpress.com/?attachment_id=99.

Moggridge, Donald E. 1992. *Maynard Keynes: An Economist's Biography*. London; New York: Routledge.

Morgan, Mary S. 2003. "Economics." In *The Cambridge History of Science: The Modern Social Sciences*, 275–305. Cambridge University Press.

Morgan, Mary S. 2011. "Seeking Parts, Looking for Wholes." In *Histories of Scientific Observation*, edited by Lorraine Daston and Elizabeth Lunbeck, 301–325. Chicago; London: University Of Chicago Press.

Morgan, Mary S. 2012. *The World in the Model: How Economists Work and Think*. Cambridge: Cambridge University Press.

Morgan, Mary S., and Marcel J. Boumans. 2004. "Secrets Hidden by Two-Dimensionality: Modelling the Economy as a Hydraulic System." In *Models: The Third Dimension of Science*, 369–401. Stanford: Stanford University Press.

Moschella, Manuela. 2012. "IMF Surveillance in Crisis: The Past, Present and Future of the Reform Process." *Global Society* 26 (1): 43–60.

Muller, Jerry. 1995. *Adam Smith in His Time and Ours*. Princeton: Princeton University Press.

Muller, Jerry. 2002. *The Mind and the Market: Capitalism in Western Thought*. New York: Anchor.

Muniesa, Fabian, Yuval Millo, and Michel Callon. 2007. "Introduction." In *Market Devices*, edited by Michel Callon, Yuval Millo, and Fabian Muniesa. Malden: Wiley-Blackwell.

Nathan, Robert R., Daniel Barnett Creamer, and Oscar Gass. 1946. *Palestine: Problem and Promise; an Economic Study*. Washington, DC: Public Affairs Press.

Nau, Heino Heinrich. 2000. "Gustav Schmoller's Historico-Ethical Political Economy: Ethics, Politics and Economics in the Younger German Historical School, 1860–1917." *European Journal of the History of Economic Thought* 7 (4): 507–531.

Nau, Heino Heinrich, and Philippe Steiner. 2002. "Schmoller, Durkheim, and Old European Institutionalist Economics." *Journal of Economic Issues* 36 (4): 1005–1024.

Nettelbeck, Colin. 2009. "Kassovitz's 'France D'en Bas' and Sarkozy's 'Racaille': Art and the Alienation of Politics in Contemporary France." *French History and Civilization* (2): 70–81.

Newlyn, Doreen. 2011. "A Memoir on the Creation of the Newlyn/Phillips Machine." *Economia Politica*, no. 1/2011.

Norton, Bruce. 1995. "Late Capitalism and Postmodernism: Jameson/Mandel." In *Marxism in the Postmodern Age*, edited by Antonio Callari, Stephen Cullenberg, and Carole Biewener, 59–70. New York: Guilford Press.

O'Brien, Ellen. 1989. "How the 'G' Got into the GNP." In *Perspectives on the History of Economic Thought Vol. X: Method, Competition, Conflict and Measurement in the Twentieth Century*. Brookfield: Edward Elgar.

Okigbo, Pius. 1962. *Nigerian National Accounts, 1950–57*. Enugu, Eastern Nigeria: Federal Ministry of Economic Development.

Okigbo, Pius. 1963. "Nigerian National Accounts 1950–7." In *African Studies in Income and Wealth: Papers*, edited by L. H. Samuels, 285–306. International Association for Research in Income and Wealth. Conference. Chicago: Quadrangle Books.

O'Neill, John. 1989. "Religion and Postmodernism: The Durkheimian Bond in Bell and Jameson – With an Allegory of the Body Politic." In *Postmodernism/Jameson/Critique*, edited by Douglas Kellner, 139–161. Washington, DC: Maisonneuve Press.

Oshima, Harry T. 1957. "National Income Statistics of Underdeveloped Countries." *Journal of the American Statistical Association* 52 (278): 162–174.

Owen, Edward Roger John. 1982. *Studies in the Economic and Social History of Palestine in the Nineteenth and Twentieth Centuries*. Carbondale: Southern Illinois University Press.

Oxfeld, Ellen. 1993. *Blood, Sweat, and Mahjong: Family and Enterprise in an Overseas Chinese Community*. Ithaca: Cornell University Press.

Özgöde, Onur. 2015. Governing the Economy at the Limits of Neoliberalism: The Genealogy of Systemic Risk Regulation in the United States, 1922–2012. Thesis, Columbia University.

Patinkin, Don. 1973. "In Search of the 'Wheel of Wealth': On the Origins of Frank Knight's Circular-Flow Diagram." *The American Economic Review* 63 (5): 1037–1046.

Patinkin, Don. 1976. "Keynes and Econometrics: On the Interaction between the Macroeconomic Revolutions of the Interwar Period." *Econometrica* 44 (6): 1091.

Patinkin, Don. 1982. *Anticipations of The General Theory? And Other Essays on Keynes.* Chicago: University of Chicago Press.

Pauly, Louis W. 1997. *Who Elected the Bankers? Surveillance and Control in the World Economy.* Ithaca: Cornell University Press.

Pauly, Louis W. 2008. "The Institutional Legacy of Bretton Woods: IMF Surveillance, 1973–2007." In *Orderly Change: International Monetary Relations since Bretton Woods,* edited by David M. Andrews. Ithaca: Cornell University Press.

Peacock, Alan T., and Dosser, Douglas G. M. 1958. *The National Income of Tanganyika 1952–54.* London: Her Majesty's Stationery Office.

Perlman, Mark. 1996. *The Character of Economic Thought, Economic Characters, and Economic Institutions.* Ann Arbor: University of Michigan Press.

Perlman, Mark, and Morgan Marietta. 2005. "The Politics of Social Accounting: Public Goals and the Evolution of the National Accounts in Germany, the United Kingdom and the United States." *Review of Political Economy* 17 (2): 211–230.

Pesaran, M. Hashem, and George C. Harcourt. 2000. "Life and Work of John Richard Nicholas Stone 1913–1991." *The Economic Journal* 110 (461): F146–65.

Philipsen, Dirk. 2015. *The Little Big Number: How GDP Came to Rule the World and What to Do about It.* Princeton: Princeton University Press.

Phillips, A. W. 1950. "Mechanical Models in Economic Dynamics." *Economica*, New Series, 17 (67): 283–305.

Picon, Antoine. 2007. "French Engineers and Social Thought, 18–20th Centuries: An Archeology of Technocratic Ideals." www.academia.edu/3482039/French_Engineers_and_Social_Thought_18-20th_Centuries_An_Archeology_of_Technocratic_Ideals.

Pisani-Ferry, Jean, André Sapir, and Guntram B. Wolff. 2011. "An Evaluation of IMF Surveillance of the Euro Area." Blueprints. Bruegel. https://ideas.repec.org/b/bre/bluprt/629.html.

Pleyers, Geoffrey. 2010. *Alter-Globalization: Becoming Actors in a Global Age.* Cambridge: Polity.

Podet, Allen Howard. 1986. *The Success and Failure of the Anglo-American Committee of Inquiry, 1945–1946: Last Chance in Palestine.* Lewiston: Edwin Mellen Press.

Polak, Jacques Jacobus. 1954. *An International Economic System.* London: George Allen & Unwin.

Poovey, Mary. 1998. *A History of the Modern Fact.* Chicago: University of Chicago Press.

Poovey, Mary. 2008. *Genres of the Credit Economy.* Chicago: University of Chicago Press.

Press, Eyal. 2011. "The Sarkozy-Stiglitz Commission's Quest to Get Beyond GDP." *The Nation*, May 2. www.thenation.com/article/sarkozy-stiglitz-commissions-quest-get-beyond-gdp/.

Prest, Alan R. 1957. *The Investigation of National Income in British Tropical Dependencies.* Institute of Commonwealth Studies. London: Athlone Press.

Prest, Alan R. 1963. "Review of *Nigerian National Accounts, 1950–57.*, by P. N. C. Okigbo." *The Economic Journal* 73 (289): 142.

Prest, Alan R., and Ian G. Stewart. 1953. *The National Income of Nigeria, 1950–51.* London: Her Majesty's Stationery Office.

Pŕibram, Karl. 1983. *A History of Economic Reasoning.* Baltimore: Johns Hopkins University Press.

Pujol, Michele A. 1998. *Feminism and Anti-Feminism in Early Economic Thought.* Cheltenham: Edward Elgar.

Pyatt, Graham, and Alan Roe. 1977. *Social Accounting for Development Planning with Special Reference to Sri Lanka.* Cambridge: Cambridge University Press.

Radhakrishnan, Rajagopalan. 1989. "Poststructuralist Politics: Towards a Theory of Coalition." In *Postmodernism/Jameson/Critique*, edited by Douglas Kellner, 301–332. Washington, DC: Maisonneuve Press.

Radice, H. 1984. "The National Economy: A Keynesian Myth?" *Capital and Class* 22: 111–140.

Rajan, Raghuram, and Luigi Zingales. 2003. "The Great Reversals: The Politics of Financial Development in the Twentieth Century." *Journal of Financial Economics* 69 (1): 5–50.

Rao, V. K. R. V. 1940. *The National Income of British India 1931–1932.* London: Macmillan.

Rao, V. K. R. V. 1943. *An Essay on the Nature and Purpose of Economic Activity.* New Delhi: University of Delhi.

Rao, V. K. R. V. 1953. "Some Reflections on the Comparability of Real National Incomes of Industrialized and Under-Developed Countries." *Review of Income and Wealth* 3 (1): 178–210.

Rauchway, Eric. 2015. *The Money Makers: How Roosevelt and Keynes Ended the Depression, Defeated Fascism, and Secured a Prosperous Peace.* New York: Basic Books.

Ravela, Christian. 2013. "States of Dispossession: U.S. Political Culture, State Form, and Race from 1930 to the Present." Thesis, University of Washington.

Rijken van Olst, H. 1953. *The National Income and National Accounts of the Republic of Panama, 1944–1952.* United Nations ST/TAA/K/Panama/1. New York: United Nations.

Rivkin, Ellis. 1952. "Review of *Review of The Jews and Modern Capitalism*, by Werner Sombart, M. Epstein, and Bert F. Hoselitz." *The Journal of Economic History* 12 (2): 174–175.

Robbins, Lionel. 1932. *An Essay on the Nature and Significance of Economic Science.* London: Macmillan.

Robinson, Austin. 1987. "General Discussion." In *Keynes and Economic Development: The Seventh Keynes Seminar Held at the University of Kent, Canterbury, 1985*, edited by A. P. Thirlwall, 136–145. Basingstoke: Macmillan.

Rosen, Sam. 1979. "National Income and Outlay in Palestine, 1936. (Book Review)." *Journal of Economic Literature* 17 (3): 1046–1048.

Rothbard, Murray N. 1993. *Man, Economy, and State: A Treatise on Economic Principles.* Auburn University: Ludwig von Mises Institute.

Rothbarth, Erwin, and John Maynard Keynes. 1939. "The Income and Fiscal Potential of Great Britain." *The Economic Journal* 49 (196): 626–639.

Ruppin, Arthur. 1949. *Building Israel; Selected Essays, 1907–1935.* New York: Schocken Books.

Ruskin, John. 1891. *Munera Pulveris. 1891*. New York: Charles E. Merrill.

Ruskin, John. 1906. *"A Joy for Ever": (And Its Price in the Market) Being the Substance (with Additions) of Two Lectures on the Political Economy of Art, Delivered at Manchester, July 10th and 13th, 1857*. London: George Allen.

Ryder, William H. 2009. "A System Dynamics View of the Phillips Machine." Conference paper, 27th International Conference of the System Dynamics Society. www.systemdynamics.org/conferences/2009/proceed/papers/P1038.pdf.

Sarkozy, Nicolas. 2007a. "Discours À Toulon (07/02/07)." http://sites.univ-provence.fr/veronis/Discours2007/transcript.php?n=Sarkozy&p=2007-02-07.

Sarkozy, Nicolas. 2007b. "Discours de Dakar 26 July 2007." Original French text: https://fr.wikipedia.org/wiki/Discours_de_Dakar English translation from www.africaresource.com/essays-a-reviews/essays-a-discussions/437-the-unofficial-english-translation-of-sarkozys-speech.

Sassen, Saskia. 2001. *Spatialities and Temporalities of the Global: Elements for a Theorization*. Durham, NC: Duke University Press.

Sassen, Saskia. 2012. "Global Finance and ITE Institutional Spaces." In *The Oxford Handbook of the Sociology of Finance*, edited by Karin Knorr Cetina and Alex Preda, 13–32. Oxford: Oxford University Press.

Sassen, Saskia. 2014. *Expulsions: Brutality and Complexity in the Global Economy*. Cambridge, MA: The Belknap Press.

Sauvy, Alfred. 1952. "Trois Mondes, Une Planète." *L'Observateur*, August 14.

Sayre, Robert, and Michael Löwy. 1984. "Figures of Romantic Anti-Capitalism." *New German Critique* (32): 42–92.

Schäfer, Armin. 2006. "Resolving Deadlock: Why International Organisations Introduce Soft Law." *European Law Journal* 12 (2): 194–208.

Schneider, David Murray. 1980. *American Kinship: A Cultural Account*. Chicago: University of Chicago Press.

Schumaker, Lyn. 2001. *Africanizing Anthropology: Fieldwork, Networks, and the Making of Cultural Knowledge in Central Africa*. Durham, NC: Duke University Press.

Scott, David. 1995. "Colonial Governmentality." *Social Text* (43): 191–220.

Scott, James C. 1999. *Seeing Like a State: How Certain Schemes to Improve the Human Condition Have Failed*. New Haven: Yale University Press.

Seers, Dudley. 1952. "The Role of National Income Estimates in the Statistical Policy of an Underdeveloped Area." *The Review of Economic Studies* 20 (3): 159.

Seers, Dudley. 1976. "The Political Economy of National Accounting." In *Employment, Income Distribution, and Development Strategy: Problems of the Developing Countries: Essays in Honour of H.W. Singer*, edited by Alec Cairncross and Mohinder Puri, 193–209. New York: Holmes & Meier.

Seikaly, Sherene. 2015. *Men of Capital: Scarcity and Economy in Mandate Palestine*. Stanford: Stanford University Press.

Shah, Khushal Talaksi, and Kaikhusrau Jijibhai Khambata. 1924. *Wealth & Taxable Capacity of India*. Bombay: D. B. Taraporevala Sons.

Shah, Nayan. 2001. *Contagious Divides: Epidemics and Race in San Francisco's Chinatown*. Berkeley: University of California Press.

Shalhoub-Kevorkian, Nadera, Antonina Griecci Woodsum, Himmat Zu'Bi, and Rachel Busbridge. 2014. "Funding Pain: Bedouin Women and Political Economy in the Naqab/Negev." *Feminist Economics* 20 (4): 164–186.

Shamir, Ronen. 2013. *Current Flow: The Electrification of Palestine*. Stanford, California: Stanford University Press.

Shoham, Hizky. 2013. "'Buy Local' or 'Buy Jewish'? Separatist Consumption in Interwar Palestine." *International Journal of Middle East Studies* 45 (3): 469–489.

Shohat, Ella, and Robert Stam. 2012. *Race in Translation: Culture Wars around the Postcolonial Atlantic*. New York: NYU Press.

Shumway, David. 1989. "Jameson/Hermeneutics/Postmodernism." In *Postmodernism/ Jameson/Critique*, edited by Douglas Kellner, 172–202. Washington, DC: Maisonneuve Press.

Simmel, Georg. 1950. *The Sociology of Georg Simmel*. Edited by Kurt H. Wolff. New York: Simon and Schuster.

Simmel, Georg. 2004. *The Philosophy of Money*. London: Routledge.

Singer, Hans. 1987. "What Keynes and Keynesianism Can Teach Us about Less Developed Countries." In *Keynes and Economic Development: The Seventh Keynes Seminar Held at the University of Kent, Canterbury, 1985*, edited by A. P. Thirlwall, 70–87. London: Palgrave Macmillan.

Skidelsky, Robert. 1992. *John Maynard Keynes: The Economist as Saviour 1920–1937*. New York: Viking Penguin.

Skidelsky, Robert. 2001. *John Maynard Keynes. Volume 3, Fighting for Freedom, 1937–1946*. New York: Viking Penguin.

Smith, Adam. 1976. *The Theory of Moral Sentiments*. Glasgow Edition of the Works and Correspondence of Adam Smith 1. Oxford: Oxford University Press.

Smith, Adam. 1979. *An Inquiry into the Nature and Causes of the Wealth of Nations*. Oxford: Oxford University Press.

Sombart, Werner. 1951. *The Jews and Modern Capitalism*. Translation of *Die Jüden und das Wirtschaftsleben* [1911] by M. Epstein. Glencoe: The Free Press.

Speich Chassé, Daniel. 2008. "Traveling with the GDP Through Early Development Economics' History." SSRN Scholarly Paper ID 1291058. Rochester, NY: Social Science Research Network. http://papers.ssrn.com/abstract=1291058.

Speich Chassé, Daniel. 2011. "The Use of Global Abstractions: National Income Accounting in the Period of Imperial Decline." *Journal of Global History* 6 (1): 7–28.

Speich Chassé, Daniel. 2014. "Technical Internationalism and Economic Development at the Founding Moment of the UN System." In *International Organizations and Development, 1945–1990*, edited by Marc Frey, Sönke Kunkel, and Corinna R. Unger, 23–45. Basingstoke: Palgrave Macmillan.

Speich Chassé, Daniel. 2016. "The Roots of the Millennium Development Goals: A Framework for Studying the History of Global Statistics." *Historical Social Research* 41 (2): 218–237.

Stevenson, Michael. 2011. "The Search for the Fountain of Prosperity." *Economia Politica*, no. 1/2011.

Stiglitz, Joseph E., Amartya Sen, and Jean-Paul Fitoussi. 2009. "Report by the Commission on the Measurement of Economic Performance and Social Progress." www.insee.fr/fr/ publications-et-services/dossiers_web/stiglitz/doc-commission/RAPPORT_anglais.pdf.

Stiglitz, Joseph E., Amartya Sen, and Jean-Paul Fitoussi. 2010. *Mismeasuring Our Lives: Why GDP Doesn't Add Up*. New York: The New Press.

Stocking, George W. 1995. *After Tylor: British Social Anthropology 1888–1951*. Madison: University of Wisconsin Press.

Stone, Richard. 1951. "The Use and Development of National Income and Expenditure Estimates." In *Lessons of the British War Economy*, edited by Daniel Norman Chester, 83–101. National Institute of Economic and Social Research. Economic and Social Studies; 10. Cambridge: Cambridge University Press.

Stone, Richard. 1978. "Keynes, Political Arithmetic and Econometrics." *Proceedings of the British Academy* 64: 55–92.

Stone, Richard. 1986. "Social Accounting: The State of Play." *The Scandinavian Journal of Economics* 88 (3): 453.

Stone, Richard. 1994. *The Role of Measurement in Economics: The Newmarch Lectures, 1948–49.* Aldershot: Gregg Revivals.

Stone, Richard, David G. Champernowne, and James E. Meade. 1942. "The Precision of National Income Estimates." *The Review of Economic Studies* 9 (2): 111–125.

Studenski, Paul. 1958. *The Income of Nations; Theory, Measurement, and Analysis.* New York: New York University Press.

Suzuki, Tomo. 2003. "The Epistemology of Macroeconomic Reality: The Keynesian Revolution from an Accounting Point of View." *Accounting, Organizations, and Society* 28 (5): 471–517.

Szereszewski, R. 1968. *Essays on the Structure of the Jewish Economy in Palestine and Israel.* Jerusalem: Maurice Falk Institute for Economic Research in Israel.

Szporluk, Roman. 1991. *Communism and Nationalism: Karl Marx versus Friedrich List.* New York: Oxford University Press.

Takagi, Shinji, Tomás Reichmann, International Monetary Fund, and Independent Evaluation Office. 2006. *Multilateral Surveillance.* Washington, DC: Independent Evaluation Office of the IMF.

Tamari, Shai M. 2008. *Conflict Over Palestine: Zionism & the Anglo-American Committee of Inquiry, 1945–1947.* Thesis, University of North Carolina, Chapel Hill.

Taylor, Ruth E. 2001. "Death of Neurasthenia and Its Psychological Reincarnation." *The British Journal of Psychiatry* 179 (6): 550–557.

Tellmann, Ute. 2003. "The Truth of the Market." *Distinktion: Journal of Social Theory* 4 (2): 49–63.

Tellmann, Ute. 2009. "Foucault and the Invisible Economy." *Foucault Studies* (6): 5–24.

Thomas, Dominic Richard David. 2013. *Africa and France Postcolonial Cultures, Migration, and Racism.* Bloomington: Indiana University Press.

Thompson, Graham F. 1998. "Encountering Economics and Accounting: Some Skirmishes and Engagements." *Accounting, Organizations and Society* 23 (3): 283–323.

Tily, Geoff. 2009. "John Maynard Keynes and the Development of National Accounts in Britain, 1895–1941." *Review of Income and Wealth* 55 (2): 331–359.

Tooze, J. Adam. 2001. *Statistics and the German State, 1900–1945: The Making of Modern Economic Knowledge.* Cambridge: Cambridge University Press.

Toye, John. 2006. "Keynes and Development Economics: A Sixty-Year Perspective." *Journal of International Development* 18 (7): 983–995.

Toye, John. 2009. "Herbert Frankel: From Colonial Economics to Development Economics." *Oxford Development Studies* 37 (2): 171–182.

Tress, Ronald C. 1948. "The Diagrammatic Representation of National Income Flows." *Economica,* New Series, 15 (60): 276–288.

Trevor-Roper, Hugh R. 1951. "A Fertile Error: The Jews and Modern Capitalism." *Commentary,* July 1.

Tribe, Keith. 1995. *Strategies of Economic Order: German Economic Discourse 1750–1950.* Cambridge: Cambridge University Press.

Tribe, Keith. 1997. *Economic Careers Economics and Economists in Britain 1930–1970.* Routledge Studies in the History of Economics. London: Routledge.

Tribe, Keith. 2002. *Historical Schools of Economics: German and English.* Keele Economics Research Papers.

Tsing, Anna Lowenhaupt. 1993. *In the Realm of the Diamond Queen Marginality in an out-of-the-Way Place*. Princeton: Princeton University Press.

Tsing, Anna Lowenhaupt. 2000. "Inside the Economy of Appearances." *Public Culture* 12 (1): 115–144.

Tsing, Anna Lowenhaupt. 2005. *Friction: An Ethnography of Global Connection*. Princeton: Princeton University Press.

Tufan. 2015. *A Critical Analysis of Richard Crossman, Palestine Mission: A Personal Record (London: Hamish Hamilton, 1947)*. Accessed December 5. www.academia. edu/7719294/A_critical_analysis_of_Richard_Crossman_Palestine_Mission_A_Personal_Record_London_Hamish_Hamilton_1947_.

United Nations. 1953. *A System of National Accounts and Supporting Tables*. Studies in Methods, no. 2. New York: United Nations.

United Nations. 1955. *Methods of National Income Estimation*. Its Studies in Methods: Series F, no. 8. New York: Statistical Office of the United Nations.

United Nations. Statistical Office. 1947. *National Income Statistics of Various Countries*. United Nations. [Document] ST/STAT. Lake Success: United Nations.

United Nations. Statistical Office. 1948. *National Income Statistics of Various Countries, 1938–1947*. United Nations Pub. Sales No. 1948. XVII. 2. Lake Success: United Nations.

Van Arkadie, Brian, and Charles Raphael Frank. 1966. *Economic Accounting and Development Planning; an Introduction to General Principles of Accounting, Input-Output Tables and National Income Accounts and Their Application to Planning Economic Development, with Special Reference to the Problems of Tropical Africa*. Nairobi: New York: Oxford University Press.

Vanoli, André. 2005. *A History of National Accounting*. Amsterdam: IOS Press.

Vanoli, André. 2010. "Is National Accounting Accounting? National Accounting between Accounting, Statistics and Economics." *Comptabilités* (1). http://comptabilites.revues. org/226.

Walters, Bernard. 1995. "Engendering Macroeconomics: A Reconsideration of Growth Theory." *World Development* 23 (11): 1869–1880.

Ward, Michael. 2004. *Quantifying the World: UN Ideas and Statistics*. Bloomington: Indiana University Press.

Waring, Marilyn. 1988. *If Women Counted: A New Feminist Economics*. San Francisco: Harper and Row.

Waring, Marilyn. 1999. *Counting for Nothing: What Men Value and What Women Are Worth*. Toronto: University of Toronto Press.

Waterman, Anthony M. C. 2003. "Romantic Political Economy: Donald Winch and David Levy on Victorian Literature and Economics." *Journal of the History of Economic Thought* 25 (1): 91–102.

Welch, Patrick. 2000. "Thomas Carlyle on the Use of Numbers in Economics." In *Forum for Social Economics*, 29: 61–74.

White, Hayden. 1982. "Getting out of History." *Diacritics* 12 (3): 2–13.

Williams, Raymond. 1977. *Marxism and Literature*. Oxford: Oxford University Press.

Williams, Raymond. 1987. *Culture and Society: Coleridge to Orwell*. London: Hogarth.

Winch, Donald. 1996. *Riches and Poverty: An Intellectual History of Political Economy in Britain, 1750–1834*. Ideas in Context 39. Cambridge: Cambridge University Press.

Winch, Donald. 2009. *Wealth and Life: Essays on the Intellectual History of Political Economy in Britain, 1848–1914*. Cambridge: Cambridge University Press.

Wood, Cynthia. 1997. "The First World/Third Party Criterion: A Feminist Critique of Production Boundaries in Economics." *Feminist Economics* 3 (3): 47–68.

Wood, Cynthia. 2003. "Economic Marginalia: Postcolonial Readings of Unpaid Domestic Labor and Development." In *Toward a Feminist Philosophy of Economics*, edited by Drucilla Barker and Edith Kuiper, 304–320. London: Routledge.

Wrigley, Christopher C. 1954. "The National Income of Nigeria, 1950–51 (Book Review)." *The Economic History Review* 7 (2): 274–275.

Yanovsky, Moshe. 1965. *Anatomy of Social Accounting Systems*. London: Chapman and Hall.

Yonay, Yuval P. 1998. *Struggle over the Soul of Economics: Institutionalist and Neoclassical Economists in America Between the Wars*. Princeton: Princeton University Press.

Young, Robert. 1990. *White Mythologies: Writing History and the West*. London: Routledge.

Zein-Elabdin, Eiman O. 2004. "Articulating the Postcolonial (with Economics in Mind)." In *Postcolonialism Meets Economics*, edited by Zein-Elabdin and S. Charusheela, 21–39. New York: Routledge.

Zein-Elabdin, Eiman O. and S. Charusheela, eds. 2004. *Postcolonialism Meets Economics*. New York: Routledge.

Index